Rousseau's God

Rousseau's God

THEOLOGY, RELIGION,
AND THE NATURAL GOODNESS
OF MAN

John T. Scott

The University of Chicago Press   Chicago and London

The University of Chicago Press, Chicago 60637
The University of Chicago Press, Ltd., London
© 2023 by The University of Chicago
All rights reserved. No part of this book may be used or reproduced in any manner whatsoever without written permission, except in the case of brief quotations in critical articles and reviews. For more information, contact the University of Chicago Press, 1427 E. 60th St., Chicago, IL 60637.
Published 2023
Printed in the United States of America

32 31 30 29 28 27 26 25 24 23   1 2 3 4 5

ISBN-13: 978-0-226-82548-9 (cloth)
ISBN-13: 978-0-226-82550-2 (paper)
ISBN-13: 978-0-226-82549-6 (e-book)
DOI: https://doi.org/10.7208/chicago/9780226825496.001.0001

Library of Congress Cataloging-in-Publication Data

Names: Scott, John T., 1963– author.
Title: Rousseau's God : theology, religion, and the natural goodness of man / John T. Scott.
Description: Chicago ; London : The University of Chicago Press, 2023. | Includes bibliographical references and index.
Identifiers: LCCN 2022035681 | ISBN 9780226825489 (cloth) | ISBN 9780226825502 (paperback) | ISBN 9780226825496 (ebook)
Subjects: LCSH: Rousseau, Jean-Jacques, 1712–1778—Religion. | Theology. | Religion. | Philosophical anthropology. | Philosophy and religion.
Classification: LCC B2138.R4 S46 2023 | DDC 220.6—dc23/eng/20220909
LC record available at https://lccn.loc.gov/2022035681

For Adrienne

CONTENTS

List of Abbreviations ix

INTRODUCTION 1

CHAPTER 1
TRUTH AND UTILITY 20

CHAPTER 2
THE THEODICY OF THE
DISCOURSE ON INEQUALITY 56

CHAPTER 3
PRIDE AND PROVIDENCE IN THE
LETTER TO VOLTAIRE 85

CHAPTER 4
PSYCHIC UNITY AND DISUNITY AND
THE NEED FOR RELIGION 108

CHAPTER 5
INTRODUCTION TO THE
"PROFESSION OF FAITH" 131

CHAPTER 6
THE THEOLOGICAL TEACHING OF THE
"PROFESSION OF FAITH" 149

CHAPTER 7
THE CRITIQUE—AND REVIVAL—OF
RELIGION IN THE "PROFESSION OF FAITH" *188*

CHAPTER 8
ON CIVIL RELIGION *201*

CONCLUSION *229*

Acknowledgments 233
Notes 235
Bibliography 251
Index 259

ABBREVIATIONS

For those writings by Rousseau on which I focus, I use the abbreviated titles and do so parenthetically within the text. For other writings by Rousseau, I use an abbreviated title and identify the edition from which the work is drawn. All translations from primary and secondary sources are my own unless otherwise noted. I sometimes alter translations without so noting, using the Pléiade edition of the *Oeuvres complètes* unless otherwise noted.

CC   *Correspondence complète.* Ed. Ralph A. Leigh. 50 vols. Oxford: Voltaire Foundation, 1965–91.
CW   *The Collected Writings of Rousseau.* Ed. Roger D. Masters and Christopher Kelly. 13 vols. Hanover: University Press of New England, 1990–2010.
OC   *Oeuvres complètes.* 5 vols. Bibliothèque de la Pléiade. Paris: Gallimard, 1959–95.

Beaumont   *Letter to Beaumont.* In *CW*, vol. 9.
Contract   *On the Social Contract; or, Principles of Political Right.* In *The Major Political Writings of Jean-Jacques Rousseau*, trans. and ed. John T. Scott. Chicago: University of Chicago Press, 2012.
Emile   *Emile, or On Education.* Trans. Allan Bloom. New York: Basic Books, 1979.
Inequality   *Discourse on the Origin and Foundations of Inequality among Men.* In *The Major Political Writings of Jean-Jacques Rousseau*, trans. and ed. John T. Scott. Chicago: University of Chicago Press, 2012.
Mountain   *Letters Written from the Mountain.* In *CW*, vol. 9.
Reveries   *Reveries of the Solitary Walker.* In *CW*, vol. 11.

Sciences	*Discourse on the Sciences and the Arts.* In *The Major Political Writings of Jean-Jacques Rousseau,* trans. and ed. John T. Scott. Chicago: University of Chicago Press, 2012.
Voltaire	*Letter to Voltaire.* In *CW*, vol. 3.

Introduction

On the evening of June 8, 1762, Rousseau learned that an order for his arrest had been issued. His recently published work, *Emile, or On Education*, had been condemned by the Parliament of Paris, in large part for the discussion of theology and religion contained in the separate section of the work titled the "Profession of Faith of the Savoyard Vicar." The author was then living in Montmorency, about ten miles north of Paris, having retreated from the city to the countryside six years earlier to embark on a personal reformation. His friends and sometime hosts there, the duc and duchesse de Luxembourg, and other supporters gathered in the night to confer and counseled him to flee to England. "Jean-Jacques does not know how to hide," he declared. Nonetheless, the next morning Jean-Jacques fled. But he did not hide. After breakfasting, he climbed into a borrowed cabriolet, insisting that the folding top remain down. As he left the grounds of the estate, he passed the carriage carrying the officials arriving to arrest him. Readily recognizable in his Armenian costume of a caftan and tall fur hat, Rousseau defiantly drove straight through Paris and then headed east toward his native Geneva. Ten days later his fellow citizens condemned *Emile*, along with the *Social Contract* for good measure, burning the offending books and ordering his arrest. After canvassing his options, the fugitive headed on foot for the tiny village of Môtiers, nestled in the mountains above Lake Neuchâtel.[1] A month later he learned that a pastoral letter had been issued by Christophe de Beaumont, archbishop of Paris, censuring *Emile*. Rousseau had accomplished something of a trifecta of persecuted authors of the eighteenth century, earning the wrath of secular and religious authorities, Catholics and Protestants alike, with his controversial writings.

In his open reply to the archbishop of Paris, the *Letter to Beaumont*, Rousseau defended the publication of *Emile*, and especially the "Profession of Faith." He explained the philosophical system of which *Emile* was an expression. "The fundamental principle of all morality about which I have reasoned in all my writings and developed in this last one with all the clarity of which I was capable is that man is a naturally good being, loving justice and order; that there is no original perversity in the human heart, and that the first movements of nature are always right" (*Beaumont*, 28; see also *Letters to Malesherbes, CW*, 5:575; *Dialogues, CW*, 1:22–23, 209–13).[2] The corollary to the natural goodness of man is his corruption in society. Rousseau therefore claims that he has been able to explain the source of our wickedness without resorting to the doctrine of original sin, admitting to the archbishop that his philosophical system is directed against that gloomy doctrine. "Original sin explains everything except its own principle, and it is this principle that has to be explained. . . . Man was created good. We both agree on that, I believe. But you say he is wicked because he was wicked. And I show how he was wicked. Which of us, in your opinion, better ascends to the principle?" (*Beaumont*, 31). As for the "Profession of Faith," he makes an astonishing declaration: "I will always consider it the best and most useful writing in the century during which I published it" (46–47). His phraseology here—that he "published" the "Profession of Faith" as opposed to acknowledging that he wrote it—indicates the problematic relationship between the "Profession of Faith" and the text of *Emile*, and indeed Rousseau's entire corpus.

Why did Rousseau publish the "Profession of Faith," indeed publish it at such considerable personal risk to himself? How are the theological and religious teachings promulgated by the Savoyard Vicar related to Rousseau's philosophical system of the natural goodness of man? What does Rousseau argue in his own name concerning theological and religious issues? The questions raised by Rousseau's defense of *Emile* and the "Profession of Faith" are the subject of this book.

Rousseau's God offers a comprehensive interpretation of Rousseau's theological and religious writings, both in themselves and in relation to his philosophy and political theory as a whole. The themes of theology and religion run throughout Rousseau's writings. In the prize essay that began his career as the most famous writer of the time, the *Discourse on the Sciences and the Arts* (1751), one of the central complaints against the deleterious moral effects of the sciences and the arts was how they undermined healthy religious sentiments. "But those vain and futile declaimers go about everywhere, armed with their deadly paradoxes, undermining the foundations of faith and annihilating virtue. They laugh disdainfully at those old-fashioned words 'fatherland' and 'religion' and consecrate their talents and their philosophy to destroying and degrading all that is sacred among men" (*Sciences*, 25). In the *Discourse on Inequality* (1755) Rousseau proclaims the central tenet of his philosophical system, the natural goodness of man, and claims that this doctrine serves to "justify nature," making the work a theodicy or physiodicy. He made the intention of his second *Discourse* manifest in his *Letter to Voltaire* (1756), directed against Voltaire's "Poem on the Lisbon Earthquake," where he defended the natural goodness of man and of nature itself. Rousseau turned more overtly to theological and religious themes in *Emile* (1762), with its lengthy "Profession of Faith," and the *Social Contract* (1762), the longest chapter of which is "On Civil Religion." He defended the content of the theological and religious thought expressed in these writings and explained his intentions in publishing them in the *Letter to Beaumont* (1763) and *Letters Written from the Mountain* (1764). Finally, the questions of God and providence, fate and hope, preoccupy Rousseau in his last, autobiographical writings.

When I speak of Rousseau's *theological* and *religious* thought I differentiate between these two related subjects as *theory* is related to *practice*. That is, theology is a branch of philosophy devoted to reasoning about God, providence, and so on, whereas religion concerns the beliefs, doctrines, and practices involved in the worship of the divinity. Rousseau writes on both subjects, sometimes separately and sometimes together. Most notably, this division structures the two parts of the "Profession of Faith." The first part contains the Vicar's theological reasonings based on his understanding of nature and human nature, of the existence and nature of the divinity, and of the human soul, freedom, and conscience in relation to the divinity. The second part is devoted to a critique of religious beliefs and practices such as revelation, miracles, and scripture. By contrast, whereas the "Profession of Faith" contains an extensive discussion of theology, the chapter "On Civil Religion" in the *Social Contract* limits itself to a single sentence on the positive doctrines necessary for a civil religion and instead focuses on the utility (or lack thereof) of religious beliefs and practices from the perspective of politics. Since one of Rousseau's main strategies across his writings is to limit theological doctrines to a minimum so as to maximize potential assent to them, and this in order to make them practically efficacious, his theological and religious views cannot be entirely separated.

The overall argument of my inquiry is that there is a complicated relationship between Rousseau's philosophy of the natural goodness of man, on the one hand, and his theological and religious thought, on the other, which revolves around what can be framed as two oppositions:

first, between the attributes or needs of *natural man* and *social or moral man*; second, between the criteria of *truth* and *utility*.

As for the first opposition, I argue that Rousseau's solution to the problem of evil and therewith his justification of God and nature extends only to *natural man*, that is, humans considered as physical beings existing under the physical laws of nature, such as he portrays human nature in the pure state of nature. I later add a caveat to this argument by examining how in *Emile* Rousseau takes up the task of educating a developed social or moral being in such a way as to maintain his natural goodness and psychic unity, if on another plane than that of natural man, and thereby extend his theodicy and physiodicy beyond physical man *simpliciter*. Yet this justification is insufficient for *social man* as he ordinarily develops in society, that is, from the perspective of developed humans who, in part owing to *amour-propre*, demand justification and consolation for the internal divisions they experience and the injustices they believe they suffer. Rousseau must therefore supplement the natural or physical providence that applies to *physical man* with a teaching concerning divine particular providence required by *social or moral man*, even though that teaching is at best doubtful in his view. This leads to the second set of oppositions.

Rousseau argues that theological and religious doctrines must be assessed by two criteria, *truth* and *utility*, criteria that he importantly also insists cannot be assumed to be consistent with one another. The theological and religious views he expresses throughout his writings, whether in his own name or in the voice of the Savoyard Vicar or others, are offered by him as less *true* than *useful*. They are presented as *true* up to a point and with an eye to the limits of human knowledge, but beyond that point as beliefs or opinions that fulfill our psychological need for hope and consolation. They are advanced as *useful* in various ways depending on the context: psychologically, morally, or politically. In sum, I therefore see a consistency of substance and aim across his theological and religious writings both in themselves and in relation to his philosophy. Let me clarify that I am not arguing that the theological and religious views he advances are "merely" useful, and that in two respects. First, they are not "merely" useful, because under certain assumptions they may also be true. For example, if Rousseau is a deist who believes in the divinity, such a belief would from his perspective be both true and useful. Second, whatever their truth value, they are not "merely" useful in the sense of manipulative or simply instrumental, but are instead intended to be salutary with regard to human virtue and happiness, or one might say "truly" salutary.

The Natural Goodness of Man and the Problem of Religion

Rousseau famously proclaims that a single principle unifies all of his works and comprises a "system": the natural goodness of man. But no less important for understanding his philosophy, and especially his theological and religious writings, is the corollary of his "great principle": society makes men wicked. The juxtaposition of our natural goodness and current wickedness is clear in Rousseau's first assertion of his principle, in the *Discourse on Inequality*: "Men are wicked; sad and continual experience spares the need for proof. Yet man is naturally good—I do believe I have demonstrated it" (*Inequality*, note IX, 127). Indeed, in my own view, the power of Rousseau's writings is most fully felt in his diagnosis of the evils we experience in ourselves and in our relations with others. He gives full-throated and eloquent voice to the corrupting effects of personal dependence, the psychic disunity we experience as we are torn between our inclinations and duties, the perils of feeling our existence through the opinions of others, the false veils of politeness and civility with which we are swathed, the pains of unrequited love and disappointing friendships, and so on.[3] The psychic disunity and the evils experienced by developed humans are what, according to Rousseau, lead them to turn to religion to explain their predicament and to offer consolation and hope. Or so I will argue.

Locating Rousseau within the seventeenth- and eighteenth-century debates over theology and especially the problem of evil, and the scholarly literature on them, helps bring out what is important and perhaps unique about his theological and religious writings. Since my business here is not to canvass these debates, my attention to this issue will necessarily be brief. Fortunately, others have gone before me.

Particularly helpful is how Ernst Cassirer situates Rousseau within Enlightenment debates over the problem of evil. According to Cassirer, most Enlightenment thinkers, and particularly French thinkers including Voltaire and the Encyclopedists, held a critical and skeptical attitude toward religion, or at least toward superstition and religious authorities, a stance captured by Voltaire's battle cry, *Écrasez l'infâme!* In turn, they tended to embrace or at least proclaim their allegiance to a deism that led to a rather optimistic or even casual attitude toward the problem of evil, whether on the level of the cosmos or the individual. Such thinkers include Locke, Shaftesbury, Toland, and Leibniz, and the English among them especially influenced the French thinkers of the eighteenth century. According to Cassirer, and other scholars as well, it was the Lisbon earthquake of All Saints' Day 1715 that shook Voltaire, usually so urbane and insouciant about the problem of evil, with his optimism tumbling down along with that of many of his fellow travelers.[4] The intellectual aftershocks of the Lisbon earthquake may be overstated, but it is an apt place to dwell, since I devote a chapter of this book to Rousseau's *Letter to Voltaire* and their engagement over the problem of evil. The paradox of Rousseau's reply to Voltaire's "Poem on the Lisbon Earthquake" is that he defends a form of optimism against what he sees as Voltaire's pessimistic indictment of providence, while at the same time acknowledging that the evils we suffer as human beings are all too real. This paradoxical combination of optimism and realism, not to say pessimism, runs through Rousseau's exposition of the system of the natural goodness of man and his corruption in society throughout his writings.

Once again, Cassirer is helpful on this issue. When he turns in his survey of the problem of evil in the Enlightenment to the "thoroughly original trend of thought" seen in Rousseau, Cassirer repeats what he has written in his study devoted to Rousseau's thought concerning his novel solution to the problem of evil—namely, by locating the source of evil in society and thus in men themselves,[5] an interpretation I take up in chapter 2. But he also offers another helpful lens through which we can see Rousseau's unique place in seventeenth- and eighteenth-century thought. Cassirer says of Rousseau: "He is the first thinker in the eighteenth century to take Pascal's accusation against men seriously and to feel its full force. Instead of softening it, instead of attributing it to the self-torturing mood of a brooding misanthropist, as Voltaire had done, Rousseau grasps its cardinal point."[6] Once again, this gets to the heart of Rousseau's thought: while he agrees with Pascal about the psychic division, misery, and evil we experience, he denies the sublime misanthrope's argument that this evil lies in original sin, and in fact proclaims the natural goodness of man against what he will call that "gloomy doctrine" (*Beaumont*, 31).

Pascal is probably best located in the Augustinian tradition, so casting our eyes back to the bishop of Hippo will help situate Rousseau. In book VIII of his *Confessions*, where he recounts the critical moment of his conversion, Augustine relates how he was listening to man telling of how he, too, struggled to understand the Scriptures and to abandon his wicked ways. "But while he was speaking, O Lord," he says, "you were turning me around to look at myself. For I had placed myself behind my back, refusing to see myself. You were setting me before my own eyes so that I could see how sordid I was . . . but there was no place where I could escape from myself." He summarizes the condition of his soul: "My inner self was a house divided against itself." Augustine, needless to say, traces the source of this division to original sin. Finally, shortly afterward comes the conversion scene when he hears a little girl repeating, "'Take it up and read, take it up and read,'" and picks up the Gospels to read: "If you wish to be perfect, go, sell your possessions, and give the money to the poor, and you will have treasure in heaven; then come, follow me" (Matthew 19:21 [NRSV]).[7] And so was he converted. Of course, Rousseau, too, wrote his own *Confessions*. I note that book VIII of the work is the occasion for him to tell a story parallel to Augustine's conversion narrative: a story of reading a very different text, the announcement of the prize essay competition by the Academy of Dijon in the *Mercure*, which marked his own conversion in the "Illumination of Vincennes" in which he glimpsed the principle of the natural goodness of man and his corruption in society (*Confessions*, CW, 5:294–95). In short, Rousseau turns Augustine on his head.[8]

As for Pascal, he is eloquent on our house being divided against itself. To take one example among many: "Be aware, proud men, what a paradox you are to yourselves. Humble yourself, powerless reason! Be silent, foolish nature! Learn that humanity infinitely transcends humanity and hear from your Master your true condition of which you are unaware.... It is astonishing however that the mystery furthest from our understanding is the transmission of sin, the one thing without which we can have no understanding of ourselves."[9] Rousseau admits the effect, that our psychic division make us a paradox to ourselves, but denies the cause, original sin.

For Rousseau, or so I shall argue, the doctrine of the natural goodness of man does not suffice for developed human beings, at least only with rare exceptions. Proclaiming to divided and wicked beings that they are naturally good and unified offers little consolation, especially if the potential remedies for our condition are as difficult and as fragile as they seem to be. Rousseau therefore turns to salutary theological and religious teachings to offer consolation and hope to the virtuous and a check on the wicked. The question of to what extent these teachings cohere with his philosophy of the natural goodness of man, that is, the extent to which Rousseau holds them to be true as well as useful, is, of course, the subject of this study. For the present, I limit myself to suggesting that the tensions between his philosophy and these theological and religious teachings explain certain inconsistencies or even contradictions other interpreters have found in his thought.

The question of the unity of Rousseau's thought has long been an issue faced by interpreters. For the most part, the question has revolved around the consistency of his various writings—for example, the supposed individualism of the *Discourse on Inequality* as opposed to the alleged collectivism of the *Social Contract*. Most of these debates have largely been settled or rendered stale over the past fifty years and more. What questions remain largely open concern the metaphysical and epistemological basis of Rousseau's thought, including with regard to his philosophical and theological writings, but also with regard to such issues as the status of the general will.[10] I restrict myself to the metaphysical and epistemological issues.

A number of interpreters have been struck by the inconsistency between what they see as the philosophical commitments of the *Discourse on Inequality* and his earlier writings in general and those of his later writings, principally *Emile* and the "Profession of Faith" in particular. On the one hand, they argue that the *Discourse* is naturalistic, monist, or even materialist in its basis, while *Emile* and the "Profession" are dualist.[11] Or, as one scholar has framed the issue, Rousseau seems to move from an early Epicureanism to a later Stoicism in his thought.[12] Often what is at issue in this debate, even if the participants in the debate do not acknowledge it, is the question of whether the views concerning metaphysical dualism, freedom, conscience, and the like, expressed by the Savoyard Vicar in the "Profession," represent Rousseau's own views on these matters. Of course, this is one of the main subjects of the present study. By distinguishing what the Vicar says about these matters from Rousseau's own stated views, I find that Rousseau is consistent across his writings about the metaphysical and epistemological basis of his thought.

Let me conclude this review of Rousseau's complex position within seventeenth- and eighteenth-century philosophical and theological debates with what a recent and influential scholar of Enlightenment thought has to say about Rousseau. Jonathan Israel finds Rousseau difficult to fit into his rubric of the radical versus moderate Enlightenment. Part of his difficulty lies in squaring the deism, the immortality of the soul, and so on, expressed by the Savoyard Vicar, which he takes without comment to be Rousseau's own views, with other elements of his thought. He therefore speaks of Rousseau's "hybrid status as a political thinker who combined elements of radicalism with the moderate Enlightenment, or rather Spinoza with Locke."[13] Indeed, Rousseau seems to haunt Israel, who concludes his *Radical Enlightenment* by writing: "What is especially remarkable about Rousseau's thought is its Janus-headed mixing of elements from both radical and mainstream Enlightenment."[14] We can all agree, I think, that Rousseau's thought is, if anything else, complex.

Truth and Method

Here I offer some remarks on the interpretive commitments that guide my study and differentiate it from other treatments of the subject. What many studies of Rousseau's theological and religious teaching have in common is the assumption that he is expressing his own sincere views, whether in his own authorial voice or through the "mouthpiece" of the Savoyard Vicar in the "Profession" or Julie in the *New Heloise*. In contrast, I do not assume that the views he expresses in his writings are necessarily the same as his own. Indeed, I suggest that it is something of a fool's errand to attempt to uncover his sincere religious beliefs. I will explain my reasons for taking this approach below. Frankly, I do not find the question of Rousseau's own beliefs, whatever they may be, a productive one for understanding the substance and aim of his thought. Rather, I am concerned with what he has to say about theological and religious subjects in his writings, what aims he has as an author in addressing these subjects, and how what he says on these subjects helps us better understand his philosophy as a whole.

Admittedly, Rousseau makes it tempting to assume that the theological and religious views he expresses in his own name or otherwise, indeed the views he proclaims on any subject, are truly and sincerely his own. Central to his authorial persona is the stance of someone revealing the truth hidden from our eyes by the false appearances of society and the machinations of those in power. "Where could the painter and apologist of nature, so disfigured and calumnied now, have found his model if not in his own heart?" (*Dialogues, CW*, 1:214). Voltaire was fond of comparing Jean-Jacques to Diogenes, barking from his barrel, but Rousseau might have embraced the comparison by taking up the lantern in search of a man only to find that he and he alone, in fact, was that man. He adopted as his motto *Vitam impendere vero*—"To consecrate one's life to the truth"—and throughout his writings he insisted on his truthfulness and especially his sincerity. Finally, he upped the ante in his autobiographical writings. How could anyone who revealed he enjoyed being spanked, stole ribbons, exposed himself to young women, and abandoned his children not be telling the truth?

Many readers have taken Rousseau's authorial persona to be the man himself. There are various versions of this approach. Among the most influential and insightful is Jean Starobinski's interpretation of Rousseau as someone seeking to recapture a "transparency" lost among the "obstacles" that prevent us from seeing or communicating it. Starobinski's psychoanalytically informed reading attends to "the emotional sources and unconscious underpinnings of his thought," especially as expressed in the *Confessions* and the stories Rousseau tells of his own fall from innocence. There is, then, a unity of intention in his writings: "to preserve or restore a compromised state of transparency." The hallmark of Rousseau's writings for Starobinski is therefore "sincerity" as a form of self-reconciliation, and he argues that Rousseau's goal is to make his soul transparent to the reader. Finally, on the matter of truth-telling, Starobinski states: "We have moved from the realm of (historical) *truth* to that of *authenticity* (the authenticity of *discourse*)."[15] Thomas Kavanagh takes a kindred path in his tellingly titled *Writing the Truth*, in which he presents Rousseau as an author struggling to reveal the truth of his soul through the distorting mediation of language and especially writing. "Resolved to avoid a rhetoric that converts discourse into the counterproof of everything it proclaims, insisting that the prescriptural plenitude of sincerity is the only message he offers to his reader," Kavanagh writes, "Rousseau undertakes an impossible project." When he takes up the great lawgiver of the *Social Contract*, who must "persuade" rather than "convince" and who resorts to deception by pretending that his laws come from the gods, Kavanagh rejects the possibility of esotericism, specifically as represented by Leo Strauss: "As useful as Strauss's intuition is, it should be apparent that the position he describes is antithetical to Rousseau's. Rather than hide his truth behind a veil . . . , Rousseau strives instead to proclaim it with an urgency and a directness that challenges his readers' most fundamental political concepts."[16] Other similar interpretations could be cited centering on Rousseau's sincerity and authenticity, among them those of Marshall Berman, Charles Taylor, and Jason Neidleman.[17] None of the studies discussed so far focuses on Rousseau's theological and religious thought.

As for studies of his theological and religious thought that presume Rousseau is expressing his own sincerely held views, many of them blend biography and textual exegesis, beginning with Rousseau's upbringing in Calvinist Geneva, focusing on the crisis of faith provoked by the *philosophes* and his renewed religiosity, and then examining the *Letter to Voltaire*, "Moral Letters," *Julie*, and the "Profession of Faith" as a series of "professions" expressing Rousseau's own theological sentiments and religious commitments. This approach is most famously taken by Pierre-Maurice Masson in his landmark three-volume study, *La religion de J.-J. Rousseau* (1916). The same approach is taken by Ronald Grimsley in one of the few full-scale books devoted to the subject, *Rousseau and the Religious Quest* (1968), in which he calls Rousseau "the sincere thinker."[18] Other studies that touch on the subject but follow the same generally biographical approach include Charles Hendel's *Jean-Jacques Rousseau:*

Moralist (1934), Helena Rosenblatt's *Rousseau and Geneva* (1997), and Timothy O'Hagan's *Rousseau* (1999).

The focus of most studies of Rousseau's theological and religious thought has been the "Profession of Faith," whether as an analysis of the writing itself or as part of a more general consideration of his thought, and most of these studies assume that the Savoyard Vicar speaks for Rousseau. At first glance there appears to be good reason for making this assumption. First, Rousseau himself states that the results of the Vicar's inquiry are "approximately" (*à peu près*) the same as his own settled views (*Reveries*, 22–23), although he does not elaborate on the similarities (or the differences). Elsewhere he writes that the professions of faith by the Vicar and Julie in the *New Heloise* are "sufficiently in accord that one can explain one of them by the other, and from this agreement it can be presumed with some likelihood that if the author who published the books that contain them does not adopt both of them in their entirety, he at last favors them greatly" (*Mountain*, 39). He nonetheless does not explain in what way the author might be presumed to "favor" them. Second, interpreters point to the similarity of many of the arguments made by the Vicar to what Rousseau writes elsewhere—for example, in the *Letter to Voltaire* and the *New Heloise*, as well as unpublished writings such as the "Moral Letters" and the letter to Franquières. How similar in fact these different writings are to one another in both substance and aim will be a main subject of my inquiry.

Why, then, did Rousseau put the "Profession" into the mouth of a Catholic priest and separate it from the main text of *Emile* as a work supposedly written by someone else? I will take up this question more thoroughly in chapter 5, but a sketch here will be helpful. Most interpreters assume that Rousseau did so as a precaution. For example, the editor of the Pléiade edition writes: "He is seeking to attenuate his responsibility."[19] In this interpretation, the Vicar is a "chimerical character" (Beaumont), a "fictional character" (Dent), a "*persona ficta*" (O'Hagan) behind which Rousseau attempts to hide, or a "mouthpiece" (Douglass, Grimsley, Masson) or "spokesman" (Gouhier) for his views. Thus, many scholars simply elide Rousseau and the Vicar and take the character to speak for the writer. They do so not only with regard to Rousseau's theological and religious commitments, but also, and more problematically in my view, with regard to philosophical subjects such as metaphysical dualism, freedom, sociability, and conscience, using the Vicar's arguments to supplement and illuminate what Rousseau writes elsewhere.[20] Other scholars are more cautious, acknowledging the separate status of the "Profession" and its speaker—for example, when Roger Masters suggests that the "Profession" contains a "detachable metaphysics" that Rousseau proffers but does not embrace because he wants to make his philosophical system as metaphysically neutral as possible.[21] Still others, fewer in number, point to substantive differences between the Vicar's arguments and what Rousseau himself writes, sometimes very significant differences, and therefore seek to understand the different arguments and aims of the "Profession" as compared to Rousseau's system of the natural goodness of man.[22] I will end the suspense my reader must feel by revealing that I count myself among the minority. I argue that a careful examination of the "Profession" reveals important differences in substance and aim in comparison to *Emile* and Rousseau's other philosophical writings.

Finally, Rousseau's personal correspondence is another type of evidence often brought forward to argue that the theological and religious arguments found in his writings, including the "Profession," generally reflect his personal views on the subject.[23] The assumption in doing so is that even if there is some room to doubt that he fully speaks his mind in his "public" writings, out of caution or some other reason, what he writes in his "private" letters must be an expression of his true beliefs, or at least a more frank expression of them. Nonetheless, this approach is to misunderstand the status of correspondence in the eighteenth century, where there was no clear line between "private" and "public" correspondence.

Scholars who study the social and literary practices of the period in relation to letter-writing argue that the private/public dichotomy that seems so natural and obvious to us today cannot be simply mapped onto the seventeenth and eighteenth centuries. They often address the subject by engaging Jürgen Habermas's well-known argument about the structural transformation of the public sphere during the period.[24] They argue that his categories often do not fit with the actual practices of the time. For example, Claire Brant writes: "Though some letter-writing fits [Habermas's] model of communicative action, others do not. The varied and often unpredictable circulation of letters confounds simple distinctions between public and private."[25] Similarly, Rachael Scarborough King argues: "Jürgen Habermas has called the eighteenth century 'the century of the letter,' recognizing the importance of letters but miscategorizing them as solely private documents where 'the individual unfolded himself in his subjectivity.'"[26] There are both historical and theoretical reasons for not embracing the binaries of private and public, manuscript and print, and so on. As for the historical reasons, first, letter-writing was influenced by the humanist tradition, which looked back to the letters by Cicero, Seneca, and Pliny, for example, as literary models to be imitated, as witnessed, for instance, in Petrarch, and so letter writers were often self-consciously working within an established tradition. Second, letters were very commonly read aloud or circulated in "epistolary communities" not limited to family and close friends. As for the theoretical reasons, the concept of "privacy" as we would understand it was only just evolving in the period,[27] and the norms of what we would understand as "private"—in letters or otherwise—only began to fully develop at the end of the eighteenth and beginning of the nineteenth century.[28] In fact, just as problematic is how to determine what to call a letter that was not "familiar," since "public" is too broad a concept to capture the actual norms and practices of the era.[29] Rather, there was more of a spectrum without clearly demarcated points along it. On the one end was a truly "familiar" letter not meant for the eyes of anyone but the recipient, perhaps a love letter. On the other end was an entirely "public" letter, such as a published work that only nominally takes the form of a letter—for example, Edmund Burke's *Reflections on the Revolution in France*. And everything in between.

Rousseau's "letters" can be arrayed along such a spectrum. As for truly "familiar" letters, there are arguably only a small number extant— for example, some early letters to Madame de Warens. Once he became a celebrated writer, he probably had to assume that nearly every letter he wrote was not entirely private. Indeed, he himself published (posthumously) his correspondence with Madame d'Epinay and others in her circle with whom he had a falling-out. The entirely "public" letters are easy to identify: the *Letter on French Music*, the *Letter to d'Alembert*, *Letter to Beaumont*, and *Letters Written from the Mountain*. These works take an epistolary form but are obviously meant for publication and public consumption. The harder cases lie in between the extremes. Witness the publication of the initially "private" letter to Voltaire as what we know as the *Letter to Voltaire*. Since Rousseau suggested to the recipient that their correspondence be published, he clearly wrote it with an eye to publicity. Moreover, he undoubtedly knew that anything sent to Voltaire was bound to be circulated by the gossipy spider at the center of the web of *philosophes*. The so-called *Moral Letters* written to Sophie d'Houdetot have a similar status, for Rousseau proposes their possible publication in the first letter. What about a more identifiably "private" correspondence, such as the 1769 letter to Franquières where Rousseau discusses his religious beliefs? The original letter is lost, but a manuscript exists in both Rousseau's hand and that of a copyist, with corrections inserted, indicating the care with which he wrote it and suggesting that he had eventual publication in mind. More importantly, interpreting this letter requires at minimum that the rhetorical situation be taken into account: responding to an unknown correspondent who has asked him to help him settle his religious doubts. Finally, as for letters to various correspondents in which Rousseau professes his belief in God and his hopes for the afterlife, they were almost all written to Protestant ministers, another rhetorical situation to be considered. What is actually more striking about these letters is how *seldom* and how *little* he professes. In short, Rousseau's letters do not provide straightforward evidence for his beliefs.

Finally, before turning to an outline of my argument, I want to be clear that, in investigating Rousseau's theological and religious writings as distinct from his own beliefs and in insisting on the distinction between what he writes in his name from what he has the Vicar or others say, I am not maintaining that he has some sort of "esoteric" theology to which he gives access to select readers and that he propounds an "exoteric" teaching in his writings for other readers. Some interpreters do argue that Rousseau is an esoteric writer, including on theological subjects.[30] Although my interpretation here is largely consistent with such readings, I am more simply and modestly arguing that it is impossible to know what his true views might be. Further, in my view, for a writer to be fully esoteric there must be both an "esoteric" and an "exoteric" teaching. In Rousseau's case, I do not detect an esoteric teaching in the subjects under examination. Yes, he may not say everything he thinks, and may say other things he holds to be at best doubtful, but this is not esotericism full stop. When I first began this project, I anticipated that I would have to tread into the hazardous waters of esoteric readings, but as I progressed I instead became increasingly impressed with how forthright Rousseau is. When he claims to believe in the divinity or the afterlife, for example, he offers these beliefs as just that: beliefs. He admits that he believes them because they offer him hope and consolation, not because they are true. He continually insists on the limits of human knowledge and the ineluctable doubtfulness of our reasonings. He is also quite frank in acknowledging that he propounds certain views because they are less true than useful—psychologically useful because of the hope and consolation they provide, morally useful because they encourage virtue and check vice, and politically useful because they promote civic virtue and preach toleration. My focus is therefore on the substance and aims of his writings on theology and religion.

Outline of the Argument

With the exception of the broad sketch in chapter 1 of Rousseau's discussion of the problematic relationship between truth and utility, including with regard to theology and religion, across several of his works, each chapter of this book focuses on a separate work or part of a work. I examine these works in chronological order because the theological and religious arguments of Rousseau's writings tend to become more explicit and more expressly devoted to the subject over time. For example, the *Letter to Voltaire* makes the theological issues largely implicit in the *Discourse on Inequality* more explicit and also provides a bridge to the more developed theological and religious teaching presented in the "Profession of Faith" in *Emile*. In analyzing these works, I draw on other writings in which Rousseau discusses theological and religious matters—for example, the "Moral Letters" and letter to Franquières. Although my focus is on Rousseau's thought, I situate his theological and religious views within the broader philosophical and theological debates of the seventeenth and eighteenth centuries where useful. Finally, I do not address Rousseau's influence on later thinkers, despite the importance of the subject, both because my focus is on Rousseau and because I am not competent to do so.[31]

Chapter 1 examines the two criteria Rousseau advances for assessing theology and religion, *truth* and *utility*, with the critical point being that he insists that these two criteria do not always coincide. I undertake this examination in three steps. First, I begin with Rousseau's argument in the *Discourse on the Sciences and the Arts* that there is a perennial disproportion between science and virtue. Most importantly, scientific or philosophic inquiry undermines virtue because it throws the opinions and beliefs on which popular morality rests into doubt. Rousseau alludes in the *Discourse* to religious sentiments as among these popular opinions and beliefs, but he is more forthright on the topic in writings in which he defends and expands on his prize essay. Second, I include a brief discussion of Rousseau's answer in the *Reveries of the Solitary Walker* to the question of under what conditions someone, and especially an author, is obliged to tell—or to withhold—the truth. His ruminations on the moral requirements of truth and lying provide the context for his claim that his settled moral views were "approximately" the same as what is found in the "Profession of Faith." Third, I turn to an analysis of the *Letter to Beaumont* and Rousseau's defense of the publication of *Emile* and the "Profession." My analysis touches on three important subjects that will occupy me in this book. First, Rousseau explains to the prelate that the system of the natural goodness of man and his corruption in society, which underlies and unifies all of his writings, amounts to a rejection of the doctrine of original sin. His admission helps us understand one important way in which his philosophy is related to specifically theological issues. Second, he proposes that theology and religion be assessed by two criteria that are not necessarily congruent: truth and utility. As I have explained, these two criteria guide Rousseau in how and why he presents his theological and religious thought as he does, and therefore guide my interpretation of his writings on the subject. Third, Rousseau proclaims that he is a Christian, and what becomes clear in the *Letter to Beaumont*, and elsewhere, is that the religion of the Gospel as he understands it is equivalent to natural religion, which can be discovered by reason alone. My interest here, as always, lies in understanding what he *writes* about his purported religious beliefs, not what he may actually believe.

Chapter 2 presents an interpretation of the *Discourse on Inequality* as a theodicy or, more accurately, a physiodicy. Other readers of Rousseau, beginning with Kant and including scholars such as Ernst Cassirer, Frederick Neuhouser, and others, have also argued that Rousseau offers a novel solution in his writings to the problem of evil. What distinguishes my interpretation is my argument that Rousseau finds the solution in the beginning, so to speak, with natural man in what he terms the "pure state of nature," whereas other interpreters argue the solution lies, so to speak, in the end through a historical and ethical progress of humans as fully ethical agents. I focus on Rousseau's portrait in the first part of the work of "physical man" existing under the physical laws of nature as the key to his argument for the natural goodness of man and his justification of nature. Insofar as the *Discourse* can be considered a theodicy or physiodicy, then, it is limited to humans considered as physical beings and to general providence, whether literally considered in terms of divine providence or metaphorically in terms the "providence" of nature. This argument will inform my analyses of Rousseau's more specifically theological and religious writings throughout this study by enabling me to separate Rousseau's arguments concerning general providence and particular providence, and especially the reasons why he feels the need to supplement the physical providence of the *Discourse* with teachings of particular divine providence.

In chapter 3 I turn to the *Letter to Voltaire*, in which Rousseau situates his argument in the *Discourse on Inequality* concerning the natural goodness of man and his justification of nature within a theological argument concerning natural and divine providence. Rousseau wrote his letter in 1756 in response to Voltaire's "Poem on the Lisbon Earthquake," countering the pessimistic poet with his unique brand of optimism. I argue that close analysis of the *Letter* shows that Rousseau offers a double teaching concerning providence. In the first teaching, he reaffirms the general providence of nature in terms of physical causes and effects in a manner that is consistent with his depiction in the *Discourse on Inequality* of natural man in the pure state of nature. In the second teaching, he supplements the first naturalistic teaching with an account of a beneficent God with particular providence for the individual. The turning point between these two teachings comes when he mentions pride—*amour-propre*. Rousseau thereby indicates that he has added this second teaching because he considers it useful and even necessary for developed and corrupted human beings.

Chapter 4 examines Rousseau's account of the development of human nature in the *Discourse on Inequality* and in *Emile* with several aims in mind. My analysis of the *Discourse* in the first section of the chapter is limited to two topics: first, establishing that his discussion of freedom, perfectibility, and psychological development does not entail metaphysical dualism and is instead naturalistic and phenomenological and, second, examining how psychic disunity and corruption come about in the normal course of human development. In the second section I turn to *Emile*, and these same two topics: first, examining how the educational program of *Emile* is designed to maintain psychic unity in an individual and thereby to preserve the natural goodness of man, if on a different plane than natural man, and, second, arguing that his account of human development in the work, including the conscience, is once again naturalistic and phenomenological. My analysis of these topics is both backward-looking and forward-looking. It looks back to my argument in chapter 2 concerning the natural goodness of man and offers a caveat to my claim there that Rousseau's theodicy or physiodicy is restricted to physical man in physical nature by showing how it can be extended to developed social or moral beings insofar as they can develop in accordance with the natural goodness of man. It looks forward to my examination in the following three chapters of the "Profession of Faith," which does advance a dualist metaphysics. Whereas for Rousseau human beings are naturally unified beings whose divisions or contradictions come from without and are not intrinsic aspects of our being, in the Vicar's telling we are naturally divided beings, consisting of two "principles" associated with body and soul. This psychic disunity creates a psychological need for certain religious beliefs.

Chapter 5 is the first of three chapters devoted to the "Profession of Faith" and is meant to be preparatory for analyzing the theological and religious arguments advanced by the Savoyard Vicar. In order to understand the aim and audience of the "Profession," I examine its place in *Emile* and its narrative elements, which are very rarely examined by scholars. I argue that the information provided by these narrative elements—the dramatis personae of the Vicar and the youth who listens to his speech, the rhetorical situation, the dramatic setting, and so on—

reveals that the "Profession" has a different aim and audience than the main text of *Emile*. Namely, I argue that the teaching of the "Profession" is appropriate for the those like the Vicar and the youth who experience psychic disunity, an audience that would therefore include the readers of *Emile*. Finally, I suggest that the "Profession" is presented by Rousseau as a separate text because, unlike the system of the natural goodness of man, which is given by the author as authoritative and true, both Rousseau and the Vicar invest the reader or auditor with the authority to judge its truth and utility for themselves. This emphasis on individual judgment is central to Rousseau's theological and religious writings.

The "Profession" proper is divided into two parts, and chapter 6 is devoted to the theological arguments contained in the first part of the Vicar's speech. I follow the Vicar through his speech: the initial doubt into which he is thrown, his decision to rely on his own understanding and sentiment rather than on the authority of others, his examination of the examining "self," his turn outward to understand the physical universe, the articles of faith he derives concerning the existence and nature of the divinity and the immateriality of the soul, the extension of God's care to particular individuals to rectify the imbalance of good and evil in the moral world, and the conscience. Throughout this analysis I explore how the Vicar's arguments compare with what Rousseau writes in his own name on these subjects, especially within *Emile*. Particularly important for this examination is my argument that the Vicar's metaphysical dualism derives from his experience of psychic division and is meant to address it, and that in this he differs decisively from Rousseau's own account, in *Emile* and elsewhere, of psychic unity and a naturalistic explanation of the elements of the Vicar's argument, notably concerning conscience.

Chapter 7 is dedicated to the second part of the "Profession" and the critique of religion propounded by the Vicar as well as his praise of the morality of the Gospel. While I sketch the main points of the Vicar's argument and relate them to what Rousseau writes elsewhere, my main interest is in the avowed aims of the inquiry: to recognize the limits of what we can know as the truth in matters of revelation, miracles, Scripture, and related subjects with the declared aim of the utility of the inquiry in making readers less pridefully presumptuous and more tolerant in religion. As for the praise of the Gospel, both by the Vicar and by Rousseau himself, the main point is what I argued in chapter 1 with regard to the *Letter to Beaumont*—namely, that in their reading the central teaching of the Gospel is equivalent to the moral truth accessible to reason alone. Finally, and in keeping with the "Profession" as a whole, a related aim of the second part is to grant individuals the authority to judge for themselves.

In chapter 8 I turn to the chapter "On Civil Religion" in the *Social Contract* and analyze its substance and aims in relation to Rousseau's theological and religious thought and his political theory more generally. In my interpretation of the chapter I examine why Rousseau prefaces his brief discussion of the topic of the chapter—the dogmas required by civil religion—with a lengthy sketch of the history of religions and an analysis of the available alternatives—the religion of the citizen, the religion of man, and the religion of the priest—from the perspective of politics. I suggest that this historical sketch and schematic analysis reveal the ultimately irresolvable situation in which we find ourselves with regard to the relationship of politics and religion. In short, Rousseau offers his civil religion as the best available means to address the motivational problem of politics while promoting religious toleration, or, in other words, as the best available way to square the circle of truth and utility.

Finally, in the conclusion I summarize my examination of Rousseau's theological and religious writings in light of his philosophy of the natural goodness of man and his corruption in society. I argue that the tensions between them can be explained by the two oppositions that run through his thought and my analysis of it: first, the different psychic attributes and psychological needs of *natural man* as opposed to *social or moral man*, and second, and following from this first opposition, the criterion of *truth* as opposed to *utility*.

CHAPTER 1

Truth and Utility

Throughout his writings Rousseau is concerned with both the truth of his philosophical system of the natural goodness and the utility of his writings. For example, he opens the Preface to his *Discourse on the Sciences and the Arts* by congratulating the Academy of Dijon for posing a question concerning "metaphysical subtleties," but rather "with one of those truths that pertain to the happiness of the human race" (*Sciences*, 7). If there are truths that are useful for human happiness, there may be other truths that are useless or even pernicious. Indeed, one of the principal lessons of his prize essay is that truth and utility are not always aligned, and even that there is a persistent disproportion between science and virtue.

Nowhere is the tension between truth and utility more problematic than in Rousseau's writings on theology and religion. The problems exist on at least two levels. First, within his thought itself, there is a problematic relationship between his philosophical system, on the one hand, and his discussions of theology and religion, on the other. Simply put, the natural goodness of man and the goodness of nature do not provide a theological and religious doctrine sufficient for humans once they develop into moral beings and are corrupted in society. Rousseau must therefore provide doctrines that provide hope and consolation, that promote virtue and prevent vice, and that are in some tension with his philosophical system. Second, and following from this first problematic relationship, Rousseau's aim of presenting his thought with both truth and utility in mind—as well as the tension between them—poses obvious difficulties for the interpreter of his writings in sorting out their truth and utility.

This chapter takes up these two problematic aspects of Rousseau's theological and religious writings in a general manner, in part to prepare for the detailed analyses of these writings in subsequent chapters. The first section examines Rousseau's argument in the *Discourse on the Sciences and the Arts*, and in his defenses of the work, concerning the disproportion between science and virtue. The second section offers a reading of his own self-examination in the *Reveries of the Solitary Walker* regarding how not telling the truth, or even what we would ordinarily term lying, is permitted or even required of an author. In brief, Rousseau adopts utility as the criterion for telling the truth as well as for departing from the truth. With the general issue of truth and utility in mind, I turn in the third section to its application to Rousseau's theological and religious writings, focusing on Rousseau's defense of the publication of *Emile*, and especially the "Profession of Faith of the Savoyard Vicar," against the condemnation by the archbishop of Paris. The *Letter to Beaumont* takes up a number of subjects central to my analyses of Rousseau's theological and religious writings: first, the relationship between his philosophical system of the natural goodness of man and traditional theological questions; second, the defense of publishing *Emile* and the "Profession" and his other writings in terms of their utility; third, an extensive discussion of his own supposed religious views, which he presents as true and useful.

The Disproportion between Science and Virtue

The *Discourse on the Sciences and the Arts* was the first fruit of Rousseau's discovery of the principle that he later explained animated and unified all of his subsequent works. Writing some dozen years after the momentous event on the way to visit Diderot, imprisoned in the chateau of Vincennes, he described the effect on him of reading the prize essay question proposed by the Academy of Dijon: "Oh Sir, if I had ever been able to write a quarter of what I saw and felt under that tree, how clearly I would have made all the contradictions of the social system seen, with what strength I would have exposed all the abuses of our institutions, with what simplicity I would have demonstrated that man is naturally good and that it is from these institutions alone that he becomes wicked" (*Letters to Malesherbes*, CW, 5:575). Although Rousseau later acknowledged the flaws in his prize essay, he repeatedly maintained that it was inspired by the "Illumination of Vincennes" and was part of his "system" (see *Letters to Malesherbes*, CW, 5:575; see also *Beaumont*, 28–29; *Dialogues*, CW, 1:22–23, 209–13). The relationship between the first *Discourse* and Rousseau's later works has nonetheless been a subject of scholarly debate, with some interpreters accepting the author's testimony and others arguing that the work at best contains elements of his later thought in inchoate form.¹ For the present purposes I need not wade into this debate. Instead, I want to focus on Rousseau's first articulation in the *Discourse* of a problem central to his treatment of theology and religion throughout his writings: the disproportion between science and virtue.²

Writing exactly in the middle of the century of Enlightenment, Rousseau famously argued in answer to the question posed by the Academy of Dijon that the advancement of the sciences and the arts corrupts morals. He further argues that this phenomenon is not restricted to his times, but is universal. "Virtue has been seen to flee in proportion as their light dawned on our horizon, and the same phenomenon has been observed in all times and in all places" (*Sciences*, 15).³ Rousseau's argument in the *Discourse* concerning the relationship between the advancement of the sciences and the arts, on the one hand, and moral virtue, on the other, is more complex than it first appears.⁴ Nonetheless, these first appearances are not altogether incorrect and, whatever further layers or complications to his argument, Rousseau consistently maintains that there is disproportion between science and virtue, truth and practice.

What I am terming a "disproportion" between science and virtue can be more fully articulated as what Rousseau argues is a tension between science or philosophy, on the one hand, and popular morality, on the other. Religious opinions and practices are necessarily implicated in this disproportionate relationship because, in Rousseau's view, they are among the principal bulwarks of popular morality. Philosophy or science undermines popular morality, including civic virtue, for two reasons. First, popular morality and therewith religious opinions are just that, opinions, and the inquiring eye of philosophy undermines those opinions by casting them into doubt. Second, according to Rousseau, philosophy as it is almost universally conducted is animated by pride, and the prideful philosopher is indifferent to the effects of his philosophizing on popular morality. In this section I examine the disproportion between science and virtue with particular reference to religion as it comes to light in the *Discourse* and then in Rousseau's defenses of the work.

The issue of the problematic relationship between philosophic inquiry and popular opinion is raised from the very outset of the *Discourse*. In the Preface Rousseau writes that he is addressing a question that "is concerned with one of those truths that pertain to the happiness of the human race," but he acknowledges that his inquiry into this truth will challenge reigning opinion. "I foresee that I will not easily be forgiven for the side I have dared to take. Clashing head-on with everything that nowadays attracts men's admiration, I can expect only universal blame, and it is not for having been honored with the approbation of a few wise men that I should count on that of the public." In short, he will blame the sciences and the arts in a century in which they are widely admired. Yet he immediately generalizes the problematic relationship between science and public opinion, just as he will do with regard to his argument about the relationship between the sciences and the arts and morality. "In all times there will be men destined to be subjugated by the opinions of their age, their country, their society. Someone who today plays the freethinker and the philosopher would, for the same reason, have been a fanatic at the time of the League" (7). In addition to seeing Rousseau's first formulation of the disproportion between science and virtue, we here glimpse the first hint about the relationship between philosophy and religion. Philosophic "freethinking" will turn out to be as sectarian as religious fanaticism.

What is the relationship between science and virtue? In the Exordium Rousseau addresses the paradox of blaming the sciences and praising ignorance before a learned tribunal. "It is not science I abuse, I told myself; it is virtue I defend before virtuous men" (9). Given his indication of the side he will take in the question, it may come as a surprise that the body of the discourse proper begins with a praise of enlightenment.

> It is a grand and beautiful spectacle to see man emerging, as it were, out of nothingness through his own efforts; dissipating by the light of his reason the shadows in which nature has enveloped him; rising above himself; soaring by his mind to the celestial regions; traversing with the steps of a giant, like the sun, the vast expanse of the universe; and, what is even grander and more difficult, returning into himself in order there to study man and to know his nature, his duties, and his end. All these marvels have been revived in the past few generations. (11)

Several critics suggested that the opening praise of enlightenment contradicted the argument of the work.[5] Yet in response Rousseau never gainsaid the progress of the sciences and the arts, and he was at pains to deny he had. Instead, the question involves their effect on morals. Rousseau begins with what he calls in the Preface "the opinions of their age, their country, their society"—namely, the opinion that there is a harmonious relationship between science and virtue.[6] The opening description of this "grand and beautiful spectacle" paints two movements of this Promethean image: man soaring through his reason into the physical universe and then an "even grander and more difficult" task of man returning to himself "to know his nature, his duties, and his end." These two movements capture the two parts of the Academy's question: the restoration of the sciences and the arts, on the one hand, and the state of morals, on the other. As Rousseau proceeds in the *Discourse* he gradually undermines the initial impression of the apparent harmony between science and virtue.[7]

In order to unsettle the assumption of harmony between science and virtue, Rousseau catalogues the vices hidden behind the appearance of virtue: "Suspicions, offenses, fears, coolness, reserve, hatred, betrayal continually conceal themselves behind that uniform and deceitful veil of civility, behind that much lauded urbanity we owe to the enlightenment of our age" (13). Having done so, he is finally ready to state his argument:

> When there is no effect, there is no cause to seek: but here the effect is certain, the depravity real, and our souls have been corrupted in proportion as our sciences and our arts have advanced toward perfection. Shall it be said that this is a misfortune particular to our age? No, Gentlemen: the evils caused by our vain curiosity are as old as the world. The daily rise and fall of the ocean's waters have not been more regularly subjected to the course of the star that gives us light during the night than has the fate of morals and integrity to the progress of the sciences and the arts. Virtue has been seen to flee in proportion as their light dawned on our horizon, and the same phenomenon has been observed in all times and all places. (14–15)

The disproportion between science and virtue is not restricted to his own time, but is a perennial problem. He states this as a scientific fact, likening the relationship between science and virtue to the relationship between the moon and the tides. Ironically, then, Rousseau employs science to criticize science in the name of virtue.

But that is not how philosophy is customarily employed. While cataloguing historical examples of how the rise of the sciences and the arts has been accompanied by moral corruption, Rousseau remarks on those rustic peoples who remained virtuous: "They were not unaware that in other lands idle men spent their lives arguing over the sovereign good, over vice and virtue, and that prideful reasoners, bestowing the greatest praise on themselves, lumped together other peoples under the contemptuous name of barbarians. But they considered their morals and learned to disdain their doctrine." Actuated by pride, philosophers debate virtue and vice rather than act in accordance with morality. Rousseau nonetheless objects to the abuse of philosophy, not to philosophy itself.[8] Hence his evocation shortly after stating his thesis of Socrates as "the wisest of men" who was among the few who "resisted the general torrent and protected themselves against vice while in the abode of the Muses" (17–18). However, if a Socrates can philosophize while remaining virtuous, a whole people cannot. "Peoples: know once and for all, then, that nature wanted to keep you from science just as a mother tears a dangerous weapon from the hands of her child.... Men are perverse; they would be even worse if they had had the misfortune to be born learned" (20).

The first part of the *Discourse* is largely devoted to historical examples of peoples that become corrupt with the introduction of the sciences and the arts, or what Rousseau terms "historical inductions" based on "uncertain chronicles." He therefore turns in the second part of the work to examine "the sciences and the arts in themselves" by employing "philosophic research" to see whether these inductions hold (21–23). He locates the cause of the corrupting effects of the sciences and the arts in the passions that give rise to the sciences and the arts in the first place:

> Indeed, whether one leafs through the annals of the world, whether one supplements uncertain chronicles with philosophical research, human knowledge will not be found to have an origin that corresponds to the idea one would like to have of it. Astronomy was born from superstition; eloquence from ambition, hatred, flattery, lying; geometry from avarice; physics from vain curiosity; *all of them*, even moral philosophy, from human pride. The sciences and arts therefore owe their birth to our vices. (23; emphasis added)

We can now distinguish between the sciences and the arts "in themselves" and the sciences and the arts as a popular or social phenomenon. In this regard, I note that Rousseau consistently writes of the "advancement" of the sciences and the arts when speaking of their relationship to moral corruption. This distinction helps explain his complex argument in the *Discourse* and elsewhere concerning the disproportion between science and virtue—namely, that there is such a disproportion under certain conditions. First, he maintains that there is a disproportion between science and virtue when the sciences and the arts are pursued as part of a popular or social phenomenon. Second, he argues that the sciences and the arts in themselves can be pursued by certain individuals without corrupting their virtue, meaning that in such cases there is no disproportion between science and virtue—in the case of Socrates, for example. At the very end of the first part of the work he asks two rhetorical questions: "What! Could integrity be the daughter of ignorance? Could science and virtue be incompatible?" (20). His answer to both: yes and no.

Having identified the corrupt sources of the sciences and the arts in the passions, above all in human pride, Rousseau turns to the social and political conditions under which these passions operate. "What would we do with the arts without the luxury that nourishes them?" The sciences arise in similarly dubious circumstances. "If our sciences are vain in the object they propose for themselves, they are still more dangerous through the effects they produce. Born in idleness, they nourish it in their turn, and the inseparable loss of time is the first injury they necessarily do to society." Then, returning to the arts: "The misuse of time is a great evil. Other evils still worse accompany the letters and the arts. One of them is luxury, born like them from men's idleness and vanity. Luxury rarely proceeds without the sciences and the arts, and never do they proceed without it" (23–25). Rousseau thereby points to the social conditions, notably inequality, that foster the corrupt passions that are the source of the sciences and the arts and then give rise to their further corrupting effects on society. In short, the advancement of the sciences and the arts and moral corruption rise in proportion to one another as the concurrent and mutually reinforcing effects of man's corruption in society.

What about the disproportion between science and virtue, then? The specific danger of science to popular morality and civic virtue is part of Rousseau's analysis. When he turns to the sciences after first remarking how the arts are nourished by luxury, he remarks on the difficulty of ascertaining the truth through scientific investigation given all the doubts involved, or what he terms "a dangerous Pyrrhonism" (14). "How many errors, a thousand times more dangerous than the truth is useful, must be braved in order to reach it!" Here we glimpse one of the reasons he argues that there is a disproportion between science and virtue: philosophy sows dangerous doubt and error, and, further, the truths it does discover are of dubious utility. He expands on the supposed uselessness of philosophic inquiry by listing a series of scientific discoveries, such as the fact that the orbits of the planets are the ratios of the areas covered in equal times, or Kepler's law, an example that should make us recall the initial praise of enlightenment of man "soaring by his mind to the celestial regions" and then returning into himself to seek his duties. Rousseau now suggests that the seemingly harmonious relationship between science and virtue is at best uncertain: "Answer me, I say, you from whom we have received so much sublime knowledge: even if you had never taught us any of these things, would we be any less populous, less well-governed, less formidable, less flourishing or more perverse? Reexamine, then, the importance of your productions," philosophic productions that "procure us so little utility" (24–25).

The supposed uselessness of science from the perspective of politics and morals would render it risible. Yet the doubts it sows already suggest one way in which science might be corrosive to popular morality. To this Rousseau adds the pride and irresponsibility with which philosophers typically commune with their muse. Having remarked on the idleness in which the sciences are born and then nourish, he exclaims:

> What am I saying, idle? And would to God they were indeed! Morals would be healthier and society more peaceful. But those vain and futile declaimers go about everywhere, armed with their deadly paradoxes, undermining the foundations of faith and annihilating virtue. They laugh disdainfully at those old-fashioned words "fatherland" and "religion" and consecrate their talents and their philosophy to destroying and degrading all that is sacred among men. Not that at bottom they hate either virtue or our dogmas: it is public opinion to which they are hostile, and in order to bring them back to the altars, it would be enough to banish them among the atheists. O rage for distinction! What will you not do? (25)

Presumably these philosophers are "vain and futile" because of the emptiness and uncertainty of their inquiries, as well as "vain" in the sense of prideful. They appear to be motivated by the desire for recognition, for they "declaim," and they are either indifferent or hostile to the effects of their "deadly paradoxes" on the foundations of religious faith and virtue—that is, public opinion. They are even indifferent to religious belief, equal opportunity atheists or believers depending on which side lies distinction, both in the sense of distinguishing themselves from public opinion and in the sense of seeking reputation. In sum, insofar as philosophy necessarily entails questioning opinions, there is in principle a disproportion between science and popular virtue. Insofar as philosophy is conducted for prideful motives and in open hostility to public opinions, it is also inimical in practice to the foundations of religious faith and popular morality.

The popularization of the sciences and the arts is Rousseau's principal concern with regard to their effects on morals. We are no longer concerned with virtues and instead cultivate talents. "We have physicists, geometers, chemists, astronomers, poets, musicians, painters. We no longer have citizens." Since we now have the sciences and the arts, they should be confined to select societies such as the Academy of Dijon, drawing a remedy from the very poison. In this context, then, he returns to the inimical effects of philosophy. "What is philosophy?" he asks. "What do the writings of the best-known philosophers contain? What are the teachings of those friends of wisdom? To listen to them, wouldn't one take them for a troop of charlatans crying out, each from his spot on the public square: 'Come to me, it is I who alone does not deceive'?" In other words, the philosophers are sectarians who seek victory over their opponents and acclaim from the public. Most of the philosophic teachings Rousseau mentions concern religion and morality, with one claiming there is no other God than the world (Spinoza), another that there are neither virtues nor vices (Mandeville), and still another that men are wolves and can devour one another in clear conscience (Hobbes). "O great philosophers! Why do you not save these profitable teachings for your friends and your children? You would soon reap the reward, and we would no longer fear finding any of your sectarians among our own" (32–33). Philosophers are more interested in recruiting sectarians than they are with the effects of their teachings.

Rousseau's concern with how philosophy or science is pursued as a public activity comes to light in the closing pages of the *Discourse* in a way that reveals the complex nature of his understanding of the disproportion between science and virtue. First, when he asks, "What do the writings of the best-known philosophers contain?" he is particularly concerned with their writings as writings, that is, as works available to any reader. "Did paganism, given over to all the aberrations of human reason, leave to posterity anything that could be compared to the shameful memorials that printing has prepared for it under the reign of the Gospel?" Thanks to typography "the dangerous reveries of the likes of Hobbes and of Spinoza will last forever." But let me also draw attention to his mention of "the reign of the Gospel" in his question. To be sure, this phrase is meant to counterbalance the earlier mention of the times of paganism, but it also calls attention to the fact that the Gospel is a written work and that the tenets of Christianity are promulgated through writing. As we shall see later, one of his concerns in investigating religions is the interpretation of Scripture and the utility of the Gospel as he interprets it. At any rate, the invention of printing has exacerbated the problem of the disproportion between science and virtue by making the products of philosophy or science indiscriminately available to the public. "What shall we think of those compilers of works who have indiscreetly broken down the door of the sciences and let into their sanctuary a populace unworthy of approaching them . . . ?" (33–34).

Yet if the public cannot safely pursue the sciences without corruption, Rousseau now declares that a few individuals can do so, meaning that there is no disproportion between science and virtue in some rare cases. He had earlier mentioned Socrates as his ancient example in this regard, and now he names three modern exemplars: Bacon, Descartes, and Newton. "If some men must be allowed to give themselves over to the study of the sciences and the arts, it is only those who feel they have the strength to walk alone in their footsteps and go beyond them. It belongs to this small number to raise monuments to the glory of the human mind" (34–35). Where there is no disproportion between science and virtue because of the genius of mind and strength of soul of those who practice the sciences and the arts, Rousseau commends the pursuit. Indeed, he engages in it himself.

Alas, such "preceptors of the human race" are rare individuals. In closing, then, Rousseau adopts the persona of a humble member of the people: "As for us, common men, to whom heaven has not imparted such great talents and has not destined for so much glory, let us remain in our obscurity.... O virtue! Sublime science of simple souls, are then so many efforts and preparations needed to know you? Are not your principles engraved in all hearts, and is it not enough to learn your laws to return into oneself and to listen to the voice of one's conscience in the silence of the passions?" (34–36). To recur to the opening Promethean image at the head of the body of the *Discourse*, for most people the passions actuated by the desire to soar by the mind into the celestial regions are antithetical to virtue, but it is not necessary thus to soar into those regions in order to return into oneself to be virtuous. Where there exists a disproportion between science and virtue, Rousseau counsels the untutored practice of virtue.

Within the general argument of the *Discourse* concerning the disproportion between science and virtue we glimpse how religious beliefs and practices are implicated in this disproportion, but it is not Rousseau's main theme in the work. His concern with religion in this respect is more salient in his defenses of the *Discourse*, notably in the *Observations by Jean-Jacques Rousseau of Geneva on the Reply Made to His Discourse*, which appeared later in the same year as the *Discourse* itself. Although published anonymously, Rousseau and everyone else knew the work was by Stanisław Leszczyński, the titular king of Poland and father-in-law to the French king. The *Observations* was Rousseau's lengthiest piece in the polemical exchange over the *Discourse*, and it is best known for a passage in which he arranges the "genealogy" of the advancement of the sciences and the arts in relation to moral corruption, arguing that inequality is the ultimate progenitor of both the sciences and the arts and moral corruption (*Observations*, CW, 1:48). What is more pertinent to the present inquiry is Rousseau's lengthy treatment of the relationship between philosophy and religion.[9]

In the portion of the *Observations* preceding his turn to the question of religion, Rousseau restates his view of what I have termed the disproportion between science and virtue. He does so by clarifying his argument in the *Discourse* by way of reply to a number of Stanislaus's remarks on what he sees as its paradoxical argument. For example, the king was among those who viewed the opening praise of enlightenment in the *Discourse* as inconsistent with the main argument of the work or as willfully paradoxical, remarking that such praise must have been "costly" for Rousseau to make and then, worse, to retract (in *CW*, 1:29). Rousseau responds that he offered his praise of enlightenment in all sincerity, and then clarifies the argument of the *Discourse*. "Science is very good in itself, that is evident." However, despite its purity, it engenders doubts, uncertainties, absurd systems, and these corrupting effects are due to the fact that "science—as beautiful and sublime as it is—is not made for man; that he has too limited a mind to make much progress in it, and too many passions in his heart not to put it to bad use." Further, it distracts men from their primary duties and ignites their passions to vice. The "cultivation of the sciences corrupts the morals of a nation," he states, noting that he had carefully distinguished in his argument between the "truly learned" or "a few privileged souls" and "an entire people."[10] He explains that "the study of the Universe ought to exalt man toward his Creator, I know, but it exalts only human vanity." Instead of relying on science or philosophy to discover morality, we need only listen to our internal guide to "lead us innocently" (*Observations, CW*, 1:37–42). In short, Rousseau asserts that he never claimed that knowledge and virtue are necessarily incompatible, or that ignorance was required for virtue, but he instead maintains that he argued that there is a disproportion between science and virtue for the vast majority of people.

Rousseau's specific attention to the relationship between philosophy and religion occurs in a lengthy excursus in which he replies to some remarks concerning religion by Stanislaus (or, more likely, his assistant in the enterprise, the Jesuit Father Menou). These remarks come at the end of the first part of Stanislaus's *Reply*, and so in response to the end of the first part of Rousseau's *Discourse*. Tellingly, this is the point in the *Discourse* at which Rousseau addresses "peoples": "Peoples: know once and for all, then, that nature wanted to keep you from science just as a mother tears a dangerous weapon from the hands of her child" (*Sciences*, 20). We can therefore anticipate that Rousseau's discussion of religion in response to Stanislaus concerns the relationship between philosophy and popular religious belief. Stanislaus objects that the abuses of philosophy and its deleterious effects on morals can be defeated by religion. "It is pride and obstinacy that produce schisms and heresies. It is Pyrrhonism and incredulity that favor independence, revolt, passions, all the heinous crimes." Stanislaus writes. "Such adversaries do honor to religion. To defeat them, it has only to appear; by itself, it is capable of confounding them all." And Stanislaus has a broad understanding of this invincible religion: Scripture, theology, moral philosophy, and the study of nature. His assumption is that these various approaches to religion are all in harmonious accord, a "pure enlightenment" that supports religion and virtue alike (in *CW*, 1:32). In reply, Rousseau turns to examine the main premise of Stanislaus's argument concerning the supposed harmony between science and religion.

The investigation on which Rousseau now embarks takes the form of a historical sketch of the relationship between Christianity and philosophy. A brief recap will suffice. According to him, the sciences were not part of the Jewish religion, and the disputes between the Pharisees and Sadducees had little to do with science and everything to do with pride. More importantly, philosophy had no place in the simple faith of the Gospel preached by Jesus and the apostles. Alarmed by the success of the preaching of the Gospel and their loss of revenue, the pagan priests first leagued themselves with the secular authorities to persecute the Christians and then made common cause with the pagan philosophers, "who did not find their advantage in a religion that preaches humility." Infused with the same pride as their persecutors, the Christians themselves became "furious persecutors among themselves." Worse, the Christians took up the arms of philosophy in their disputes, including in the dispute over whether they should even make use of philosophy in the dispute. After the respite of the Dark Ages, with the revival of letters these disputes were renewed, as ever animated by pride and the desire for victory. Finally, reaching the present day, Rousseau finds the sciences and the arts flourishing: "Science spread and faith vanishes. Everyone wants to teach how to do good, and no one wants to learn. We have all become scholars and we have ceased to be Christians." Having completed his tour, Rousseau summarizes the lesson we are to learn: we should abandon the books of philosophy and "prideful science" and instead practice the morality of the Gospel with "Christian humility" (*Observations, CW*, 1:44–48).

The particular danger posed to popular morality by prideful philosophy mixed with religion is suggested by a lengthy note Rousseau includes in the excursus. The note is added to his discussion of the Christians who first turned to philosophy to defend their faith. He begins the note by claiming that Justin Martyr and others who availed themselves of philosophy "upheld precisely the same sentiment" as he himself does—namely, that philosophy and faith should be kept separate. As for the philosophers, Rousseau emphasizes their sectarian character and their disdain for popular opinion. After quoting a lengthy passage (in Latin) from Diogenes Laertius in which a Cyrenaic philosopher brags about how the "wise man" scorns common morality and "the public opinion of fools and simpletons," he maintains that such contempt for popular morality and opinion is common to *all* philosophers. Rousseau adduces as proof of his claim the supposed fact that "all" philosophers, ancient and modern, have practiced esoteric communication.[11] "And what shall we say about the distinction between the two doctrines so eagerly received by all the Philosophers, and by which they professed in secret sentiments contrary to those they taught publicly?" Indeed, he extends this claim to non-Western philosophy when he notes that the Chinese also follow "the esoteric doctrine."[12] He maintains that Pythagoras and all the other philosophers gave lessons in atheism to their disciples in secret while professing adherence to the established religion in public. One might attribute the motive for this esotericism to the desire not to meet the fate of Socrates, but Rousseau instead suggests the motive is pride: to distinguish themselves from the crowd and from other philosophical sects. He concludes the note: "But Philosophy will always defy reason, truth, and even time, because it has its source in human pride, stronger than all those things" (*Observations*, CW, 1:45–46n).

The argument in the *Observations* concerning the pernicious effects of philosophy can be seen as a special case of the more general argument of the *Discourse* (and *Observations*) concerning the effect of the advancement of the sciences and the arts on morals, but it is much more directly related to the issue of religion, and especially Christianity, than anything in the *Discourse* itself. If his position in the *Observations* about the incompatibility of philosophy and religious faith and popular morality *in practice* is clear, it is unclear whether he believes they are incompatible *in principle*. Perhaps some light is shed on this question by noting his emphasis in the *Observations* on the sectarian character of philosophy, and also by remarking on the fact that in the *Discourse* he speaks of the morally corrupting effects of the *advancement* of the sciences and the arts. That is, in both cases he is considering philosophy or science as a *social* phenomenon, not philosophy in itself. If so, his position would seem to be that, for all intents and purposes, philosophy and religious faith and popular morality are incompatible, not because philosophy per se is deleterious but because in all but the most unusual cases philosophers are actuated by pride.

Finally, Rousseau's critique of philosophy in relation to popular morality is particularly clear in another of his early writings, the "Preface" to his play *Narcissus*, which is in effect a defense of the *Discourse on the Sciences and the Arts*. Confronting head-on the charge that he is inconsistent or hypocritical for criticizing the sciences and the arts in his prize essay while himself continuing to work as a practicing scientist and artist, Rousseau repeats his argument. "Among a people the taste for letters always proclaims a beginning of corruption which it very promptly accelerates," for this taste "in a whole nation" derives from idleness and the desire to distinguish oneself. "The taste for letters, philosophy and the fine arts destroys love of our primary duties and of genuine glory," substituting civility for virtue. This taste further enervates our bodies and souls. "The taste for philosophy loosens in us all the bonds of esteem and benevolence that attach men to society, and this is perhaps the most dangerous of the ills engendered by it." The philosopher "concentrates into his person all the interest that virtuous men share with their fellows: his contempt for others turns to the profit of his pride: his amour-propre increases in the same proportion as his indifference to the rest of the universe. For him, family, fatherland become words devoid of meaning: he is neither parent, nor citizen, nor man; he is a philosopher" ("Preface" to *Narcissus*, CW, 1:191–92). While some "sublime geniuses" admittedly know how to "pierce through the veils in which the truth is enveloped" free of vanity, jealousy, and the other passions, they are rare souls: "For if all men were Socrates, science would not be harmful to them, but they would have no need of it" (195). The harm of science to a people derives from the fact that opinions and customs are the basis of popular morality.

> Every people which has morals, and which consequently respects its laws and does not at all want to refine its ancient practices, ought to secure itself against the sciences, and above all against the learned, whose sententious and dogmatic maxims would soon teach it to despise its practices and its laws; which a nation can never do without being corrupted. The smallest change in customs, even if it is advantageous in certain respects, always turns to the disadvantage of morals. For customs are the morality of the people; and as soon as it ceases to respect them, it no longer has any rule except its passions nor bridle than the laws, which can sometimes hold back the wicked, but never make them good. (195)

Customs are the morality of the people, and among those customs are religious beliefs and practices. As Rousseau would later write in defense of *Emile* and the *Social Contract*, "Religion is useful and even necessary for peoples" (*Mountain*, 140). If religion is useful and even necessary for peoples, then to what extent is the philosopher obligated to respect popular morality, including religious beliefs, for example, by remaining silent about the truth of established beliefs if they are salutary, or even justified in promoting salutary opinions despite their dubiety?

On Truth and Lies in the Moral Sense

Rousseau's understanding of his authorial responsibilities with respect to the public effects of his writings flows directly from the disproportion between science and virtue he identifies in the *Discourse on the Sciences and the Arts*. This understanding guides him in all of his published works, and I would also suggest in his unpublished writings and letters as well. The interpretive problem is as simple to state as it is difficult to resolve: How can an author whose motto is *Vitam impendere vero*—"To consecrate one's life to the truth"[13]—justify his departures from the truth? The interpretive problem is only made more difficult when we consider that Rousseau insisted on taking responsibility for his works by openly and insistently proclaiming his authorship, an unusual practice in an era when most books appeared anonymously or pseudonymously, including almost all the major philosophic and literary writings of the Enlightenment. Christopher Kelly has addressed these issues in his excellent *Rousseau as Author*. I limit myself here to a brief discussion of Rousseau's ruminations in the *Reveries of the Solitary Walker* on how not telling the truth, and even plain lying, are consistent with, and even dictated by, his responsibilities as an author.

Rousseau's reflections on how withholding the truth or even lying are consistent with his motto of dedicating himself to the truth are found in the "Fourth Walk" of the *Reveries*, but we must begin with the "Third Walk" because the two promenades are explicitly yoked together. The pairing of the two walks is indicated by the fact that Rousseau begins the "Third Walk" with an epigraph containing a saying by Solon, "I continue to learn while growing old" (*Reveries*, 17), and then returns to the aphorism at the very end of the "Fourth Walk" (40).[14] (Interestingly, Plutarch also repeats Solon's saying at the beginning and end of his *Life of Solon*, and, perhaps meaningfully for interpreting Rousseau's discussion of lying, the second occasion occurs with Plutarch remarking on Solon's unfinished "account or myth" [*logon ē mython*] of Atlantis.[15]) Importantly for our purposes, the subject of the "Third Walk" is Rousseau's reminiscence of settling his religious views in the wake of the doubts sown by his former friends the *philosophes*, while the "Fourth Walk" contains his reflections on the moral question of truth and lies.[16] We may suppose, then, that his reflections pertain to matters concerned with theology and religion.

In the "Third Walk" Rousseau relates how he decided to settle his opinions at the age of forty and never again review or revise them. The time of reckoning as he tells it therefore occurred immediately following the "Illumination of Vincennes" and the publication of the prize essay that made him famous. He describes the setting for his external and internal reform: "A great revolution which had just taken place in me; another moral world which was unveiling itself to my observations; men's insane judgments, whose absurdity I was beginning to feel," and so on (19–20). The problem was the company he kept.

> I was living then among modern philosophers who hardly resembled the ancient ones. Instead of removing my doubts and ending my irresolution, they had shaken all the certainty I thought I had concerning the things that were most important for me to know. Ardent missionaries of atheism and very imperious dogmatists, there was no way that they would, without anger, put up with anyone daring to think other than they did about any point whatsoever. (21)

Perhaps Rousseau specifies that the modern philosophers do not resemble the ancients because the latter at least paid homage to public opinion and popular morality by restricting their inimical doctrines to private communication. At any rate, he claims of his former friends: "They had not persuaded me, but they had troubled me. Their arguments had shaken me without having ever convinced me" (21).

The task of reviewing his opinions was an arduous one, Rousseau writes, casting himself as a Theseus caught in the darkness of a labyrinth, but he persisted. "After the most ardent and sincere seeking that has perhaps ever made by any mortal, I determined for my whole life all the sentiments important for me to have; and though I may have deceived myself in my conclusions, I am at least sure that my error cannot be imputed to me as a crime, for I made every effort to keep myself from it." The source of at least some of his possible self-deceptions is revealing: "To be sure, I have no doubt but what the prejudices of childhood and the secret wishes of my heart made the scale lean to the side of the most consoling for me. It is difficult to keep ourselves from believing what we so ardently desire," and he gives as an instance the "hope or fear" we have concerning the afterlife (21–22). To recur to the language of persuasion and conviction, by his own admission his reasonings on these matters lacked the full force of rational conviction considering the doubtfulness inherent in the subject matter, and at least some of the conclusions he reached were the result of the persuasive force of prejudices, hopes, fears, and consolation. We will see him employ similar language concerning the scale of deliberation inclining to the more consoling side in the *Letter to Voltaire*, the "Profession of Faith," and elsewhere.

Having described the process of settling his opinions, he compares his reckoning to what is contained in the "Profession of Faith." Scholars often refer to this passage to justify the assumption that the Savoyard Vicar speaks for Rousseau. Let us scrutinize the passage.

> The result [*résultat*] of my painful seeking was approximately [*à peu près*] that which I set down [*je l'ai consigné*] afterward in the "Profession of Faith of the Savoyard Vicar," a work unwarrantedly prostituted and profaned among the present generation but which may one day make a revolution among men, if good sense and good faith are ever reborn among them. (22–23)

What is the "result" or "outcome" of his painful seeking? Rousseau's word choice is ambiguous. Does he refer to the specific "articles of faith" that the Savoyard Vicar posits—for example, concerning the existence of the divinity and the afterlife? Or does he refer to the process of introspection itself, including the doubts inherent in the endeavor and its results, limitations that both Rousseau and the Savoyard Vicar admit? As Charles Butterworth notes, "The whole account of the reform is limited to a discussion of *how* these thoughts were reached. There is no description of their substance nor any defense of their logical soundness."[17] In either case, Rousseau states that the "result" was "approximately," or "more or less," what is contained in the "Profession." How close he does not say. Finally, his choice of phrasing of having "set down" the "result"—*je l'ai consigné*—is potentially interesting. The verb *consigner* has the main sense of "to report" something, but the use of the *passé composé* in particular evokes the alternative sense of having "consigned" or "confined" something or someone somewhere, as in "consigned/confined to barracks," a phrasing that has the effect of distancing himself from what is reported in the "Profession." At any rate, Rousseau is studiously cagey about just how close his own religious and other views are to those professed by the Savoyard Vicar.

In the remainder of the "Third Walk," Rousseau relates that although he was sometimes "troubled" by the doubts he entertained concerning the views he had adopted—"How many times in these moments of doubt and uncertainty was I ready to abandon myself to despair!"—he never abandoned them. "Serene in this disposition, I find in it, along with self-contentment, the hope and consolation I need in my situation." Returning at the end of the promenade to Solon's aphorism, he reflects some twenty-five years after his painful quest that, since he refuses to resubmit his views to renewed scrutiny, unlike the sage he does not continue to learn while growing old. To learning he opposes practicing virtue, the task to which he does devote himself in his dotage (25–27). The disproportion between science and virtue persists.

Turning now to the "Fourth Walk," Rousseau reports there that the ruminations on truth and lies set forth in the promenade were occasioned one day by his reading of two texts. The first text was from the author he says most "benefits" him, that is, the author he finds most useful: Plutarch. The text is "How to Profit from One's Enemies," in which the author counsels profiting from self-examination in the face of criticism by an enemy. The second text was a pamphlet by someone he takes to be an enemy, a certain Abbé Rosier. The title page of the pamphlet included an epigraph that he takes to mock his own motto of dedicating his life to truth, and so he takes the implied criticism as the occasion to examine himself in accord with the maxim "Know thyself" inscribed on the Temple of Delphi (28). Rousseau's choice of the text from Plutarch is interesting for the present purpose because the work provided the legend to the frontispiece of the *Discourse on the Sciences and the Arts*. Recall that the frontispiece depicts Prometheus bringing the sciences and arts to mankind, with three figures in the engraving: Prometheus, a man, and a satyr who is attempting to grasp the torch. The legend reads: "Satyr, you do not know it." Below the legend Rousseau refers the reader to a passage in the essay in which he elaborates on the legend by quoting from the unidentified source: "'The satyr,' an ancient fable goes, 'wanted to kiss and embrace the fire the first time he saw it, but Prometheus called out to him: Satyr, you will mourn the beard on your chin, for it burns when it is touched'" (*Sciences*, 2, 23n). As a number of interpreters have noted, the continuation of the passage in Plutarch's essay complicates the warning to the satyr, for Prometheus goes on to reveal that the fire "gives light and warmth, and is an implement serving all the arts providing one knows how to use it well."[18] In other words, the legend drawn from Plutarch speaks directly to the disproportion between science and virtue that is the subject of Rousseau's prize essay.

The self-examination prompted by this enemy's mockery of his motto leads Rousseau to confront the fact that despite his dedication to truth he had frequently passed off his "inventions" as true, and moreover he felt no remorse for his "fabrications" despite having a heart that abhors falsehood. How to resolve this apparent contradiction? "I remember having read in a philosophy book that to lie is to conceal a truth we ought to make manifest," he begins his inquiry. "From that definition, it indeed follows that to withhold a truth we have no obligation to declare is not a lie. But does he who, not being content with not telling the truth in such a case, says the opposite, lie or not? According to the definition, we could not say that he lies." In other words, both passively withholding the truth and actively stating a falsehood are not cases of lying where the truth is not owed. Rousseau therefore asks (1) when and how we owe the truth; (2) whether there are cases when we may innocently deceive. The answer to the first question is in essence that a truth is owed when it is useful. The corollary to this answer is that truths that are not useful are not owed, and therefore may be concealed. "Nothing of that which is good for nothing can be owed; for a thing to be owed, it is necessary that it be, or that it may be, useful" (29–30).

Are there cases where we may innocently deceive? Rousseau's answer to the second question is more complex. He begins with a distinction: "Not to say what is true and to say what is false are two very different things." Building on his answer to the first question, he argues that falsehood properly speaking is to say what is not true in the case where the truth is useful, and thus where the falsehood is injurious. In turn, "not to say what is true" is the case where the truth is not useful or is indifferent, and therefore not saying the truth is indifferent or not injurious. Indeed, "not to say what is true" might be useful, and even more useful than telling the truth, for "particular and individual truth is not always a good; it is sometimes an evil, very often an indifferent thing." In fact, Rousseau argues that, because in society private interests are often opposed to one another and are also often opposed to the public interests, it would in fact be injurious always to adhere to telling the truth (30–31). The criterion for knowing when to tell or withhold the truth is once again utility.[19]

And utility is also the criterion for knowing when "not to say what is true," or—despite Rousseau's distinctions—in ordinary parlance, when to lie. "To lie without profit or prejudice to ourselves or another is not to lie: it is not a lie; it is a fiction." What about cases where the fiction is intended to be beneficial? "Fictions which have a moral purpose are called allegories or fables; and as their purpose is or ought to be only to wrap useful truths in easily perceived and pleasing forms, in such cases we hardly care about hiding the *de facto* lie, which is only the cloak of truth; and he who merely sets forth a fable as a fable in no way lies" (32). Rousseau first offers the example of stories and novels, and we might think in this regard of his *Julie*, and especially the Second Preface, or "Conversation about Novels," in which he playfully entertains the question of whether the letters he claims to have found and assembled as the work's editor (and not author) are "real" or "fictional" (*Julie, CW,* 6:8–22). We should note that he will also claim that he is the editor (and not the author) of the "Profession of Faith." Is that writing a "fable," too?

Returning to the *Reveries*, he states that to insistently offer such a fiction as "real truths" (*vérités réelles*) is undeniably to tell "true lies" (*vrais mensonges*). Nonetheless, nobody has any considerable scruples about these lies or seriously reproached someone for telling them. His example in this context is the story the *Temple de Gnide*, and Rousseau respects the anonymity of the author by not naming Montesquieu. The author presents the work as a translation of a Greek manuscript that fell into his hands, a transparent falsehood but also an innocent or even beneficial one if the work has a moral purpose, which Rousseau thinks it does not because its religious façade only thinly veils its lascivious contents (32–33). Is Rousseau's choice of a story with a religious theme (and an erotic context) designed to make us think of the "Profession of Faith"?

Returning to his ruminations, Rousseau argues that truthfulness does not consist in faithfully citing facts concerning indifferent matters, especially when such truth-tellers color the facts when it concerns themselves. Rather: "The man I call *truthful* does just the opposite. In perfectly indifferent things, the truth the other man then respects so strongly concerns him very little; and he will scarcely have scruples about amusing a group of people with contrived facts from which no unjust judgment results." But he will be "solidly *truthful*, even against his self-interest" where it is a question of profit or hurt, and so on, to himself or others. Such a lover of truth may well alloy his speech with falsehoods when they concern indifferent matters, but will be scrupulously truthful when it is useful. What about a lie that is useful? Rousseau closes his rumination by returning to the *Temple de Gnide*. "If the *Temple de Gnide* is a useful work, the story about the Greek manuscript is only a very innocent fiction; it is a lie very worthy of punishment if the work is dangerous" (33–34). The test is utility.

"Such were my rules of conscience about lying and truth," and so Rousseau completes his reasonings and returns to himself. He carefully avoids harmful lies and even white lies. But he admits that he often resorts to falsehoods—for example, when his slow mind fails to keep up with the conversation. "When I absolutely have to speak and amusing truths do not come to mind soon enough, I concoct fables so as not to remain mute." He offers fictions about indifferent matters, and more importantly he substitutes a "moral truth" for the factual truth, "that is to say, to portray effectively the affections natural to the human heart and always to set forth some useful instruction, to make of them, in a word, moral tales or allegories." Rather than identifying the "useful instructions" he has set forth, Rousseau tells some stories about occasions on which he lied—for example, to protect someone, in this case a friend who accidentally caused the young Jean-Jacques's fingers to be crushed.

"*Magnanima menzogna! O quando è il vero / Si bello che si possa a te preporre?*" he exclaims (35–38).[20] Rousseau concludes his recollections: "From all these reflections, it follows that the commitment I made to truthfulness is founded more on feelings of uprightness and equity than the reality of things, and that in practice I have more readily followed the moral dictates of my conscience than abstract notions of the true and the false. I have frequently concocted fables, but very rarely lied." Adopting his motto has given Rousseau an almost unbearable burden, perhaps never permitting him to "let fictions or fables come out of a mouth *and a pen* which had been specifically consecrated to the truth." In other words, he has let fictions or fables issue from his pen. He concludes his walk by saying with Solon that he has indeed learned something in old age from these reflections (39–40; emphasis added). Namely, he has learned the justification for his departures from the unalloyed truth because of their utility.

Truth and Utility in the *Letter to Beaumont*

In defending the publication of *Emile* and especially of the "Profession of Faith of the Savoyard Vicar" against the condemnation by the archbishop of Paris, Rousseau announces his dedication to the truth: "I have promised to speak it in every useful thing as long as it is in me" (*Beaumont*, 52). Evidently his authorship of the "Profession of Faith" is not among the "useful" things about which he has promised to speak the truth, for he does not acknowledge his authorship of the "Profession" and instead maintains he is its editor. The *Letter to Beaumont* offers us a perspective on two central issues in this book. First, it throws light on the relationship between his philosophical system of the natural goodness of man and traditional theological and religious teachings, especially original sin. Second, Rousseau's extended discussion of the tension between truth and utility in matters of theology and religion lends precision to the general issues of the disproportion between science and virtue and the question examined thus far of what an author owes in terms of telling the truth. One might say schematically that the first issue concerns Rousseau's defense of what he writes in his own name in *Emile*, that is, the truth of his philosophical system, and that the second issue encompasses his defense of the publication of the "Profession of Faith," that is, the utility of promulgating certain theological doctrines and religious practices. In addition, Rousseau expounds his own supposed religious views, although here too his emphasis is on their utility. I take up each of these issues in turn.

THE PRINCIPLE OF THE NATURAL GOODNESS OF MAN AGAINST THE DOCTRINE OF ORIGINAL SIN

Settled in the mountain village of Môtiers after his flight into exile, Rousseau wrote a reply to the *mandement* issued against his book by the archbishop of Paris, with the open letter dated November 18, 1763, then published in February of the following year. "Why must I have something to say to you, your Grace?" he begins. "What common language can we speak, how can we understand one another, and what is there between you and me?" (*Beaumont*, 21).[21] The wide gulf between the powerful prelate and the fugitive author is already indicated by the full title: *Jean-Jacques Rousseau, Citizen of Geneva, to Christophe de Beaumont, Archbishop of Paris, Duke of St. Cloud, Peer of France, Commander of the Order of the Holy Spirit, Patron of the Sorbonne, Etc.* (19).[22] David armed with his pen alone against Goliath with all his titles and entitlements.

Rousseau opens the *Letter to Beaumont* by stating that he is obliged to reply because, despite the lack of a common language between them and the gulf between their stations, the archbishop had attacked not only his book but himself.[23] "Yet I must reply to you. You force me to do so yourself. If you had attacked only my book, I would have let it pass, but you also attack me personally" (21). The personal attack with which Beaumont begins his pastoral letter consists in accusing Rousseau of willful inconsistency and perfidious intention: "From the bosom of error, there arose a man full of the language of philosophy without being a genuine philosopher," Beaumont proclaimed, "a mind endowed with a multitude of knowledge that did not enlighten him, and that spread darkness in other minds; a character given to paradoxes of opinions and conduct. . . . He made himself the preceptor of the human race in order to deceive it, the public monitor in order to lead everyone astray, the oracle of the century in order to complete its destruction" (in *CW* 9:3–4). Rousseau's response to this attack consists in maintaining the consistency of his works and in defending his intentions in publishing his writings.

Characterizing himself as something of an accidental author thrust into the public realm, Rousseau claims that his works, beginning with the *Discourse on the Sciences and the Arts* up through *Emile*, are consistent, and this despite the contradictory judgments they have received. "I have written on various subjects, but always with the same principles: always the same morality, the same belief, the same maxims, and if you will the same opinions. . . . Now I am impious. Soon perhaps I will be devout" (21–22). Rousseau thus shows himself to be aware that his writings raise questions about his true opinions, including on matters of religion. He questions the jurisdiction of the archbishop of Paris and the Parliament of Paris in condemning the writings of a Genevan published in Holland, but his main point is that all of his previous writings contained the same "maxims" and circulated freely without condemnation. "Yet all these books, which you have read, since you judge them, are imbued with the same maxims. The same modes of thought are not more disguised in them. If the subject was not suited to developing them to the same extent, they gain in force what they lose in extent, and the author's profession of faith is found expressed there with less reserve than that of the Savoyard Vicar." Note that we already have two "professions of faith": Rousseau's own as author of *Emile* and his other works and that of the Vicar. A page later he is even more emphatic: "I will defend myself, then, but I will defend my honor rather than my book. I am examining not the profession of faith of the Savoyard Vicar, but the Pastoral Letter of the Archbishop of Paris, and it is only the bad things he says about the editor that force me to talk about the work" (26–27). Rousseau is the "editor" of the "Profession," not the author. These are the first of several instances where he will insist upon the distinction between himself and the Vicar.

The "maxims" that animate the works are soon revealed. "The fundamental principle of all morality, about which I have reasoning in all my writings and developed in this last one with all the clarity of which I was capable, is that man is a naturally good being, loving justice and order; that there is no original perversity in the human heart, and that the first movements of nature are always right." The correlate to the natural goodness of man is his corruption in society. Rousseau claims that he has been able to explain the source of our wickedness without resorting to the doctrine of original sin, admitting to the archbishop that his philosophical system is directed against that gloomy doctrine. He casts doubt on the doctrine on scriptural grounds, stating: "First, it is not at all certain, in my view, that this doctrine of original sin, subject as it is to such terrible difficulties, is contained in the Scriptures either as clearly or as harshly as it has pleased the rhetorician Augustine and our theologians to construct it." He also does so on theological grounds, saying that the doctrine "greatly obscure[s] the justice and the goodness of the supreme Being." However, his main argument is philosophical: "Original sin explains everything except its own principle, and it is this principle that has to be explained. . . . Man was created good. We both agree on that, I believe. But you say he is wicked because he was wicked. And I show how he was wicked. Which of us, in your opinion, better ascends to the principle?" (28–31).

In his pastoral letter the archbishop had indeed remarked on how the principle animating *Emile* contradicted the doctrine of original sin. As proof he cites a passage in which Rousseau wrote: "Let us set down . . . as an incontestable maxim that the first movements of nature are always right. There is no original perversity in the human heart" (in *CW*, 9:4). The archbishop ceases quoting at this point, but the passage continues in the original with the point Rousseau underscores in his reply: "There is not a single vice to be found in it of which it cannot be said how and whence it entered" (*Emile*, 92). He acknowledges that the archbishop is correct in his criticism—of what he writes in his own name, that is. Where Beaumont is incorrect is in attributing to him what the Vicar says, and he once again distinguishes between himself and the Vicar (31–32). I note for now that nowhere in the "Profession" do we find any discussion of the natural goodness of man. Yet Rousseau remains emphatic about what he writes in his own name: "If man is good by his nature, as I do believe I have demonstrated, it follows that he remains so as long as nothing foreign to himself spoils him. . . . On this principle, I establish negative education as the best or rather as the only good one" (35).

Among the lessons omitted in the "negative education" meant to forestall the entrance of vice is premature religious instruction, an omission that drew Beaumont's particular ire, and it is on this subject that Rousseau most strenuously insists on the distinction between himself and the Vicar. He quotes a passage from the archbishop's pastoral letter in which Beaumont is quoting *Emile*, a passage that the archbishop characterizes as what "he [i.e., Rousseau] says through the organ of a chimerical character." And Rousseau even goes to the trouble of correcting Beaumont's misquotation of the passage. Having done so, he points out that the archbishop incorrectly attributes a passage that he himself wrote in his own name to the Vicar. "Before I transcribe your comment here, allow me to state mine," he replies. "It is that this supposedly chimerical character is myself and not the Vicar. That this passage which you believed to be in the profession of faith is not, but in the body of the book. Your Grace, you read very superficially and you cite very negligently the writings you stigmatize so harshly. I find that a man in office who censures ought to examine his judgments more carefully" (38). We would do well to heed Rousseau's censure when interpreting the "Profession."

For the remainder of the first half of the *Letter to Beaumont*, and before turning to the question of how to assess religions according to the criteria of truth and utility, Rousseau addresses the archbishop's objections to the theological reasonings in the book. Whose book? I am being intentionally ambiguous here in my phrasing, for in objecting to these "theological reasonings" Beaumont once again conflates Rousseau and the Vicar, and our author will yet again point out the prelate's error. The first objections to which he replies concern certain cautionary remarks he makes in the text running up to the "Profession"—in his own name—concerning reasoning in matters of theology. Referencing his account in the *Discourse on Inequality* of the slow course of human development and especially the gradual development of reason, Rousseau defends his claim that our ideas concerning the divinity develop only slowly and precariously, and are liable to distortion because of human pride (39–41). He then takes up Beaumont's objections to doubts concerning the nature of the divinity and the doctrine of creation ex nihilo expressed by the Vicar within the "Profession." Once again, then, Rousseau chastises the archbishop for conflating what he writes in his own name with what the Savoyard Vicar says in his speech, stating of Beaumont's objections: "Be this as it may, that is not the issue between us, and without supporting the sentiments of the Vicar, my only task here is to point out your errors" (45). Rousseau neither embraces nor eschews what the Vicar says on these matters.

ASSESSING RELIGIONS ACCORDING TO TRUTH AND UTILITY

Up to this point in the *Letter to Beaumont*, Rousseau has been concerned with defending the consistency of his writings, all of which he proclaims are based on the principle of the natural goodness of man and his corruption in society. We might characterize his subject up to this point as concerned with truth, that is, the philosophical truth he has discovered and expounded in his writings. To anticipate, such truth-telling may also be useful—for example, in challenging the "disheartening doctrine of our harsh theologians" (31n)—but the emphasis is on the truth. It is at this point in the letter, then, that Rousseau shifts subject, announcing: "Your Grace, we are about to reach the most important discussions" (46). These discussions concern the potential conflict between the two criteria by which religions should be assessed: truth and utility. Continuing to maintain the fiction that he is the "editor" of the "Profession," Rousseau's defense for "publishing" the writing centers on its utility. He does not pronounce on its truth.

"After having attacked my system and my book, you also attack my religion," he begins, "and because the Catholic Vicar raises objections against his Church, you seek to depict me as the enemy of my own [religion], as if to propose difficulties about a sentiment were to renounce it, as if all human knowledge did not have its difficulties." There are two religious accounts to examine: Rousseau's own religious views ("my religion") and those contained in the "Profession" ("the Catholic Vicar").[24] In the next paragraph Rousseau offers his defense: "My ready reply to you is to declare with my usual frankness my sentiments in matters of religion, just as I have professed them in all my writings and just as they have always been in my mouth and my heart" (46).

Apparently, Rousseau's "usual frankness" does not extend to admitting his authorship of the "Profession of Faith," and he defends having "published" the writing in terms of its utility. "I will tell you, furthermore, why I published the profession of faith of the Vicar, and why, despite such an uproar, I will always consider it the best and most useful writing in the century during which I published it." Nothing less than the most useful writing of the entire century. As for himself: "I shall speak of my religion, because I have one, and I shall speak of it loudly because I have the courage to do so and because it would be desirable for the good of men if it were that of the human race." Once again, his emphasis is on the utility of his professed religious views—for nothing less than the entire human race. At this point Rousseau encourages the impression that he is a Protestant, in contrast to the Catholic Vicar—for example, by stating: "Fortunate to be born into the most reasonable and holy religion on earth" (46–47). I will return to the question of what Rousseau states in the *Letter to Beaumont* and elsewhere about his religious views, but to anticipate I can say that the standard of what is "reasonable" about Protestantism or any other religion will effectively redefine what it means to be a Christian for Jean-Jacques. In any case, for now, he recommends both the Vicar's religion and his own for their utility.

The system of the natural goodness of man and his corruption in society, which Rousseau articulates and defends in the first half of the *Letter to Beaumont*, and which he expounds for both its truth and utility, provides the standard for assessing religions. Having turned to this "most important discussion," then, he explains the genesis of his philosophical system. "I very much desire, your Grace, to follow my usual method here, and give the history of my ideas as my only reply to my accusers. I believe that I cannot better justify all I have dared to say than by saying again everything I have thought" (51–52). The "history of my ideas" is a version of his discovery of the principle of the natural goodness of man and his corruption in society he first glimpsed on the road to Vincennes. Relating how after long observation of men revealed a contradiction between what they said and what they did, he states that he found the source of the contradiction in the fact that "being and appearing were two things as different for them as acting and speaking." He therefore sought the cause.

> I found it in our social order which—at every point contrary to nature, which nothing destroys—tyrannizes over nature constantly and constantly makes nature demand its rights. I followed this contradiction to its consequences, and saw that by itself it explained all the vices of men and all the ills of society. From which I concluded it was not necessary to assume that man is wicked by his nature, when it is possible to indicate the origin and progression of his wickedness. These reflections led me to new research about the human mind considered in the civil state, and I found then that the development of enlightenment and of vices always occurred in the same ratio, not in individuals but in peoples, a distinction I have always carefully made and that none of those who have attacked me has ever been able to conceive. (52)

The contradictions between being and appearance, actions and speeches, follow from the contradiction between nature and man's natural goodness, on the one hand, and the "civil state" and man's corruption in society, on the other. The question, then, is how or to what extent this corruption can be remedied or ameliorated within a given society. This question will be the touchstone for Rousseau for how religions should be assessed and what a responsible author is permitted to write on the subject.

The account Rousseau provides of his discovery of the source of the contradictions he perceived clearly evokes the first fruit of the "Illumination of Vincennes," the *Discourse on the Sciences and the Arts*. In this light, then, his approach in the *Letter to Beaumont* to the question of how to assess religions in light of the contradiction between nature and society, and of what an author may responsibly write on the subject, is a particular case of a more general problem of the disproportion between science and virtue, truth and utility. He imagines Beaumont raising an objection to the self-professed "friend of the truth" during a tête-à-tête in the privacy of his study: "But this frankness is misplaced with the public! But not every truth is good to state!" Rousseau's reply is instructive about the relationship between truth and utility and about his views of what an author can responsibly say publicly on these questions: "There are prejudices that must be respected? That may be, but it is when everything else is in order, and it is impossible to remove these prejudices without also removing what compensates for them. Then the evil is left for love of the good. But when the state of things is such that there can be no change that is not for the better, are prejudices so respectable that reason, virtue, justice, and all the good that truth could do for men must be sacrificed to them?" He does not answer his own rhetorical question.

On the one hand, he clearly does not believe that the present state of things is "in order" such that "prejudices"—that is, popular opinions—must be respected for the greater good. On the other hand, he does not say whether the present state of things meets the threshold justifying a wholesale questioning of "prejudices" in the name of truth. "As for myself," he states in this context, "I have promised to speak [the truth] in every *useful* thing as long as it is in me" (51–52; emphasis added).

The very fact that he published the "Profession" suggests a selective approach on Rousseau's part of challenging certain inimical "prejudices," such as those resulting in intolerance, and replacing them with healthier... what? Truths? Prejudices? What are men to be taught? After stating that "public education" has "essential defects" due to the passions and the "prejudices" of both those who teach and those who learn, he writes: "Now whatever one does, the interest of the public men will always be the same, but the prejudices of the people, being without any fixed basis, are more variable. They can be modified, changed, increased, or diminished. It is only on this side, therefore, that education can gain some hold, and it is there that the friend of truth should aim. He can hope to make the people more reasonable but not those who lead it more honest" (53). In short, Rousseau as a self-proclaimed "friend of the truth" will not necessarily teach the truth to the people, but will instead shape their "prejudices" to make them "more reasonable." The relationship between the truth and what is "reasonable" is not clear, but the fact that he persists in using the language of "prejudice" suggests that the criterion for what is "reasonable" has less to do with truth than utility.

Turning specifically to the "prejudices" relating to religion, Rousseau argues that established religions with all their professions of faith, doctrines, and forms of worship penetrate neither the minds nor hearts of those who follow them without believing them and therefore have little influence over their conduct. In other words, his concern is how beliefs shape morals. "Your Grace, I must speak straightforwardly to you," he writes, and yet in the next sentence he in fact does not appear to speak in his own name. "The true believer cannot put up with all these affectations; he feels [*sent*] that man is an intelligent being who must have a reasonable form of worship, and a sociable being who must have a morality made for humanity." The "true believer" will first seek the religion suited to "man" as an intelligent and sociable being. When "national formulas" are needed as well, he will then examine the "foundations, relations, and properties" of various religions. In short, "after saying what pertains to man, we will then say what pertains to the citizen" (53–54).

Is Rousseau the "true believer" who feels that man is an intelligent and sociable being who seeks the religion suited to "man" and "citizen"?

Interestingly, in an earlier draft, instead of "the true believer" he wrote "the friend of the truth" (*OC*, 4:969 [*a*]). In the final version he therefore appears to distance himself from the sentiments of this "true believer." And rightly so, for Rousseau himself does not hold that man is a "sociable being." Or, arguably, an "intelligent being" either, at least by nature or originally. And this is precisely the dilemma. According to Rousseau, by his nature man is neither a social being nor a citizen. Even if we were to discover the religion suited to man qua man, or what Rousseau along with other philosophers terms "natural religion," it does not necessarily follow that this religion suits man as he now lives in societies or polities. This dilemma follows directly from the core principle of Rousseau's thought: man is by nature good and corrupted in society.

Returning to speaking in his own name, then, Rousseau articulates the criteria according to which religions should be assessed in the critical passage in the *Letter to Beaumont* to which I have referred.

> I therefore see two ways to examine and compare the various religions. One is according to what is *true and false* in them, either concerning the natural or supernatural facts on which they are established, or concerning the notions that reason gives us of the supreme Being and of the form of worship he wants from us. The other is according to their *temporal and moral effects* on earth, according to the good or evil they can do for society and the human race. One must not begin, in order to prevent this double examination, by deciding that these two things always go together, and that the truest religion is also the most social. That is precisely what is in question. (54; emphasis added)

In short, truth and utility do not necessarily coincide for a given religion. Rousseau offers a similar evaluative stance in another defense of *Emile*, though more so of the *Social Contract*: the *Letters Written from the Mountain*. "I distinguish two parts of religion, in addition to the form of worship, which is only ceremonial. These two parts are dogma and morality. I divide dogmas further into two parts, namely the one which in setting forth the principles of our duties serves as foundation for morality, and the one which, purely of faith, contains only speculative dogmas." From this division, he continues, are derived two sets of evaluative criteria: whether they are "true, false, or doubtful" and whether they are "good, bad, or indifferent." Judgment of speculative dogmas belongs to reason alone, he asserts, whereas dogmas concerned with morality, such as justice and the duties of man and citizen, are within the cognizance of government (*Mountain*, 139–40).

Using the somewhat more elaborate schema from the *Letters Written from the Mountain*, we might display the evaluative criteria in the following table.

	Dogmas		Morality
	Speculative	*Moral*	
	True	True	Good
	Doubtful	Doubtful	Indifferent
	False	False	Bad

If it were the case for a given religion that both the speculative and moral dogmas were true and the moral effects of the religion were good, then there would be no difficulty. We might assume that the archbishop believes this to be true of Catholicism. Yet this congruence is precisely what Rousseau doubts. Rousseau and Beaumont would both reject a religion that was false in its speculative and moral dogmas and bad (or unsocial) in its moral consequences. Cases where the dogmas are doubtful and the effects are indifferent are not particularly interesting. The interesting cases are the tough ones: when the moral effects of a religion are good, or at minimum indifferent, but its speculative and moral dogmas are doubtful, or even false.

Rousseau does not explicitly entertain these interesting cases of incongruence between truth and utility in the *Letter to Beaumont*, but he does so in the chapter "On Civil Religion" (IV.8) in the *Social Contract*. According to him, pagan civil religions were false in their dogmas but largely good in their political effects. In turn, the "religion of the priest," including Catholicism, is false in its dogmas and bad in its effects. Finally, the "religion of man," or the true Christianity of the Gospel, is true in its dogmas but bad in its effects. In short, there is an incongruence between the truth of the "religion of man" and the utility of the "religion of the citizen." I take up Rousseau's treatment of civil religion in chapter 8. To return to the *Letter to Beaumont*, Rousseau is emphatically concerned with the moral, social, and political effects of religions, or their utility; but whether or to what extent he is concerned with the truth of their dogmas, and especially speculative dogmas, is less certain.

Having stated that religions must be evaluated according both to their truth and to their utility, Rousseau now walks the tightrope he has stretched between the perspectives on religion: "After saying what pertains to *man*, we will then say what pertains to the *citizen*." He does so by making a maneuver reminiscent of the passage in the *Discourse on Inequality* when he first asserts that man is distinguished from the other animals by being a free agent, only then to say that this claim entails "difficulties" that make it disputable, and hence to modify his position by stating that it is perfectibility that is the distinctively human attribute (*Inequality*, 71–72). Namely, having stated that it is an open question whether truth and utility coincide or diverge in matters of religion, he first writes: "It seems certain, however, I admit, that *if* man is made for society, the truest religion is also the most social and the most human. For God wants us to be as he made us, and if it were true that he had made us wicked, it would be disobeying him to want to cease being so" (*Beaumont*, 54; emphasis added). But, of course, according to Rousseau man is naturally good and he is not "made for society," but in fact becomes wicked as he becomes sociable. Undoubtedly with these very considerations in mind, then, he changes course. "But for all its probability, this sentiment is subject to great difficulties from the historical account and the facts that contradict it" (ibid.). What he means by the "historical account" and the "facts" is unclear. Does he mean the account in the *Discourse on Inequality* of man's natural goodness and corruption in society, and therefore that the "sentiment" that "man is made for society" is false? Or does he mean that, putting aside the question of man's natural goodness, history reveals that man is not sociable—for example, in the sense that Hobbes has in mind when he claims that man is not "born fit for society"?[25] Perhaps he has both of these possibilities in mind. In any case, history and the facts reveal that man as he comes to be in society is wicked and therefore needs a religion appropriate to his condition.

The cause of the abuses committed in the name of religion witnessed by history, especially fanaticism and persecution, are the very same sources of human wickedness itself: "It is *amour-propre* and pride that are the cause." In order for unreasonable forms of worship to persist, reason itself must be silenced. Letting reason speak is therefore a way of battling unreasonable religions. "From that alone," Rousseau explains, "it follows that a great good is accomplished for peoples in this delirium by teaching them to reason about religion, for it is bringing them close to the duties of man, removing the dagger from intolerance, giving back to humanity all its rights. But it is necessary to go back to principles that are general and common to all men" (55). These principles are not to be found in books, which are the works of men, but in nature. Note that Rousseau's argument here is, so to speak, negative: removing false speculative and moral doctrines, or what he earlier termed "prejudices," will remove the cause of the bad moral or social effects of religions. He does not make the positive argument that such reasoning in matters of religion will attain true dogmas. To anticipate, the Savoyard Vicar will admit that his own reasonings are doubtful and that the "articles of faith" he propounds are just that, matters of faith. This is the inquiry into religions that pertains to "man."

What about what pertains to the "citizen"? "Why does one man have the right of inspection over another man's belief, and why does the state have it over the belief of the citizens?" Rousseau answers his own question: "It is because it is assumed that what men believe determines their morality, and that their conduct in this life is dependent on their ideas about the life to come.... In society, everyone has the right to find out whether another person believes himself obligated to be just, and the sovereign has the right to examine the reasons on which each person bases this obligation." In this context, he imagines banishing the theologians and bringing together the faithful from the major monotheistic religions. "'Let us take utility, therefore, as a rule, and then establish the doctrine that is most related to it. In that way we can hope to come as close to the truth as is possible for men. For it can be presumed that what is most useful to his creatures is what is most pleasing to the Creator.'" Having done so, he imagines them reducing their differences to a set of minimal dogmas: "about divine providence, the economy of the life to come, and all questions essential to the good order of the human race." His phrasing here suggests that all these dogmas are "questions essential to the good order of the human race." These are the tenets of "the human and social religion which every man living in society is obliged to accept." Within these limits all religious beliefs and practices are "legitimate" and deserve to be tolerated as long as they tolerate others (57–61). Readers of the *Social Contract* will recognize the basic outlines of his discussion there of civil religion. At any rate, what is evident is that the social utility of these doctrines is of paramount concern.

Such is the inquiry and the conclusions Rousseau asserts he has promulgated in his writings. "My writings will remain despite you, to your shame," he admonishes Beaumont: "The less prejudiced Christians will search them with surprise for the horrors you claim to find there. They will see in them, along with the morality of their divine master, only lessons of peace, harmony, and charity." As for the "Profession," he proclaims: "Only agree, your Grace, that if France had professed the religion of the Savoyard priest—that religion which is so simple and so pure, which makes people fear God and love men—rivers of blood would not have flooded French fields so often" (65–66). He offers a similar assessment of the writing in the *Letters Written from the Mountain*. "Let us suppose for a moment that the profession of faith of the Vicar had been adopted in a corner of the Christian world, and let us see what good and evil would result from it. This will be neither attacking nor defending it;

it will be judging it by its effects" (*Mountain*, 142ff.). Not surprisingly, the effects will be good morals and toleration. Such is what he earlier characterized in the *Letter to Beaumont* as "the best and most useful writing in the century during which I published it."

ROUSSEAU'S RELIGION

When he turned to speak to Beaumont of "the most important discussions" with his "usual frankness," Rousseau lauded the "Profession" for its utility and proclaimed: "I shall speak of my religion, because I have one, and I shall speak of it loudly because I have the courage to do so and because it would be desirable for the good of men if it were that of the human race" (47). Rousseau's own religion is also useful. By pairing his remarks about the Vicar's profession of faith and his own profession, indeed in the same paragraph, he seems simultaneously to ask us to distinguish between them and invite us to assume they are the same or at least similar. My analysis of the "Profession" will have to wait until later chapters, but for now three observations will suffice. First, both the Vicar and Rousseau restrict themselves to natural religion—that is, what theological doctrines might be deduced by human reason alone. Second, both insist on epistemological modesty in such reasoning— namely, the difficulty and doubtfulness of such reasonings. Third, both embrace the moral doctrines of the Gospel as they interpret it as both true and useful. Let me turn now to what Rousseau claims in the *Letter to Beaumont* and elsewhere concerning his own religious views. Let me remind my reader again of what I wrote in the introduction—namely, that I do not attempt to ascertain what he actually believes in the views he professes, and instead I examine only what he *writes* about his supposed religious beliefs in his authorial persona or personae and what he states about his intentions in offering them.

"Your Grace, I am Christian, and sincerely Christian, according to the doctrine of the Gospel," Rousseau begins his own profession of faith. What he means by Christianity "according to the doctrine of the Gospel" is immediately apparent: no doctrines or articles of faith beyond what is minimally necessary, but instead an emphasis on duties and good works. "As for myself," he continues, "well convinced of the essential truths of Christianity, which serve as the foundation of all good morality," he will follow the "spirit of the Gospel," leaving aside all doctrinal "subtleties" and practicing charity. He emphasizes how these beliefs offer "the consolations of this life" and "hope for the life that must follow it." He explains that, as opposed to those "nominal Christians" who are ready to believe what must be believed or say what must be said, he thinks "that what is essential in religion consists in practice" (*Beaumont*, 47–48).

We can reframe Rousseau's profession in terms of the evaluative criteria for assessing religions: truth and utility. Let us use the fuller set of criteria articulated in the *Letters Written from the Mountain*. First, as for speculative dogmas, Rousseau does not even speak to the truth, doubtfulness, or falsity of the speculative dogmas of the brand of Christianity to which he adheres. His only mention of the divinity in this context concerns the admonition to love God above all things and to love thy neighbor—moral teachings rather than speculative doctrines. Second, as for dogmas concerning moral principles, he does state that he is "well convinced of the essential truths of Christianity, which serve as the foundation of all good morality." Let me call attention to his phrasing: "*des vérités essencielles au Christianisme, lesquelles servent de fondement à toute bonne morale.*" This portion of the sentence could be alternatively rendered "the essential truths of Christianity, those which serve as the foundation of all good morality." In other words, the "essential truths" of Christianity are those truths that pertain to morality. Third, it is the good moral effects of this religion that Rousseau emphasizes here and elsewhere: "What is essential in religion consists in practice." The "spirit of the Gospel" that nourishes his heart consists in loving God above all things and loving his neighbor as himself, resulting in charitable behavior.

The religion Rousseau professes is natural religion, and thus he presents himself less as a believer than an inquirer. "I do not have, it is true, that faith I hear so many people of such mediocre probity boast about; that robust faith which never doubts anything, believes without question everything presented to it for belief, and puts aside or dissimulates the objections it does not know how to resolve." He explains: "I do not have the good fortune to see in revelation the evidence they find there, and if I decide in favor of it, it is because my heart leads me to do so, because it offers me nothing except what is consoling, and because the difficulties in rejecting it are no less great" (49). In other words, to recur again to the evaluative criteria, revelation is doubtful: he will neither affirm nor deny its truth or falseness, and the Vicar will do the same. If he inclines toward any revelation, he does so because he finds it "consoling." Interestingly, in an earlier version of this passage Rousseau used the language of the lawgiver in the *Social Contract*: "My reason could have been more *convinced*, but my heart could not have been more *persuaded*" (*CW*, 9:91; emphasis added). We will see Rousseau make similar remarks, for example in the *Letter to Voltaire*, about leaning toward one belief rather than another when reason cannot decide because of the consoling effects that persuade him to do so.

The criterion of the "reasonableness" of a religion helps explain Rousseau's statements that he is a Christian and more specifically a Protestant. "Fortunate to be born into the most reasonable and holy religion on earth, I remain inviolably attached to the worship of my Fathers," he explains to Beaumont. "Like them, I take Scripture and reason for the unique rules of my belief" (47–48). However, he takes Scripture for a rule only insofar as it accords with reason, neither affirming nor denying what reason cannot confirm. What he means when he states "I declare myself Christian" and "I have not ceased to declare myself to be a Protestant" is clearer in the *Letters Written from the Mountain*. Writing of the beneficial effects that would follow from the "Profession of Faith" being adopted "in a corner of the Christian world," he explains: "Our proselytes will have two rules of faith that make up only one, reason and the Gospel. The latter will be all the more immutable because it will base itself only on the former" (*Mountain*, 142). He is even more emphatic on this point in some of his correspondence from the same period, writing, for example: "There are not two moralities [*morales*]. That of Christianity and those of philosophy are the same."[26] And: "True Christianity is only natural religion better applied."[27] What he means by it being "better applied" (*mieux appliquée*) is not clear, but he seems to suggest that the Gospel is a more effective moral teaching than naked reason because it provides an exemplar.[28] His protestations that he remains a Protestant have a similar thrust. He says of the Reformers that they dared depart from accepted doctrine "by their own authority, by that of their reason." Every individual is competent to judge the Bible by his own reason: "Each remains the sole judge of [doctrines] for himself, and does not acknowledge any authority in them other than his own" (*Mountain*, 154–55). Such is his interpretation of the "spirit" of the Reformation, which he acknowledges is not entirely in accord with the historical record.[29] In short, Rousseau's claim that he is a Christian in accordance with the morality of the Gospel is possible because he reduces the Gospel to natural religion, or what can be known by reason alone.[30]

Rousseau argues that such a religion is *useful* for human beings in minimizing dispute over religious dogmas and practices and maximizing toleration. Let us provisionally assume that Rousseau believes that some version of natural religion is also *true*, or as close to truth as human reason can reach, while still acknowledging its limits and doubts. With the utility and potential truth of natural religion in mind, then, we can return to the issue of the relationship between Rousseau's own expressed religious views and those of the Vicar. As we saw earlier in the *Letter to Beaumont*, he both insists on distinguishing between what he writes in his own name from what the Vicar says and yet also elides these two religious views in such a way as almost invites us to assume they are the same or similar. Now we can see that his own religious views as he expresses them in the *Letter to Beaumont* and elsewhere are in fact similar to those contained in the "Profession" in at least two respects: their utility with regard to morality and their potential truth as natural religion, especially if we restrict ourselves insofar as possible to doctrines concerned with morality. In this light, whatever the specific differences over particular doctrines or other matters, Rousseau as an author subscribes to the same fundamental approach to religion with regard to its truth and utility. What Jean-Jacques actually believes, we do not know.

CHAPTER 2

The Theodicy of the *Discourse on Inequality*

"Men are wicked; sad and continual experience spares the need for proof. Yet man is naturally good—I do believe I have demonstrated it." So Rousseau claims in the *Discourse on Inequality*, having just remarked that if we go back to natural man we would perceive that "man has hardly any other evils than those he has given himself, and that nature would have been justified" (*Inequality*, note IX, 127).[1] Rousseau presents his work as a solution to the problem of evil, as a justification of nature and nature's god: as a theodicy. An immediate qualification of this characterization is necessary, and it points to the heart of the argument of this chapter. Namely, in the *Discourse* Rousseau explicitly puts aside the divinity in his examination of man's nature and history. "Religion orders us to believe that since God himself took men out of the state of nature immediately after the creation," he states. "But it does not forbid us from forming conjectures, drawn solely from the nature of man and of the beings surrounding him, about what the human race might have become if it had been left to its own devices" (63–64). While it is true that Rousseau extends the argument of the *Discourse* to include divine providence when defending the work, especially in the *Letter to Voltaire*, the subject of the following chapter, in the *Discourse* itself he makes his argument on strictly naturalistic grounds, with a sole—and problematic—reference to providence. The work is therefore more properly a justification of nature than a theodicy: a physiodicy.

Other interpreters have argued that Rousseau's thought can be considered as offering a novel solution to the problem of evil, and a brief discussion of them will help clarify my contribution. Let me begin with Kant, in part because his assessment of Rousseau's epochal contribution in this regard has been influential. Kant is famously said to have missed his regular daily walk only twice: upon the publication of *Emile* and the outbreak of the French Revolution. Whether this story is apocryphal or not, Kant's engagement with Rousseau can be seen throughout his writings.[2] Among the most explicit of these engagements is contained in what are known as the "Remarks," or notes he took on the verso pages of a copy of his *Observations on the Feeling of the Beautiful and Sublime* (1764), so shortly after he encountered *Emile*. Among those remarks is this celebrated admission: "*Rousseau* set me right. This blinding prejudice vanishes, I learn to honor human beings, and I would feel by far less useful than the common laborer if I did not believe that this consideration could impart a value to all others in order to establish the rights of humanity."[3] As for his view of Rousseau's contribution to the problem of evil and theodicy, he writes:

> Newton was the first to see order and regularity bound up with great simplicity, where before him disorder and badly matched manifoldness were to be met with, whereas since then comets travel in geometric course. Rousseau was the first to discover under the manifoldness of the available shapes of mankind man's deeply hidden nature and the concealed law according to which providence through its observation is justified. After Newton and Rousseau the objections of King Alfonso and the Manicheans are no longer valid, God is justified, and Pope's teaching is henceforth true.[4]

For Kant, then, Rousseau is the Newton of the moral world. In his view, expressed in his essay "Conjectural Beginning of Human History" (1786), Rousseau's theodicy consists in a resolution of the conflict we experience as both "physical" and "moral" creatures, which can be formulated in a historical manner. He says of Rousseau that in the two *Discourses* he "shows quite correctly the unavoidable conflict between culture with the nature of the human species as a *physical* species in which each individual was entirely to reach his vocation." Yet in *Emile* and the *Social Contract* "he seeks again to solve the harder problem of how culture must proceed in order properly to develop the predispositions of humanity as a *moral* species, so that the latter no longer conflict with humanity as a natural species."[5] The distinction between humans considered as "physical" and "moral" beings is central to my analysis of the *Discourse on Inequality*, but my interpretation of Rousseau's solution to the problem of evil goes in the opposite direction from Kant's.

Perhaps the most important scholarly version of the argument that Rousseau advances for a theodicy is Ernst Cassirer's *The Question of Jean-Jacques Rousseau* (1932), which is heavily indebted to Kant. The answer to the titular question concerning the aim of Rousseau's thought

Cassirer finds in his original solution to the problem of evil. He argues that Rousseau found the source of evil "at a point where no one before him had looked for it.... This subject is not individual man, but human society." With this realization in hand "man must become his own savior and, in the ethical sense, his own creator." In good Kantian fashion, Cassirer sees the "true destiny" of mankind for Rousseau in the proper use of freedom to legislate the moral law as individuals and in society. "Rousseau's ethics," he declares, is "the most categorical form of a pure ethics of obligation (*Gesetzes-Ethik*) that was established before Kant."[6]

A more recent reading of Rousseau's thought as a theodicy is offered by Frederick Neuhouser in his *Rousseau's Theodicy of Self-Love* (2008). Neuhouser's interpretation also has a Kantian as well as a Hegelian flavor, but he focuses more on the psychological problems and resources afforded by Rousseau's understanding of self-love. His interpretation might be characterized as having two movements. The first movement regards the problem of evil, which Rousseau addresses by distinguishing between natural *amour de soi* and developed *amour-propre*, with our evils chiefly caused by "inflamed" *amour-propre*. The second movement regards theodicy, with Neuhouser arguing that *amour-propre* is part of the solution that ultimately justifies our existence if it is properly developed in a manner where we recognize ourselves and others as equals and act as free and rational subjects.[7]

What Kant and those who largely follow him, like Cassirer and Neuhouser, have in common is that they argue that Rousseau finds the solution to the problem of evil at the end of history, so to speak. Those influenced less by Kant than Marx or other historical schools advance similar interpretations, arguing, for example, that Rousseau sees a historical transformation of human nature or at least prepares the way for those who do.[8] By contrast, I argue that the solution lies, so to speak, in the beginning—that is, in Rousseau's account in the first part of the *Discourse* of natural man in the "pure state of nature."

My analysis of the *Discourse on Inequality* has two main aims. First, I argue that the work constitutes a theodicy or, more accurately, a physiodicy in which Rousseau's principle of the natural goodness of man serves to justify nature. Second, I argue that this theodicy is limited to "physical" man existing under the physical laws of nature. To show this, I examine the relationship between the "physical" and "moral" aspects of human nature, arguing that natural man is limited to physical attributes and sketching how the initially physical attributes of human nature develop into moral attributes (e.g., physical love and moral love, *amour de soi* and *amour-propre*). In order to keep my focus here on the question of theodicy or physiodicy, however, I save a discussion of human development for chapter 4, in which I examine how and in what way the theodicy of the *Discourse* can be extended to developed human beings.

Knowing "Man" in the *Discourse on Inequality*

Like the prize-winning essay that made him a celebrity, the *Discourse on Inequality* began as an answer to the question posed by the Academy of Dijon, in this case for its 1754 prize competition. Rousseau took it upon himself to change the Academy of Dijon's question. The institution had asked: "What is the origin of inequality among men, and whether it is authorized by natural law." Rousseau reproduced the question on the page before the discourse proper, which bears the title: "Discourse on the Origin, and the Foundations of Inequality among Men" (*Inequality*, 59, 61). By the end of the Exordium Rousseau has cast off the authority of the natural law as unintelligible and inapplicable, and thus from the outset he calls into question its premise: that humans are naturally rational and moral beings. In order to answer the Academy's question about the origin of inequality among men, Rousseau argues that we must begin by knowing "man," or human nature. The aim of this section is to examine Rousseau's inquiry into human nature. First, I argue that although he presents his inquiry as a historical account of human origins and development, his investigation is more fundamentally a psychological analysis. Second, I argue that despite the change in appearance of human nature over time and especially in society, for Rousseau the physical being he finds in the "pure state of nature" remains the core of human nature, meaning that his portrait of natural man remains relevant for understanding what he terms the "present nature of man."

If we must begin by knowing man, Rousseau describes the difficulty of the task at the outset of the Preface. "The most useful and the least advanced of all human knowledge appears to me to be that of man, and I dare say that the inscription on the Temple of Delphi alone contained a more important and more difficult precept than all the hefty books of the moralists. As such I consider the subject of this discourse to be one of the most interesting questions philosophy might propose, and unfortunately for us one of the thorniest philosophers might resolve" (51). He puts aside the books of the moralists and instead raises the question of knowing human nature as a form of heeding the admonition to self-knowledge. As he explains elsewhere, "The mistake of most moralists has always been to consider man as an essentially reasonable being. Man is a sensitive being, who consults solely his passions in order to act" ("Political Fragments," *CW*, 4:70). Although by "moralists" Rousseau refers primarily to the modern natural law thinkers, he includes Hobbes,

Locke, and others in their ranks because of their common assumption that humans are naturally rational and moral beings.

The Delphic imperative raises a methodological problem the magnitude of which Rousseau believes that none of his predecessors had grasped, because of their shared assumptions concerning human nature. The difficulty consists in knowing human nature in the first place: "For how will the source of inequality among men be known unless one begins by knowing men themselves?" (51). The knowledge of "man" and of "men themselves" is complicated by the fact, asserted by Rousseau, that human nature has changed over time owing to various causes.

> And how will man ever manage to see himself as nature formed him, through all the changes that the sequence of time and of things must have produced in his original constitution, and to disentangle what he retains of his own stock from what circumstances and his progress have added to or changed in his primitive state? Like the statue of Glaucus, which time, sea, and storms had so disfigured that it resembled less a god than a ferocious beast, the human soul, altered in the bosom of society . . . has, so to speak, changed in appearance to the point of being almost unrecognizable. (51)

As others have noted, Rousseau inverts the Platonic image.[9] For Socrates the metaphor of the statue of Glaucus represents the true, unified, and godlike human soul hidden beneath the deformed appearance of the passions. Rousseau, too, finds a unified soul beneath the alterations of time, society, and the passions—"a being always acting according to certain and invariable principles" (51). But his is a being whose physical endowments alone give his soul a certain unity—an animal, not a god. Man is originally a physical being whose psychic unity follows from his purely physical attributes, a psychic unity destroyed over time as he develops into a social or moral being, ironically coming to resemble a "ferocious beast." "Man" has been transformed into "men" in the bosom of society.

Since Rousseau argues that human nature has in some sense changed over time, he gives the *Discourse* the form of a history of mankind from its origins to the present day. He characterizes his account as a whole, and especially its starting point in what he will term the "pure state of nature," as conjectural.

> Let my readers not imagine, then, that I dare flatter myself with having seen what appears to me so difficult to see. I have begun some lines of reasoning, I have hazarded some conjectures, less in the hope

of resolving the question than with the intention of clarifying it and reducing it to its genuine state. Others will easily be able to go farther along the same path, without it being easy for anyone to reach the end. For it is no light undertaking to disentangle what is original from what is artificial in the present nature of man, and to know correctly a state which no longer exists, which perhaps never did exist, which probably never will exist, and about which it is nevertheless necessary to have correct notions in order to judge our present state properly. (52)

The method is analytic. He begins from the "present nature of man" and then disentangles natural and artificial attributes to reveal our original nature. Similarly, having complained that his predecessors, philosophers of the state of nature, supposedly did not realize that their accounts contradicted Scripture, since we read there that man was never in the "pure state of nature" (a passage to which I will return), he writes:

Let us therefore begin by putting aside all the facts, for they have no bearing on the question. The research that may be undertaken regarding this subject must not be taken for historical truth, but only for hypothetical and conditional reasoning, more appropriate for clarifying the nature of things than for showing their genuine origin, and similar to the reasoning our physicists employ all the time with regard to the formation of the world. (62–63)

Rousseau refers foremost to Descartes, who hypothesizes a beginning of the world where the laws of nature imposed by God bring about natural order of their own accord, an argument he suppressed in the *Discourse on the Method*, given the fate of Galileo.[10] Rousseau's conjectures about natural man and his natural environs will be physical in nature, commencing with natural man as a physical being in the "pure state of nature."

Although he gives his account in the *Discourse* a historical form, Rousseau's remark about disentangling the natural and artificial attributes in the "present nature of man" indicates that his analysis is more fundamentally a psychological one, an inquiry into human nature. He describes his analysis as a form of meditation. "Setting aside, therefore, all scientific books that teach us only to see men as they have made themselves, and meditating on the first and simplest operations of the human soul, I believe I perceive in it two principles preceding reason." The process of introspective meditation is analogous to sight, where we "perceive" or "glimpse" (*appercevoir*) something not visible to the eye. These two "principles" turn out to be self-preservation and pity, although he does not name them here. By "principles" he means something like fundamental principles of motion, as in Descartes and Newton, and he posits the fewest number of such principles necessary to explain the phenomena: the motion of the human soul, in both its original and developed forms. "It is from the concurrence [*concours*] and combination that our mind is capable of making of these two principles, without it being necessary to introduce that of sociability, that all the rules of natural right appear to me to flow" (54–55). Sociability is a "principle" that others, notably Pufendorf, thought necessary to save the phenomena, but Rousseau strips it away along with reason as non-natural.

Recognizing the more fundamental psychological inquiry underlying the historical cast Rousseau gives to his account of human nature and development changes the terms of the debate over the issue of in what way he intends his account as conjectural or hypothetical. A minority of interpreters have argued that Rousseau puts forward the pure state of nature as a hypothesis concerning our original condition—a historical condition—which is capable, at least in principle, of being empirically tested. Thus, they view the anatomical, ethnographic, and other evidence he adduces, particularly in the notes to the work, as an effort to provide potential if inconclusive data for his hypothesis.[11] This reading takes seriously the historical dimension of the account of human origins and development and puts particular emphasis on a reading of Rousseau's understanding of the distinctive attribute of man, perfectibility, as making humans nearly infinitely malleable and therefore essentially historical beings.

Most interpreters nonetheless assume that Rousseau's account of the pure state in particular is strictly hypothetical, a thought experiment of some sort.[12] One recent example that is particularly useful for clarifying my interpretation, in part because it is also concerned with the issue of theodicy, is Neuhouser. Neuhouser characterizes the pure state of nature as "'true' (but fictitious)," a hypothetical construct in which Rousseau strips away all social relations of humans in order to consider the operation of natural self-love, or *amour de soi*, apart from its developed form of *amour-propre*, and especially "inflamed" versions of the passion. According to Neuhouser, Rousseau never entertains the pure state of nature as a historical or even psychological "fact."

> Rousseau means only to claim that [*amour de soi*], in contrast to *amour-propre*, is a passion human individuals could in principle possess on their own, even were they to exist outside of society (which, for Rousseau, no real human beings do).... But nothing in this account implies, even for Rousseau, that human beings can or should

exist without *amour-propre*. Contrary to popular primitivist readings of the Second Discourse, Rousseau does not envision human existence without *amour-propre* any more than he envisions it without love, reason, or language—all of which are just as "artificial" as *amour-propre* and no less essential to human reality.[13]

Neuhouser therefore takes Rousseau's characterization of his inquiry as hypothetical quite literally, and sees him as undertaking it, to borrow Rousseau's own characterization, "less in the hope of resolving the question than with the intention of clarifying it and reducing it to its genuine state" (52). The picture of the natural condition of man is in the service of philosophical clarification.[14]

Let me now stake out a position somewhere between these two interpretations in order to address the question of what function Rousseau's account of the pure state of nature plays in the *Discourse* and his thought as a whole. As mentioned, although Rousseau does indeed present his account in the form of a history of the human species from the pure state of nature to the civil state, this account is more fundamentally a psychological analysis of human nature and development. The hypotheses or conjectures he makes concern foremost the result of an analysis that begins with the "present nature of man," and thus Rousseau is serious about this analysis as revealing the truth about the core of human nature, then and now, as opposed to it being wholly an exercise in philosophical clarification. To be sure, as Céline Spector argues, while adopting a middle position similar to my own, the "theoretical construct" of the pure state of nature also serves a polemical function in judging social inequality and institutions or, as Rousseau states, is a means by which we can "judge our present state properly."[15]

The relationship between the historical and psychological dimensions of the *Discourse* is evident at the very end of the work where Rousseau explains that "every attentive reader" will appreciate the distance from the natural state to the civil state and thereby perceive that the "human race of one age" is not "the human race of another." He elaborates this historical claim in a more psychological register: "In a word, he will explain how the soul and human passions, altering imperceptibly, so to speak change their nature; why our needs and our pleasures change objects in the long run; why, with original man gradually vanishing, society no longer offers to the eyes of the wise man anything but an assemblage of artificial men and fabricated passions that are the work of all these new relations and have no true foundation in nature" (116). Human beings are historical beings in the sense that their uniquely malleable psychological endowments are decisively shaped by their environment, and especially their social relations, and Rousseau therefore frames the *Discourse* as a history of human nature. Yet humans nature changes only "so to speak."[16] Indeed, this premise is implicit in the image of the statue of Glaucus at the outset of the Preface, for, whatever the difficulties in doing so, the human soul can be seen beneath the changes that have occurred in it. The human soul, he writes there, "has, *so to speak*, changed in *appearance* to the point of being *almost* unrecognizable" (51; emphasis added). Finally, Rousseau's method of meditating on the "first and simplest operations of the human soul" in order to "perceive" its fundamental principles is premised on the fact that he can still discover our fundamental nature beneath all of the acquisitions we have made. This assumption is evident in a passage in the *Dialogues* where, speaking of himself, he writes:

> Where could the painter and apologist of nature, so disfigured and calumnied now, have found his model if not in his own heart? He described it as he himself felt. The prejudices that did not subjugate him, the factitious passions to which he was not prey did not hide from his eyes as they did from others those original traits so generally forgotten or misjudged. These traits so novel for us and so true once they are traced could still find, deep in people's hearts, the attestation of their correctness, but they would never have sought them out themselves if the historian of nature had not started by removing the rust that hid them. (*Dialogues*, CW, 1:214)

The "original traits" of human nature can be found by removing the rust. As Rousseau explains in the *Letter to Beaumont* when recounting his discovery of the source of the wickedness that obscures our natural goodness, "I found it in our social order which—at every point contrary to nature, which nothing destroys . . ." (52). Nature still lies beneath.

The Pure State of Nature: From Theology to Physics

Rousseau complains that previous philosophers have failed to know "man" because they have not gone far enough in their analyses of human nature, and he casts his complaint in the language of the state of nature. "The philosophers who have examined the foundations of society have all felt the necessity of going back to the state of nature, but none of them has reached it." Of course, not all philosophers have employed the concept of the state of nature. To take a notable example, the philosopher Rousseau cites in the epigraph to the *Discourse*, Aristotle, did not. In saying this, then, Rousseau simultaneously pledges his allegiance to

Hobbes, Locke, and the other philosophers of the state of nature, and declares his independence. "In short, all of them, speaking continually of need, greed, oppression, desires, and pride, have carried into the state of nature ideas they have taken from society: they spoke of savage man and they were depicting civil man" (62). Similarly, in the unpublished "State of War," he explains: "[The] error of Hobbes and of the philosophers is to confuse natural man with the men they have before their eyes, and to transport into one system a being that can continue to exist only in another" (*CW*, 11:63). Rousseau will therefore "go back" further, further than the state of nature to the "pure state of nature."

After complaining that the philosophers have not reached the state of nature, Rousseau first introduces the concept of the "pure state of nature" in a curious manner that both reveals that he is aware of the theological background of the term as a concept designed to investigate man's moral nature and duties subject to natural law, and indicates how he transforms it into a condition or "system" that depicts man's essentially physical being existing under the physical laws of nature. "It did not even enter the minds of most of our philosophers to doubt that the state of nature existed," he writes, "whereas it is evident from reading the Sacred Books that the first man, having received enlightenment and precepts directly from God, was not in that state, and that, granting the books of Moses the faith that any Christian philosopher owes them, it must be denied that men were ever found in the pure state of nature." Rousseau's charge is of course facetious if it is leveled against the likes of Hobbes, who denied that Moses was even the author of the Pentateuch. Indeed, Rousseau's charge against his predecessors is not that they have proceeded in supposed ignorance of Scripture, but that they have not pressed their inquiries far enough in that direction. If Scripture informs us that man was never in the pure state of nature, he will put it aside: "Let us therefore begin by setting aside all the facts, for they have no bearing on the question."[17] His investigation will resemble "the reasoning our physicists employ all the time with regard to the formation of the world" (62–63). It does so not only in being conjectural (and prudentially so, since it conflicts with Scripture), but also because it is physical in nature and scope.[18] Rousseau naturalizes the "pure state of nature" by removing it from the framework of scriptural history and aetiology in which it was initially conceived.

The "state of nature" is a concept found in the natural law theory of Aquinas and Suarez and then in modified form in the modern natural law tradition, for example, in Hooker, Grotius, and Pufendorf, among others. They conceived of the "state of nature" as the condition prior to the Fall, the state of innocence as opposed to the state of sin and the state of grace or redemption. Some theorists also entertained a wholly speculative "pure state of nature," the state of nature without or prior to divine dispensation. Neither this strictly conjectural "pure state of nature" nor the lost "state of nature" as conceived by these thinkers could provide much guidance for political society, precisely because they were viewed either as necessarily hypothetical (i.e., conflicting with the scriptural account) or as irretrievably lost for a fallen being. The principal role of the hypotheses about these two conditions was to elucidate the character of the universally available and applicable natural law.[19]

Rousseau follows and radicalizes Hobbes and others who themselves recast the "state of nature." More conventional natural law theorists saw the drift of the philosophy of Hobbes and others away from a "moral" and toward a "physical" inquiry, and an indication of the novelty of Rousseau's investigation is that he adopts precisely the strategy they condemned. A helpful figure in this regard is Barbeyrac, whose extensive notes in his editions and translations of Pufendorf, which were the editions Rousseau used, reveal the stakes of the argument. Barbeyrac at several points complains of the deleterious influence of Hobbes and Spinoza on Pufendorf. One such instance is in Pufendorf's definition of the state of nature in his *On the Duty of Man and Citizen* (*De officiis hominis et civis*). "The natural state may be considered, in the light of reason alone," in three ways, explains Pufendorf: "in relation to God the Creator, or in the relation of each individual man to himself, or in relation to other men." From the first point of view, "the natural state of man is the condition in which he was placed by his Creator with the intention that he be the most excellent of all the animals." In this state man should therefore "recognize and worship his Creator, admire his works, and lead his life in a manner utterly different from that of the animals destitute of reason. Hence this state is in complete contrast with the life and condition of the beasts." From the second point of view, "we may consider the natural state of man, by an imaginative effort, as the condition man would have been in if he had been left to himself alone, without any support from other men, given the condition of human nature as we now perceive it." Pufendorf argues that such a state would be "more miserable than that of any beast."[20] Rousseau's explicit denial of this claim is already revealing about how the pure state of nature functions as part of his justification of nature: "I know that we are repeatedly told that nothing would have been so miserable as man in that state; and if it is true, as I believe I have proved, that he could have had the desire and the opportunity to leave it only after many centuries, this would be a charge to level against nature and not against him whom nature had so constituted" (80). Finally, from the third point of view, the natural state is to be considered as the state of men without the civil state but still having "moral relations" guided by the law of nature.[21]

In his commentary on this passage, Barbeyrac criticizes the first two usages Pufendorf enumerates, saying that the first is "beside the question" and objecting that the second "is merely a *physical state*." Barbeyrac argues that the third sense of the state of nature is the correct one, for man is by nature a moral being who has moral or social relations and exercises his reason. Similarly, in his commentary on Pufendorf's *On the Right of Nature and of Men*, Barbeyrac objects numerous times to Pufendorf's failure to distinguish the physical and moral levels of his analysis, even though Pufendorf is at pains to distinguish "moral beings" and "moral modes" from physical ones and even though he specifically writes that the "state of nature" is "so called, not due to the fact it results from the physical principles of the essence of man."[22] Rousseau adopts the physical consideration Barbeyrac rejects.[23]

Rousseau first introduces the terminology of the "physical" and "moral" attributes of human beings in the very beginning of the *Discourse*. In the Preface he defines a "moral being" within his discussion of the requirements for a being to be subject to the natural law: "a being that is intelligent, free, and considered in its relations with other beings" (53). He argues that naturally man does not meet those requirements, for man is not naturally intelligent, free in any moral sense, and does not have moral relations with other beings, including his fellow humans. The opposition between "physical" and "moral" attributes of human nature is introduced in the Exordium. "I conceive of two sorts of inequality in the human species," he explains, "one which I call natural or physical because it is established by nature, and which consists in the differences in age, health, strength of the body, qualities of the mind, or of the soul; the other, which may be called moral or political inequality because it depends upon a sort of convention and is established, or at least authorized, by the consent of men." In both his definition of a "moral being" and in the opposition he draws between "physical" and "moral" inequality, Rousseau uses the term "moral" in a broad sense that is nearly synonymous with what we would mean by "social," so attributes and relations that are not strictly physical or natural, as well as in the narrow sense of morality. Both the broad and narrow senses of "moral" should be kept in mind throughout when examining his account.

At this stage, the opposition between "physical" and "moral" is innocuous in terms of Rousseau's argument concerning human nature, though far from innocuous with regard to his argument about inequality. To ask whether there is some essential connection between natural or physical inequalities and moral or political inequalities, as his judges have done, is to pose "a question perhaps good for slaves to debate within earshot of their masters, but not befitting rational and free men who seek the truth" (61). Yet by distinguishing between these two sorts of inequalities, Rousseau foreshadows the distinction he will draw between considering "physical man" as opposed to man "from the metaphysical and moral side" (71), and likewise the difference between "physical love" and "moral love" (86), or what I will argue is the paradigmatic case for his analysis of human passions and attributes. The function of the "pure state of nature" is to examine man as a naturally good physical being stripped of the moral attributes he acquires as he develops and is corrupted in society.

The reaction of one of Rousseau's contemporaries to the *Discourse* highlights the novelty of his account of physical man and the way in which it contested traditional conceptions of human nature as well as the biblical narrative. The title of the work I have in mind is itself illuminating: *L'homme moral opposé à l'homme physique de M. R***. Lettres philosophiques, où l'on refute le Déisme du jour*. Published anonymously a year after the *Discourse*, the work was by the abbé Louis-Bertrand Castel.[24] Castel was an acquaintance of Rousseau's during his early years in Paris, and he mentions Castel in the *Confessions* as "crazy, but a good man on the whole" (*Confessions*, CW, 5:242–43). He was best known for his contributions to the *Journal des Trévoux*, his translations of Newton, his own work on optics, music, and mathematics, and his "ocular clavicord," which Rousseau ridicules in the *Essay on the Origin of Languages* (*CW*, 7:325).

As the title of Castel's work indicates, he takes particular exception to Rousseau's distinction between our physical and our moral being and his seeming glorification of our physical existence. He accuses Rousseau of seeing only the animal in man and not the image of God. "Do you thus regard man as a wholly physical being?" he asks Rousseau at the outset of his work, and later calls him "the apologist of bestialness [*bêtise*]."[25] "Nothing proves better that you harm religion," he admonishes Rousseau, "than that you positively take the state of your solitary and animal savage as being the state of primitive innocence, as being the very state of felicity itself and as a terrestrial paradise."[26] He contrasts Rousseau's solitary being in the pure state of nature with the social and familial being described in Scripture and by the natural law theorists. He particularly objects to the "brutality" of Rousseau's discussion of human sexuality, and claims that the distinction Rousseau draws between "physical" and "moral" love clearly shows how he has misunderstood human nature.[27] Finally, Castel perceptively observes that Rousseau's portrayal of man as a physical being that is somehow "good" is connected to his statement in the *Discourse* about "how little care nature has taken to bring men together" (80). Far from "justifying" nature, as Rousseau claims to do in his work, Castel claims that his misdirected thesis "calumniates nature itself, and God as well."[28] Castel recognizes that Rousseau seeks a justification of natural providence where no one had thought to look before.

Natural Man in the Pure State of Nature

Rousseau opens his account of the pure state of nature with a portrait of natural man subsisting in the natural whole, his limited physical needs easily satisfied within the physical world encompassing him. "I will suppose him formed from all time as I see him today: walking on two feet, using his hands as we do ours, directing his gaze toward the whole of nature, and surveying with his eyes the vast expanse of heaven." The upright stature of human beings was traditionally seen as a sign of our unique nature as rational animal, by Aristotle, for example,[29] but Rousseau's natural man is very different. Stripping this being of all the supernatural gifts he may have received and all the "artificial faculties" he may have acquired, he beholds an animal. "I see an animal less strong than some, less agile than others, but, all things considered, the most advantageously physically organized of all. I see him satisfying his hunger beneath an oak, quenching his thirst at the first stream, finding his bed at the foot of the same tree that had furnished his meal, and with that his needs satisfied" (65–66). Rousseau's Adam exists not only prior to any divine dispensation, as in the traditional concept of the pure state of nature, but prior to reason, sociality, and morality. He is a purely physical being under the physical laws of nature.

PHYSICAL MAN IN PHYSICAL NATURE

Immediately following his description of natural man sitting alone beneath a tree, "his needs satisfied," Rousseau describes what appears at first glance to be a provident nature. "The earth, left to its natural fertility (IV) and covered by immense forests which no axe has ever mutilated, at every step offers storehouses and shelter to the animals of every species." In this respect, then, man is considered as one species among others. But already he differs from his fellow animals: "Men, dispersed among them, observe and imitate their industry, and so raise themselves up to the level of the instinct of beasts, with the advantage that each species has only its own instinct, and man—perhaps having none that belongs to him—appropriates them all to himself, feeds himself equally well on most of the various foods which the other animals divide among themselves, and consequently finds his subsistence more easily than any of them can" (66). We have an intimation here of perfectibility, which Rousseau will soon argue is the distinctive attribute of humans. Whereas he will later characterize that faculty as the capacity to make acquisitions that cause men to fall back "lower than the beast itself" (72), here it enables them to "raise themselves up to the level of the instincts of the beast." Whatever the extent of the earth's natural fertility, man's exiguous instinct and his ability to "appropriate" the instincts of other beasts make the provisions of nature fertile in principle for an omnivorous animal with such limited needs.

A brief comparison to his predecessors among the philosophers of the state of nature is useful for grasping the thrust of Rousseau's argument. As for Hobbes, against whose account of the natural condition of mankind Rousseau repeatedly sets his own, among the aspects of the state of nature that make it a state of war of all against all is competition. While Hobbes does argue that without "industry" there is natural scarcity, his more important argument concerning competition regards the nature and extent of human passions and faculties. "Felicity is a continual progress of the desire, from one object to another, the attaining of the former being still but the way to the latter. The cause whereof is that the object of man's desire is not to enjoy once only, and for one instant of time, but to assure forever the way of his future desire."[30] In other words, scarcity exists in principle because human desire is unlimited. As we shall see, Hobbes's natural man is "evil" in Rousseau's sense of the term because his natural endowments lead not to self-preservation and well-being, but to misery and destruction. As for Locke, the comparison is suggested by the note to which Rousseau sends the reader in the passage quoted above concerning the natural fertility of the earth. In note IV he defends his claim in part by an experiment he claims to have conducted by comparing the products of two equal plots of land, one covered with chestnuts and the other sown with wheat (note IV, 122–23). This experiment recalls a comparison of uncultivated and cultivated land by Locke in his famous discussion of property to prove precisely the opposite point. Locke initially speaks of the "Plenty God had given" mankind, and his example of that plenty is the "Acorns he pickt up under an Oak." Recall that Rousseau also begins with man satisfying his hunger beneath an oak. Yet as he proceeds Locke reveals that this "plenty" is in actuality scarcity. In England an acre of cultivated land "that bears here Twenty Bushels of Wheat" so that "the Benefit Mankind receives . . . in a Year, is worth 5£" can be compared to the produce of the same acreage of comparable uncultivated land in America, the product of which he says would be "possibly not worth a Penny; at least, I may truly say, not 1/1000 the value of the cultivated land." Locke concludes that *"labour makes the far greatest part of the value* of things, we enjoy in this World," since "Nature and the Earth furnished only the most worthless Materials, as in themselves."[31] Locke's discussion of the value of labor has implications for his own view of man's relationship to nature and nature's God.[32]

Despite first appearances, nature in Rousseau's description turns out to be a rigorous schoolmistress. After suggesting that man's alimentary needs are easily fulfilled because of his own natural endowments, or lack thereof, Rousseau argues that natural men will "develop a robust and almost unalterable temperament" as a result of being habituated to inclement weather and the need to defend their lives and prey against "other ferocious beasts." Children will likewise obtain the "excellent constitution" of their parents through the same rigors, thereby perpetuating the species. "Nature makes use of them precisely as the law of Sparta did the children of its citizens: it renders strong and robust those who are well constituted and causes all the others to perish." Or, as he states in the next paragraph, natural man's body acquires "the strength and agility that necessity obliges him to acquire" (66). Rousseau's point is not that nature nurtures and protects her offspring, but instead that the natural attributes of physical man as developed and strengthened in the fight for survival enable the strong to live and the species to subsist.

This point is underscored by Rousseau through his first explicit reference to Hobbes, which occurs at this point in the text. "Hobbes claims that man is naturally intrepid and seeks only to attack and fight." By contrast, "an illustrious philosopher" (that is, Montesquieu), Cumberland, and Pufendorf disagree, affirming that "nothing is as timid as man in the state of nature." Contrary to what he seems to imply, Rousseau does not agree with Hobbes's critics. He does not doubt that natural man is frightened by anything new when "he cannot discern the physical good and evil that must be expected from it." On the rare occasions when he is threatened "he always has the option of accepting or refusing the encounter and the choice of fleeing or fighting" (67). So, Rousseau's natural man does in fact fight, but he is not looking for a fight, as in Hobbes. In short, the fact that natural man and the species subsist undermines Hobbes's inference from the passions concerning the character of the natural condition of mankind.

Finally, Rousseau concludes his initial description of physical man in physical nature by considering other possible threats to his subsistence in such a way that underscores the fact that he faces only "physical evils." The "formidable enemies" faced by natural man are childhood, old age, and disease. The first two threats are common to all the species, and therefore do not constitute an objection concerning mankind. As for disease, Rousseau claims that the threat "principally" concerns men living in society. In other words, as with childhood and old age, humans are threatened by physical ailments like all other species, but living in society multiplies them. He indulges in one of his usual diatribes against medicine and the ills owing to inequality, such as the overindulgence of the rich and the hunger of the poor: "these are the fatal proofs that most of our ills [or "evils," *maux*] are our own work, and that we would have avoided almost all of them by preserving the simple, uniform, and solitary way of life which was prescribed to us by nature" (68–69). To use the language of the debates over the problem of evil in which Rousseau will engage defending the *Discourse* in the *Letter to Voltaire*, as physical beings we are threatened by "physical evils," but in society these evils are compounded by "moral evils."

NATURAL GOODNESS AND PROVIDENCE AS PHYSICAL PHENOMENA

With his consideration of "physical man" complete for the moment, Rousseau turns to look at him "from the metaphysical and moral side" (71). I will return to this discussion later, and for the present I will merely say that Rousseau argues that natural man as a physical being has a "metaphysical and moral side" only in potentiality, a point he illustrates with a long aporetic discussion of the difficulties in understanding how language could have originated, concluding with a conundrum: "Which was more necessary, an already formed society for the institution of languages or already invented languages for the establishment of society?" (80). With that task completed, he returns to his account of physical man in physical nature and offers important reflections on the natural goodness of man and his relation to nature, as well as to providence. The crux of his reflections is that the natural goodness of man and providence in the pure state of nature are physical phenomena.

The seeming impossibility of developing language and reason without society and vice versa further underscores the natural asociality of man. Natural man lacks the motive, means, and opportunity for interactions with his fellow human beings that exceed the satisfaction of purely physical needs. "Whatever the case may be regarding these origins," Rousseau states, "it is at least clear from how little care nature has taken to bring men together through mutual needs and to facilitate their use of speech, how little it has prepared their sociability and how little it has contributed for its part to all they have done to establish social bonds" (80). Nature has taken "little care" to prepare our sociability. Is this an indictment of nature? Or, given Rousseau's characterization of the process that "make[s] a being evil while making him sociable" (90), is it instead a justification of nature's providence, at least in relation to man considered as a physical being? Or both?

Rousseau approaches these questions through an engagement with previous philosophers of the state of nature, essentially indicting them for calumniating nature and by extension providence. In this context he refers specifically to Pufendorf's claim that man in the state of nature would be miserable,[33] in a passage I mentioned earlier when discussing the background to the concept of the pure state of nature: "I know that we are repeatedly told that nothing would have been so miserable as man in that state; and if it is true, as I believe I have proved, that he could have had the desire and the opportunity to leave it only after many centuries, this would be a charge to level against nature and not against him whom nature had so constituted." His charge applies equally or more so to Hobbes and others who depict the natural condition of mankind as a state that is necessary to exit as soon as possible. According to Rousseau the claim that natural man is "miserable" is either to use a term that is "meaningless," presumably because his physical man is incapable of being "miserable" (or "happy") in any meaningful sense, or it is incorrect. "Now, I would very much like someone to explain to me what kind of misery there can be for a free being whose heart is at peace and whose body is healthy." Indeed, if we compare the state of nature to society we will see on which side misery truly lies (80–81). Rousseau reverses the assessment of Hobbes, Pufendorf, and others who see the civil state as a remedy for evils of the natural condition.

With the question of the goodness of nature on the table, Rousseau now reveals how his account of physical man in physical nature constitutes a physiodicy. "It was by a very wise providence that the faculties he had in potential were to develop only with the opportunities to exercise them, so that they were neither superfluous and burdensome to him beforehand nor belated and useless when needed. He had, in instinct alone, everything necessary for him to live in the state of nature; he has in cultivated reason only what is necessary for him to live in society" (81). This is the sole reference to providence in the *Discourse*. Although a few interpreters have pointed to this passage as evidence for Rousseau's belief in providence,[34] I suggest it is far more ambiguous. We should begin by asking what he even means by "providence." Given that he argues that man's exit from the pure state of nature is a matter of "singular and fortuitous combinations of circumstances . . . which might very well never have occurred" (70), there is no appeal to any providential plan on the part of the (unnamed) deity or any teleological bent to nature. There is also no suggestion of a providence that extends further than the general physical laws of nature. We must therefore conclude, I believe, that he is speaking of *natural* providence, that is, either of the providence of nature in terms of the general physical laws of nature or of "providence" metaphorically.

As with his earlier statement concerning how "little care" nature has taken to prepare our sociability, we can read this passage either as an exculpation, an indictment, or both. We can read it is an exculpation in the sense that he earlier states that "most of our ills [or "evils," *maux*] are our own work," as opposed to being nature's doing. In this sense, then, it is a justification of nature. Hence Rousseau's claim in note IX that if philosophers had examined natural man instead of civil man, they "would have perceived that man has hardly any other evils than those he has given himself, and that nature would have been justified" (note IX, 127). Civil man, not natural man, is the one who is miserable.

On the other hand, the fact that our passions and faculties once they develop in society make us miserable raises the very question of the problem of evil central to any attempt to construct a theodicy, and thus would amount to an indictment of providence. Even if it is true that the faculties natural man has in potential were not "superfluous and burdensome beforehand"—that is, in the pure state of nature—they do become such after he develops. Indeed, in *Emile* he writes: "All the animals have exactly the faculties necessary to preserve themselves. Man alone has superfluous faculties. Is it not very strange that this superfluity should be the instrument of his unhappiness?" (*Emile*, 81). Nonetheless this indictment can be turned into an exculpation if we view him as offering not a theodicy, but a physiodicy. Namely, if Rousseau's argument concerning providence in the *Discourse* is restricted to natural providence strictly speaking—that is, to man as a physical being in physical nature in the pure state of nature, a being provided with passions and faculties that ensure his self-preservation and well-being, especially at the level of the species. In fact, this is the core of what Rousseau means by the natural goodness of man, a subject to which he turns next.

After having evoked providence, Rousseau turns to the question of whether or in what way natural man can be said to be good or evil. "It appears at first that men in that state, since they have neither any kind of moral relation among themselves nor known duties, could be neither good nor evil, and had neither vices nor virtues—unless, taking these words in a physical sense, one were to call vices in the individual those qualities that can harm his own self-preservation and virtues those that can contribute to it, in which case it would be necessary to call the most virtuous the one who least resists the simple impulses of nature" (81). Rousseau immediately states that he will not depart from the "usual meaning" of good and evil, vices and virtues, and instead suggests another comparison between natural men and civilized men, weighing the proportion of virtues and vices among civilized men (81). Nonetheless, since he understands natural man to be a purely physical being, Rousseau also means us to take these terms in the "physical sense" he proposes. In this case, then, physical man's "natural goodness" consists precisely in the fact that the "simple impulses of nature" tend toward his self-preservation and well-being. In short: natural man's "goodness" is a physical phenomenon.

An indication of Rousseau's conception of "goodness" as a physical category is supplied by Diderot's article "Natural Right" (*Droit naturel*) for the *Encyclopédie*, which is contemporaneous with the *Discourse on Inequality*. In the article, Diderot explains: "If man is not free or if his instantaneous determinations, or even his oscillations, arise from something material that is external to his soul, he will have in them neither reasoned goodness nor wickedness, even though they may have in them animal goodness or wickedness."[35] By distinguishing "reasoned" from "animal" goodness or wickedness, Diderot alludes to the same issue Barbeyrac identified when he criticized Pufendorf's revision of natural law theory in the light of the natural right doctrine of Hobbes, as discussed above.

Rousseau develops his conception of the natural goodness of man through an engagement with Hobbes. "Above all, let us not conclude with Hobbes that since man has no idea of goodness he is naturally evil, that he is vicious because he does not know virtue" (81). His characterization is in fact a caricature. Most importantly, Hobbes explicitly denies that he is arguing that man is naturally evil. In *Leviathan*, for example, within his discussion of the natural condition of mankind, he writes of his "inference from the passions": "The desires and other passions of man are in themselves no sin. No more are the actions that proceed from those passions, till they know a law that forbids them—which till laws be made they cannot know."[36] Yet Rousseau's claim that Hobbes portrays man as "naturally evil" makes sense if we take it in the "physical" sense of the term. Namely, if Rousseau's natural man is "good" because his natural endowments tend toward his self-preservation and well-being, Hobbes's man in the state of nature is "evil" because his passions and faculties tend toward self-destruction and misery.

Once again, Hobbes failed to reach the state of nature because he did not see that the characteristics of human beings that make them evil and miserable are not natural.

> Hobbes saw very clearly the defect of all modern definitions of natural law, but the conclusions he draws from his own definition show that he takes it in a sense which is no less false. Reasoning on the basis of the principles he establishes, this author ought to say that, since the state of nature is the state in which the care of our self-preservation is the least prejudicial to that of others, this state was consequently the most conducive to peace and the best suited to the human race. He says precisely the opposite since he has improperly included in savage man's care for his self-preservation the need to satisfy a large number of passions which are the product of society and which have made laws necessary. (81–82)

"The evil man, he says, is a robust child," Rousseau writes, quoting Hobbes.[37] He objects that "to be robust and to be dependent are two contradictory assumptions in the state of nature. Man is weak when he is dependent and he is emancipated before he is robust. Hobbes did not see that the same cause that prevents savages from using their reason, as the jurists claim they do, prevents them at the same time from abusing their faculties, as he himself claims" (82). The connection of Rousseau's critique of Hobbes to the question of natural goodness or evil is clearer in *Emile*. "But when Hobbes called the wicked man a robust child, he said something absolutely contradictory. All wickedness comes from weakness. The child is wicked only because he is weak. Make him strong, he will be good" (*Emile*, 67). We see here the central importance of dependence for Rousseau's argument about how a natural good being becomes wicked.[38] Rousseau's natural man is independent, both because he is naturally asocial and because his limited needs and passions do not require others to be satisfied. If Hobbes had stripped away the acquisitions made by man in society, he would have seen the natural goodness of man.

SELF-LOVE, PITY, AND THE NATURAL GOODNESS OF MAN

If the natural goodness of man can be defined by his having by nature the passions and faculties that make him good for himself and good (or at least not harmful) to others, then it is the two "principles" Rousseau announced in the Preface he found by meditating on the first and simplest operations of the human soul that work together to make man naturally good. Rousseau is now ready to return to those two principles, and he does so by continuing his engagement with Hobbes. Hobbes failed to notice was that there is "another principle" that moves natural man—that is, a principle in addition to that of self-love. This other principle, "having been given to man in order to soften, under certain circumstances, the ferocity of his pride [*amour-propre*], or the desire to preserve himself before the birth of this pride (XV), tempers the ardor he has for his own well-being by an innate repugnance to see his fellow human being [*semblable*] suffer" (82–83). Rousseau finally names these two "principles": self-love (*amour de soi*) and pity (*pitié*).

Rousseau follows Hobbes in arguing that self-love is the primary passion that motivates human beings, but whereas in Hobbes the passion frustrates self-preservation and well-being in the state of nature, and therefore makes man "evil" in Rousseau's conception, for Rousseau the natural form of self-love tends toward natural man's self-preservation and well-being, and therefore makes man "good."[39] In the note attached to the passage quoted above, note XV, he draws the important distinction between natural self-love (*amour de soi*) and developed pride (*amour-propre*). "Self-love is a natural feeling that inclines every animal to look after its own self-preservation and that, directed in man by reason and modified by pity, produces humanity and virtue." As a physical being, man is like all the other animals in possessing a "principle," self-love, that moves him to seek his self-preservation and well-being. Once he develops reason, this same principle works in "concurrence and combination" with pity to produce humanity and virtue. Of course, Rousseau's story is that more often pity is stifled and reason is allied with pride to make man inhumane and wicked. In any case, before this development there is no virtue or vice in natural man beyond the physical sense of the terms. As for pride or *amour-propre*, he explains: "Pride is only a relative feeling, fabricated and born in society, that inclines every individual to attach more importance to himself than to anyone else, that inspires in men all the harm they do to one another." In other words, in contrast to the strictly physical principle of natural self-love, developed self-love in the form of *amour-propre* is a quintessentially moral attribute in the broad sense of "moral" as opposed to "physical." Natural self-love is "absolute" whereas developed *amour-propre* is "relative." As Rousseau writes of the sort of self-love that exists in the primitive state, "In a word, since each man scarcely views his fellow humans any differently than he would view animals of another species, he can rob the weaker of his prey or give up his own to the stronger without considering these acts as . . . anything but natural events" (note XV, 147). Natural man's relations with his fellow humans and other animals are purely physical in nature, just like the principles that motivate him.

The other principle, the one Hobbes failed to see, is pity. Although some interpreters have pointed in particular to pity as the main reason for man's natural goodness, they tend to do so by moralizing pity as compassion or benevolence.[40] Yet even if natural pity is somehow the basis for such virtues once it develops along with the imagination, such positive forms of identification and empathy are beyond natural man's capacity. As Rousseau states in the *Essay on the Origin of Languages*, "Social affections develop in us only with our enlightenment. Pity, although natural to the heart of man, would remain eternally inactive without the imagination that puts it into play" (*CW*, 7:306). He gives a similar account of pity's awakening in *Emile* (220–23). The apparent difference between Rousseau's treatment of pity in the *Discourse* and these later works has been the subject of considerable scholarly debate, but for the present all I wish to argue is that pity remains a purely physical principle in natural man, spontaneous "gut reactions," as he terms them in *Emile* (222), to witnessing another sensitive being and principally his fellow human beings (*semblables*) suffer. The fact that natural pity concerns principally our fellow human beings is important, for the main role of the principle or passion in Rousseau's account in the *Discourse* is the way in which it tends toward the preservation of the species by checking natural man from acting upon his natural self-love in a way that needlessly inflicts harm. In this sense, then, pity is "good" by promoting the self-preservation and well-being of the individual and the species.

Rousseau's treatment of pity in the *Discourse* is highly rhetorical in nature (e.g., exaggeratedly calling it "the sole natural virtue") and quite complex (e.g., providing examples that seem inapt), and close analysis reveals that pity does very little positive work for natural man, as I have argued elsewhere.[41] For the present purposes, I restrict myself to a few observations that buttress my argument concerning pity in relation to the natural goodness of man. First, as mentioned, pity as it pertains to natural man in the pure state of nature is a purely physical principle. "Such is the pure movement of nature prior to all reflection. Such is the force of natural pity," he states after giving examples of humans and even beasts exhibiting perceptible signs of possessing it. Second, he claims that it is "quite certain that pity is a natural feeling which, by moderating the activity of love of oneself in each individual, contributes to the mutual preservation of the entire species." To be sure, self-love takes precedence over pity when they do not concur, and while Rousseau states that pity "will deter every robust savage from robbing a weak child or an infirm old man of his hard-won subsistence," he also goes on to say that it will do so "if he himself hopes to be able to find his own elsewhere." In other words, the robust savage will in fact take candy from a baby if pressed. Pity moderates self-love in such a way that discourages the needless violence seen in Hobbes's state of nature, and this seems to be the main reason Rousseau includes such a lengthy discussion justifying its naturalness. Finally, at the end of this discussion he ties his treatment of self-love and pity to the issue of the natural goodness of man. These physical principles may not rise so high as the "sublime maxim of reasoned justice"—namely, the Golden Rule, but instead form the basis of "this other maxim of natural goodness, much less perfect but perhaps more useful than the preceding one, *Do what is good for you with the least possible harm to others*" (83–85). In this way, then, the physical principles of self-love and pity work together in such a way that makes man naturally good.

THE PHYSICAL AND THE MORAL

After discussing how natural self-love and pity contribute to the self-preservation and well-being of natural man at the level of both the individual and the species, Rousseau turns to a "dangerous subject," to a "terrible passion" that, "in its fury, seems likely to destroy the human race it is meant to preserve" (85–86). If the sexual passion did in fact destroy the human race, it would make natural man "evil," to refer once again to Rousseau's terminology. He therefore distinguishes between two forms of the sexual passion: "physical love" and "moral love." Sexual love is the paradigmatic example in the *Discourse* of a "physical" attribute that develops into a "moral" one.[42] I say paradigmatic because the same reasoning he uses with regard to the sexual passion applies to the other passions, as we shall see.

"Let us begin by distinguishing the moral from the physical in the feeling of love," he begins, disarming the passion of its threatening potential: "The physical is that general desire that leads one sex to unite with the other. The moral is that which gives this desire its specific character and focuses it exclusively on a single object, or which at least gives it a great degree of energy for this preferred object." "Moral love" is an "artificial feeling born of social custom," he claims, and more importantly "this feeling is based on certain notions of merit or beauty which a savage is not in a condition to have and on comparisons he is not capable of making.... He heeds solely the temperament he has received from nature and not a distaste he could not have acquired, and every woman is good for him." In other words, natural man is "limited to the physical aspect of love alone" (86). Note that Rousseau speaks of the physical and moral "aspects" of sexual love. In other words, they are not distinct passions. Rather, moral love is a developed form of physical love that develops along with reason, imagination, and the other faculties necessary to make distinctions and form preferences.

The stakes of the distinction Rousseau insists must be made between the physical and moral "aspects" of the sexual passion, and I would suggest "physical" and "moral" aspects of human nature in general, come in an earlier discussion in the *Discourse* of the sexual passion, in which he makes his point by arguing that Locke failed to do so. His argument comes in a lengthy note to a passage in his aporetic discussion of the origin of languages in which he objects that Condillac, a follower of Locke, in his account of the origin of language has assumed what is in question—namely, the naturalness of the family. In note XII Rousseau finds in Locke an objection too "plausible on its face" (*spécieuse*) for him to be allowed to conceal it, and then transcribes a long passage from the *Second Treatise* concerning the nature of human sexual and familial relations. Locke argues that the "leading, if not the only, reason" for the longer conjunction of male and female among humans as compared to other animals is "because the female is capable of conceiving, and is commonly with child again, and brings forth a new birth, long before the former is out of a dependency for support on his parents' help, and able to shift for himself," so that the father, in order "to take care for those he hath begot, and to undertake that care for a long time, is under an obligation to continue in conjugal society with the same woman by whom he had them, and to remain in that society much longer than the other creatures" (note XII, 141–42).[43]

Most importantly, Rousseau undermines the assumptions he claims Locke makes about humans' natural needs and passions, especially with regard to sex. "Locke proves at most that the man might very well have a motive for remaining attached to the woman when she has a child, but he does not at all prove that he must have been attached to her before the delivery and during the nine months of the pregnancy." Like Condillac, Locke "obviously assumes what is in question"— not only the existence of some relatively stable society, which would lead to the development of the knowledge and foresight he supposes in humans, but the very reason and foresight in the first place. "For this kind of memory, by which one individual shows a preference to an individual for the act of procreation, requires, as I prove in the text, more progress or corruption of the human understanding than it can be assumed to have in the state of animality in question here." Rousseau alludes here to the distinction he draws between physical and moral love in the main text. Locke's argument therefore falls apart, and he has committed the same error of Hobbes and others who "had to explain a fact about the state of nature—that is, about a state in which men lived isolated and in which a given man had no motive to stay by the side of a given man, nor perhaps for men to stay by one another's sides, which is far worse; and they did not think of carrying themselves back beyond the centuries of society" (note XII, 144–45). Put differently, Locke made an analytical error by failing to distinguish physical man and moral man. Hence Rousseau's first rejoinder to Locke after quoting him: "I will first observe that moral proofs do not have a great deal of force with regard to physical matters, and that they serve rather to make sense of existing facts than to ascertain the real existence of those facts" (note XII, 143). Another example of a philosopher failing to reach the state of nature.

If physical love and moral love are the paradigmatic example in the *Discourse* of physical versus moral attributes, by their very names, then another important case of how a passion transforms from an initially physical attribute to take on a moral aspect is self-love. Indeed, the development of sexual love is closely aligned to the development of self-love, to which it is related as a form of love. The natural form of self-love, *amour de soi*, and physical love are both "absolute" passions, centered on the self and restricted to a physical character. In turn, *amour-propre* and moral love are "relative" passions, concerned with one's relations to others and therefore "moral," in the broad sense of the term. While it true that in the *Discourse* Rousseau describes *amour de soi* and *amour-propre* as "two passions very different in their nature and their effects" (note XV, 147), and they have been treated as such by some scholars, they are nonetheless both forms of the "principle" that moves humans to seek their self-preservation and well-being.[44] That *amour-propre* is a developed form of *amour de soi* is clearer in *Emile*. Notably, after discussing how the sexual passion develops in such a way that the lover desires to be preferred by the beloved above all others, Rousseau explains: "Extend these ideas, and you will see where our *amour-propre* gets the form we believe natural to it, and how self-love [*amour de soi*], ceasing to be an absolute sentiment, becomes pride [*orgueil*] in great souls, vanity in small ones" (*Emile*, 215). Note that Rousseau's premise in this passage is that we are mistaken in our belief that *amour-propre* is natural, and so our failure to distinguish natural and artificial forms of the passions is yet another example of failing to "go back" far enough. Natural man shares self-love in its natural form with the animals, and what distinguishes humans is the capacity for this passion, along with the other passions and faculties, to transform into the versions we see today.

Conclusion

A full discussion of Rousseau's theory of human nature and development would require a separate book-length treatment, and so let me conclude in imitation of Rousseau when he reminds himself in *Emile* "that my business here is not producing treatises on metaphysics and morals" (235). If I were to produce such a treatise, I would argue that Rousseau's understanding of how initially physical attributes of human nature develop into moral ones is part of his attempt to articulate a nonreductionist materialist metaphysics, as Rousseau himself intended to do in an abandoned work to which he gave the telling title *La morale sensitive, ou le matérialisme du sage—Sensitive Morality, or the Wise Man's Materialism* (see *Confessions*, CW, 5:343).[45] I myself have broached this interpretation elsewhere, especially with regard to Rousseau's argument in his musical writings, including the *Essay on the Origin of Languages*, concerning the relationship between physical and moral causes and effects—for example, how the physical properties of sound can convey moral effects through imitative melody.[46] But that is not the business at hand, although I will return in chapter 4 to Rousseau's account of human nature and development to the extent my examination of his theological and religious thought requires. For the present, I want to keep my focus on my argument concerning how Rousseau's account of the pure state of nature functions as a theodicy or physiodicy. Thus, I conclude this chapter with some remarks on how the discussion in the *Discourse* of perfectibility relates to Rousseau's argument concerning the natural goodness of man as a physical being in physical nature.

The capacity for the human passions to develop, including from initially physical passions into moral ones, points to what Rousseau identifies as the distinguishing attribute of human nature: perfectibility. His argument concerning perfectibility comes in the section of the *Discourse* that I passed over, when he turns from "physical man" to man "from the metaphysical and moral side." He commences this investigation by attempting to ascertain what distinguishes human beings from the other animals—that is, what makes man more than a simply physical being. He first claims that it is "his capacity as a free agent" that distinguishes man from the animals, who are limited to instinct, but he then appears to abandon this claim due to the "difficulties" involving free will and instead argues that the "faculty of self-perfection," or "perfectibility," is the distinctive attribute of mankind (71–72). I will return in chapter 4 to freedom, perfectibility, and the metaphysical issues involved.

Rousseau glosses "the faculty of self-perfection" as "a faculty which, with the aid of circumstances, successively develops all the others and resides among us as much in the species as in the individual" (72). Rousseau presents this distinctively human "quality" by way of a contrast: "whereas an animal is at the end of a few months what it will be all its life and its species will be at the end of a thousand years." In other words, humans individually and especially as a species are capable of change over time (and place) to a degree that distinguishes them from other animals. Indeed, while animals never lose their instinct, man may lose everything "his *perfectibility* has made him acquire" and "thereby falls back lower than the beast itself." Ironically, then, perfectibility is the source of the evils we experience once we develop, or what Rousseau will term "moral" as opposed to "physical" evils. "It would be sad for us to be forced to agree that this distinctive and almost unlimited faculty is the source of all of man's misfortunes, that it is this faculty that, by dint of time, draws him out of that original condition in which he would pass tranquil and innocent days, that it is this faculty that, over the centuries, by causing his enlightenment and his errors, his vices and his virtues, to bloom, makes him in the long run the tyrant of himself and of nature (IX)" (72–73). Despite his rhetorical emphasis on the negative effects of perfectibility, Rousseau does not feel "forced to agree" entirely with this sentiment, for our acquisitions in developing include not only "errors" but also "enlightenment," "virtues" as well as "vices." As noted, in chapter 4 I take up the divergent paths of human development, which produce either disunity (error, vice, evil) or unity (enlightenment, virtue, goodness), and how they elicit different responses with regard to theology and religion.

In the passage concerning the effects of perfectibility just quoted Rousseau sends the reader to a note, a note in which he proclaims that he has demonstrated that man is naturally good and has therefore justified nature, and in fact a passage containing the quotation with which I began this chapter in arguing that the *Discourse* offers a novel theodicy or physiodicy. After citing a philosopher who has calculated that the "evils" of human life outweigh the "goods," making life a pretty poor present, Rousseau states that he is not surprised, for the philosopher was examining "civil man" instead of "natural man." "Men are wicked; sad and continual experience spares the need for proof. Yet man is naturally good—I do believe I have demonstrated it," Rousseau proclaims. Again, "men" as they become in society are wicked, but "man"—physical man in physical nature—is naturally good. If we go back all the way to the pure state of nature, we would perceive that "man has hardly any other evils than those he has given himself, and that nature would have been justified" (*Inequality*, note IX, 127).

I have always found it exceedingly strange that Rousseau states the fundamental principle of all of his writings, that man is naturally good and is corrupted in society, in a note. Let me conclude by trying to make sense of this important note in relation to the main text of the *Discourse* to which it is attached in a way that speaks to how the work operates as a theodicy or physiodicy. The place to start, I believe, is with his claim that the justification of nature consists in showing that "man has hardly any other evils than those he has given himself." In other words, almost all of the evils we experience are the result of the development of our passions and faculties made possible by perfectibility. Recall in this light, then, that this was precisely the subject of the passage to which note IX is attached. By going back to the pure state of nature, Rousseau finds a naturally good being, that is, a being whose endowments as a physical being in physical nature tend toward the self-preservation and well-being of the individual and the species. The evils we experience as we develop are, so to speak, extrinsic, from the outside as opposed to the inside in terms of our core nature. In this light, then, the subject and aim of the *Discourse* are the same as what Rousseau said of those of *Emile*. Namely, in the *Dialogues* it is characterized as "nothing but a treatise on the original goodness of man, destined to show how vice and error, foreign to his constitution, enter it from outside and imperceptibly change him" (*Dialogues, CW*, 1:213). Or, similarly, in the *Letter to Beaumont*, he expounds the fundamental principle of all of his writings and especially of *Emile*—"that man is a naturally good being, loving justice and order; that there is no original perversity in the human heart, and that the first movements of nature are always right." And he goes on to explain: "I have shown that all the vices imputed to the human heart are not natural to it; I have stated the manner in which they are born. I have followed their genealogy, so to speak, and I have shown how, through continuous deterioration of their original goodness, men finally become what they are" (*Beaumont*, 28). Once again, "men" are evil, but "man" is naturally good.

CHAPTER 3

Pride and Providence in the *Letter to Voltaire*

On the morning of All Saints' Day, November 1, 1755, a devastating earthquake struck Lisbon, and by week's end the combination of earthquake, tsunami, and fires had destroyed the city and killed as many as 50,000 people. Such was the shock of the earthquake that it provoked a crisis of philosophical faith in the century of Enlightenment.[1] As the city's remaining inhabitants cleared the rubble over the next few months, Voltaire penned a poem on the disaster from his new estate just outside Geneva, *Les Délices*. The poem was published (anonymously) in March 1756, paired with the "Poem on the Natural Law." Rousseau received a copy of the two poems in July, and he devoted six weeks to writing a reply. In the *Confessions* he would later explain: "Struck at seeing this poor man burdened, so to speak, with prosperity and glory nevertheless declaiming bitterly against the miseries of this life and always finding all to be evil, I formed the senseless project of making him return into himself and of proving to him that all was good" (*CW*, 5:360). His letter to Voltaire was dated August 18, 1756. After receiving a brief acknowledgment of receipt of his letter the following month, Rousseau suggested through intermediaries that they consider publishing their exchange, to no avail. Three years later he learned of the unauthorized publication of his letter, in Berlin by his future antagonist Johann Heinrich Samuel Formey, soon-to-be author of the *Anti-Emile*. The already tense relationship between Rousseau and Voltaire was broken, with Rousseau penning a letter dated June 17, 1760, in which he blurted out: "*Je vous hais.*" Three years later he finally consented to have his letter published, as part of an edition of his collected works and as an accompaniment to the *Discourse on Inequality*. As for Voltaire, he wrote *Candide* (1759), which Rousseau took to be his belated reply (*Confessions*, *CW*, 5:361).[2]

If the theological and religious aspects of his argument in the *Dis-*

course on Inequality I examined in the previous chapter are muted, Rousseau makes them thematic in his defense of the work in the *Letter to Voltaire*, sometimes known as the *Letter to Voltaire on Providence*. There Rousseau defends the cause of nature and God, after his own fashion, in response to Voltaire's "Poem on the Lisbon Earthquake." In so doing, he situates the fundamental principle of the natural goodness of man and his corruption in society expressed in the *Discourse on Inequality* within a theological argument concerning natural and divine providence and a discussion of the religious sentiments requisite for men and citizens in society. Examination of the *Letter* therefore enables us to understand more completely the theological dimension of the *Discourse on Inequality*. The theological and religious arguments of the *Letter* also preview Rousseau's later treatments of these subjects, notably in the "Profession of Faith" in *Emile*, published six years later. The letter therefore serves as a bridge between the *Discourse on Inequality* and *Emile* and as a prolegomenon for the future study of the "Profession." Victor Gourevitch summarizes its importance: "In short, the *Letter to Voltaire* is Rousseau's most authoritative discussion of religious issues, the discussion in the light of which careful readers will assess his numerous other discussions of these issues."[3]

The *Letter* is widely viewed as Rousseau's first extended working out of the theological arguments and religious sentiments expressed more fully in the "Profession," as well as in *Julie*, the "Moral Letters," and other writings. Indeed, in his landmark study of Rousseau's religious thought, Masson characterizes the *Letter* as Rousseau's "first profession of faith in providence," and argues that the writing exhibited "the same orientation of thought" as the "Profession."[4] Most scholars who have studied the *Letter* have followed Masson's lead, both in seeing an essential continuity of arguments and aims from the *Letter to Voltaire* to the "Profession" and also in assuming that both works contain a sincere expression of Rousseau's religious beliefs.[5] Let me take these two widely held suppositions in reverse order.

With regard to the assumption that the *Letter* is an expression of Rousseau's own beliefs, it is certainly tempting to make. For example, many interpreters point to the fact that it is a "private" letter written in the first person in his own name (unlike, say, the "Profession"), and they also rightly note that Rousseau protests at various points in the letter that he is expounding what he sincerely believes. For reasons I have already articulated, however, I will not assume that the views Rousseau propounds are simply what he himself truly believes, especially on the ground that they are contained in a private letter. First, as I argued in the introduction, we cannot take any correspondence by Rousseau or others in this period to be "private" in the sense we would understand today, and none more so than the *Letter to Voltaire*. Although it was later published without his permission, Rousseau clearly wrote the letter with an eye to eventual publication. We know this based on correspondence in which he suggested publication of his exchange with Voltaire, and we can surmise as much based on the extraordinary care he took in composing the letter, as evidenced by the multiple drafts we possess. As Gourevitch remarks, "He clearly did not think even of this *Letter* as entirely candid and private."[6] Second, therefore, as I argued in chapter 1 with respect to Rousseau's writings on theology and religion in general, we must assume that he wrote his letter to Voltaire with an eye to both the truth and utility of what he propounds, and also keeping in mind that truth and utility do not necessarily coincide.

With regard to the second main conclusion of most scholars who have examined the *Letter*—namely, that there is an essential continuity in terms of its arguments and aims between the letter and the "Profession" and Rousseau's other theological writings—I generally agree with this assessment, but for different reasons. As for the arguments advanced in the two writings concerning God, providence, and other matters, that question will have to wait until I turn to the "Profession." As for the aims, I do see considerable continuity between the writings, including their common concern with both truth and utility.

In this chapter I argue that close analysis of the *Letter* reveals that it is a complex writing in which the divinity lies in the details. Careful analysis of the structure and argument of the letter reveals that Rousseau offers a double teaching concerning providence. In the first teaching, he reaffirms the general providence of nature in terms of physical causes and effects in a manner consistent with his depiction in the *Discourse on Inequality* of natural man in the pure state of nature as a physical being living under the physical laws of nature. In addition, in this first naturalistic account of providence he argues, again consistent with the *Discourse*, that the sweet sentiment of existence alone suffices to justify our existence, and therefore to justify nature or nature's God. My reading up to this point resembles Gourevitch's interpretation of the *Letter*, which, like my own, breaks from the common assumption that Rousseau is expressing his own sincere religious views in the *Letter* and instead analyzes the arguments he advances with a critical eye.[7] Unlike Gourevitch, I also try to account of the reasons why Rousseau would then offer a second, parallel teaching concerning moral providence. In this second teaching, Rousseau supplements the first naturalistic teaching with an account of a beneficent God with particular providence for the individual. The turning point between these two teachings comes when

Rousseau mentions pride. Rousseau thereby indicates that he has added this second teaching because he considers it useful and even necessary for developed and corrupted human beings, and by implication admits that the first, naturalistic teaching concerning the general providence of physical nature does not fulfill this need. Finally, Rousseau admits that his supposed sincere belief in the doctrine of divine providence is just that, a belief, and a belief to which he claims to incline, not because of its truth, but because of the hope and consolation it provides.

The Introduction to the *Letter to Voltaire*: Nature's Rhetoric

What does the book of nature "say" to human beings, and what would humans like to have nature and its author "say" to them? Voltaire's "Poem on the Lisbon Earthquake" can be characterized as a meditation on what might be termed the rhetoric of nature. At the outset of the Preface to the poem Voltaire remarks: "The axiom 'All is well' seems a bit strange to those who are the witnesses of these disasters"—namely, the several earthquakes he enumerates.[8] We are witnesses to the spectacle of nature, in this case the terrifying spectacle of natural disasters. The poet takes a rhetorical stance in conveying what he has seen, and that from the very first line: "O unfortunate mortals! O deplorable earth!"[9] In response, Rousseau's *Letter to Voltaire* is also concerned with the rhetoric of nature and the rhetoric of poems about nature, in this case both Voltaire's poem and the poem to which Voltaire responded, Pope's "Essay on Man." In this regard both Voltaire and Rousseau follow Pope's lead, for the first stanza of his poem (after the opening dedication to Bolingbroke) opens: "Say first, of God above, or man below, / What can we reason, but from what we know?"[10] As we shall see, the most obvious instance in the *Letter* of the theme of the rhetoric of nature and the rhetoric of poems about nature occurs when Rousseau has Pope's and Voltaire's poems each make a speech to him about the lessons we are to take from what nature has said to them and the effect of these lessons on us. Rousseau's emphasis in doing so is on the rhetorical effect of the poems. As Gourevitch states, "The debate between Voltaire and himself is framed by the question of whose view of providence is the least cruel and the most consoling."[11] Rousseau is concerned as much with the utility as the truth of the theological and religious teachings conveyed by these poems.

The two poems Rousseau has received from Voltaire are the "Poem on the Lisbon Disaster" and the "Poem on the Natural Law," the latter having been written a few years earlier and originally titled the "Poem on Natural Religion." From the very first words Rousseau emphasizes that he has received two poems, despite the fact that his attention in the *Let-*

ter is confined almost exclusively to one of the poems. "Your last poems, Sir, have reached me in my solitude.... I found pleasure in them along with instruction, and have recognized the hand of the master; and I believe I owe you thanks for the copy as well as for the work itself" (*Voltaire*, 108).[12] Voltaire's poems are concerned with nature as the supposed work of the author of nature, and Rousseau treats these poems as the works of an author that themselves portray or reflect the workmanship of the author of nature. Rousseau recognizes "the hand of the master" in the "copy" he has received of "the work itself." In other words, to recur to the analogies once familiar to those subjected to standardized tests: God : Nature :: Poet : Poem. The poem is a kind of facsimile of nature, and the poem's rhetorical or emotive effect reflects the effect we experience in witnessing the spectacle of nature.

In addition to emphasizing that he has received two poems from Voltaire, Rousseau underscores the differences between them. As for the "Poem on the Lisbon Earthquake," Voltaire's answer toward the end of the poem concerning what nature testifies to those who witness the disaster is bleak: "Nature is mute, she is interrogated in vain; / We need a God who speaks to the human race."[13] The contrast to the "Poem on the Natural Law" is dramatic, as witnessed by the concluding "Prayer," which reads in part:

> O God who is misunderstood, O God whom everything [*tout*]
>   announces,
> Hear the final words my mouth pronounces; ...
> And I can think only of a God who gave me birth,
> Only of a God who has bestowed gifts on me throughout my days.[14]

Not surprisingly, then, Rousseau explains that Voltaire's two poems have elicited very different responses from him: "Besides, the more your second poem enchants me, the more freely I side against the first; for if you have not been afraid to oppose yourself, why should I be afraid to be of your opinion?" (108).

Why emphasize the fact that he has received two poems if he confines his attention to only one of them? I suggest two reasons, one substantive and the other structural. First, Rousseau's argument in the *Letter* will be that we can have very different responses to what I have termed the rhetoric of nature, a point presaged by Voltaire's very different responses in his two poems. Second, as I will show in my analysis of Rousseau's letter, there are a number of structural and other features that involve echoing phrases or doubling other elements from one part of the letter to another, and so his emphasis on having received a pair of poems introduces and initiates this structural feature, which itself points to two substantively different teachings concerning nature and providence and our response to them.

The poem that draws Rousseau's scrutiny is the "Poem on the Lisbon Disaster." The poem itself is relatively short at 180 lines, but also includes a prose Preface nearly as long as the poem itself and a number of notes, some of them quite lengthy, in which Voltaire takes up various philosophic or scientific issues. The full title of this poem reveals it to be a critique of optimism as encapsulated in Pope's axiom: "Poem on the Lisbon Disaster, Or Examination of the Axiom, 'All Is Well'" (*Poème sur le désastre de Lisbonne, ou examen de cet axiom, "Tout est bien"*). This axiom concludes Pope's *Essay on Man* (1733–34), a long epistolary poem intended to "vindicate the ways of God to man":

> All Nature is but Art, unknown to thee;
> All Chance, Direction, which thou canst not see;
> All Discord, Harmony not understood;
> All partial Evil, universal Good:
> And, in spite of Pride, in erring Reason's spite,
> One truth is clear, Whatever is, is right.[15]

Pope's axiom stands for Voltaire as the slogan of philosophical optimism, which he also associates in his poem with Leibniz. Leibniz would, of course, later be the model for Dr. Pangloss in *Candide*, in which the Lisbon earthquake makes an appearance as well.

After opening the letter by thanking Voltaire for the poems, Rousseau immediately focuses on the differences between them, and especially on their different emotive effects. "I shall not tell you that everything [*tout*] in them appears equally good to me" (108). This statement is not simply the pronouncement of a forthright critic, since at issue in Voltaire's poem and Rousseau's response is the axiom "All is well"—*Tout est bien*. Pope's "Essay on Man," Voltaire's poem on Pope's axiom, and Rousseau's *Letter to Voltaire* are all works that ask about the character of the divine or natural whole—*le tout*—and on the proper reaction human beings should have to that whole. As Voltaire writes, "Of the great WHOLE [*TOUT*] I am but a little part."[16] Our reaction can be rational or emotive, and Rousseau makes these different ways of reacting part of his analysis: "It is not without difficulty that I sometimes defend my reason against the charms of your poetry; but in order to render my admiration more worthy of your works, I force myself not to admire everything [*tout*] in them" (108). Once again, Voltaire's poems and Rousseau's letter are "wholes" that reflect on the divine or natural "whole" and our responses to it.

The emotive effect of Voltaire's poems is the focus of Rousseau's analysis. While he finds the "Poem on the Natural Law" consoling and uplifting, the "Poem on the Lisbon Disaster" saddens and depresses him. "All my grievances are therefore against your poem on the disaster of Lisbon, because I expected from it some effects more worthy of the humanity which appears to have inspired you to write it." Rather than the consoling effects required by charity, Voltaire's poem aggravates our misery. "You reproach Pope and Leibniz for condemning our misfortunes [or "evils," *maux*], in maintaining that everything [*tout*] is good, and you so amplify the picture of our miseries that you aggravate the feeling of them; instead of the consolations for which I hoped, you cause me to be afflicted." Rousseau prefers optimism for its effects, not necessarily for its truth: "This optimism, that you find so cruel, nevertheless consoles me in the very miseries which you depict to me as intolerable" (108–9).

Rousseau reinforces his emphasis on the emotive effect of Voltaire's poems when he imagines Pope's and Voltaire's poems each making a speech to him, as mentioned earlier:

> "Man, have patience," Pope and Leibniz tell me. "Your evils [*maux*] are a necessary consequence of your nature, and of the constitution of this universe. The eternal and beneficent Being who governs you would have liked to safeguard you from them. Of all the economies possible, he has chosen the one which combined the least bad with the most good, or (to say the same thing more bluntly, if it is necessary), if he has not done better, it is that he could not do better."

"What does your poem now tell me?" Rousseau asks Voltaire.

> "Suffer forever, wretches. If there is a God who has created you, no doubt he is omnipotent; he could have prevented all your evils: do not hope that they will ever end; for one would not know how to see why you exist, if it is not to suffer and die."

In making Voltaire's poems speak, he emphasizes their rhetorical effect rather than the solidity of their arguments.

In contesting Voltaire's criticism of optimism, Rousseau embraces Pope at best at arm's length. He does not base his own argument on Pope or Leibniz, or on any other version of philosophical optimism. He makes this point in another defense of the *Discourse on Inequality*, the "Letter to Philopolis," which was written nearly a year earlier than the *Letter to Voltaire* and which he did not send or publish during his lifetime. In a response to the *Discourse on Inequality* under the pen name Philopolis, his compatriot the naturalist Charles Bonnet argued against Rousseau that society was natural to human beings and that human development is willed by God in his perfect wisdom, even granting, for the sake of argument, Rousseau's claim concerning the distinctive human faculty of perfectibility. Philopolis appealed in this context to philosophical optimism: "If it were a question of justifying providence in the eyes of men, Leibniz and Pope have done so" ("Letter from Philopolis," in *CW*, 3:124). In reply, after arguing that society is natural to mankind as decrepitude is to the individual, a development that is perhaps inevitable but not to be embraced as a positive good, Rousseau addresses philosophical optimism.

> Confronted with the list of evils [*maux*] burdening men and that I maintain are their own work, you and Leibniz assure men that all is good, and that providence is therefore justified. I was far from believing that [providence] needed help for its justification from the Leibnizian philosophy or any other. Do you yourself seriously think that a system of philosophy, whatever it may be, can be more blameless than the universe, and that to exculpate providence the arguments of a philosopher are more convincing than the works of God? ("Letter to Philopolis," *CW*, 3:129)

If Leibniz and Pope argue that "everything that is, is good," then human societies must be consistent with the general good, even if they necessarily include particular evils. Rousseau replies that particular evils are nonetheless real evils for those who experience them, and he argues that he has demonstrated that societies are among the particular evils that need never have existed for the general good. As for Leibniz and Pope, "it is clear that, properly understood, optimism has no effect either for or against me" (129). Unlike the a priori metaphysical system of Leibniz, both Voltaire and Rousseau approach the question of the order of nature and providence through a posteriori observation of nature and an assessment of the goods and evils of human life.

The speech Rousseau has Voltaire's poem make to him claims that God is doubtless omnipotent and yet condemns human beings to suffer, thus raising the central problem of theodicy: how to reconcile God's power and goodness given the existence of evil. Voltaire raises the issue in his poem and very quickly runs through some of the attempts in philosophy and theology to address it. Rousseau follows his lead in addressing them as well: "I do not know what such a doctrine could possess that is more consoling than optimism and even fatalism. As for me, I acknowledge it appears to me even crueler than Manichaeism."

That the optimism exhibited in Pope's poem is consoling Rousseau has already said. His remark that even fatalism would be more consoling than Voltaire's poem implies that Voltaire believes that God in his omnipotence could eliminate evil but chooses not to do so, thus privileging divine omnipotence over divine goodness, indeed without even speaking of goodness. In turn, Manichaeism avoids the dilemma by positing two principles, one good and another evil, and Rousseau finds such a doctrine more consoling than Voltaire's apparently uncaring deity. "If perplexity concerning the origin of evil forces you to alter one of the perfections of God," he asks Voltaire, "why do you wish to justify his power at the expense of his goodness? If it is necessary to choose between two errors, I like the first one even better" (109). Indeed, in *Emile* Rousseau will state (significantly, in a discussion of the natural goodness of man): "Of all the attributes of the all-powerful divinity, goodness is the one without which one can least conceive it" (*Emile*, 67). As we shall see, in a sense this is precisely what he will argue in reply to Voltaire: that the goodness of nature and the author of nature consist in the general lawlike regularity of nature as a whole, even if those laws entail particular evils.

The Teaching Concerning Natural Providence

We might expect Rousseau to turn at this point to a discussion of divine providence, but he does not. In fact, he does not speak of God again until much later in his letter. Instead of discussing divine providence and the problem of theodicy, he first appeals to the justification of our existence he has elaborated in the *Discourse on Inequality*. In other words, rather than defending the goodness of the deity, he brings forward as witness the natural goodness of man. The doctrine of the natural goodness of man is his answer to the problem of theodicy. Only then does he turn to the question of providence, but in a wholly naturalistic manner in which he limits his discussion to the physical laws of nature and man's place within nature. Taken as a whole, then, his discussion of the natural goodness of man and then the goodness of nature constitutes the first, naturalistic teaching concerning providence.

JUSTIFYING OUR EXISTENCE: THE NATURAL GOODNESS OF MAN

Rousseau begins his justification of nature and human nature by tying it to the *Discourse on Inequality*. "You do not wish, Sir, that your work be regarded as a poem against providence; and I shall indeed restrain myself from giving it this name, although you have characterized as a book against the human race a writing wherein I pleaded the cause of the human race against itself" (109). He refers both to what Voltaire writes in his poem and to what Voltaire wrote in a letter to him concerning the *Discourse*. As for the "Poem on the Lisbon Disaster," Voltaire summarizes his intention toward the end:

> One day all [*tout*] will be good, this is our hope;
> All is good today, this is the illusion.
> The wise deceive me, and God alone is right [*a raison*].
> Humble in my sighing, resigned to my suffering,
> I do not rise up against Providence.[17]

Of course, it is difficult not to read Voltaire's poem as an indictment of God for our suffering, as a poem against providence, even if Rousseau will not so accuse him.[18] Let that be as it may. As for Voltaire's letter to Rousseau concerning the *Discourse*, it famously begins: "I have received, Sir, your new book against the human race.... You paint with very true colors the horrors of human society from which ignorance and weakness anticipate so many comforts. Never has so much intelligence been used to seeking to make us stupid [*bêtes*]" (Voltaire to Rousseau, August 30, 1755, in *CW*, 3:102). Like Voltaire in the "Poem on the Lisbon Disaster," Rousseau in his *Discourse* depicts the evils human beings suffer. The difference, he explains, lies in his intention: "My purpose was excusable, and even praiseworthy, as I believe, for I showed to men how they caused their miseries themselves, and consequently how they might avoid them" (109). In other words, in the *Discourse* Rousseau pleads the cause of the human race against itself by solving the problem of evil through his central principle of the natural goodness of man and his corruption in society.

The next several paragraphs of the *Letter to Voltaire* might be characterized as Rousseau's interpretation of the *Discourse on Inequality* with an eye to the problem of evil. He begins by appealing to the traditional distinction between moral evil and physical evil, but he reaffirms them in terms of the "system" of the natural goodness of man. "I do not see that one can seek the source of moral evil other than in man free, perfected, and thereby corrupted; and, as for physical evils, if sensitive and impassive matter is a contradiction, as it seems to me, they are inevitable in any system of which man is a part" (109). As we saw in the previous chapter, a central argument of the *Discourse on Inequality* concerns the distinction between the "physical" and the "moral" when analyzing human beings and their attributes. As physical beings, humans suffer physical evils such as illness and death because of the nature of material beings. Or as Rousseau states in the letter, physical evils are "inevitable in any system of which man is part." Even if physical man suffers physical evils, he is nonetheless naturally good. For the present, however, he restricts his focus to human beings and he does not discuss the physical order of nature as a whole. As for moral evils, he attributes them to what he argued in the *Discourse* was the distinctive human faculty of perfectibility: "man free, perfected, and thereby corrupted." Moral man becomes corrupted or evil and is himself the source of the moral evils as well as many of the physical evils he suffers. In keeping with his portrait in the *Discourse* of the original nature of human beings as physical beings whose moral attributes exist only in potential, Rousseau for the moment puts aside moral evil and reduces the problem of evil to its physical aspect. In doing so, he also follows Voltaire, who essentially entirely ignores moral evils in his poem.[19]

As for physical evils, then, he claims: "I believe I have shown that with the exception of death, which is an evil almost solely because of the preparations which one makes preceding it, most of our physical evils are still our own work." Rousseau's main point is that most of the physical evils we suffer are actually caused by ourselves and are therefore essentially moral evils. Staying with the example of the earthquake, he notes that humans built the tall buildings in Lisbon that collapsed and caught fire. "How many unfortunate people have perished in this disaster because of one wanting to take his clothes, another his papers, another his money. Is it not known that the person of each man has become the least part of himself, and that it is almost not worth the trouble of saving it when one has lost all the rest?" Earthquakes occur in the uninhabited wilderness, but no one speaks of them because we only take account of the "Messieurs" of the city. Perhaps some of those killed died quickly and avoided the agonies of a protracted death at the hands of their heirs, solicitors, and medical doctors. "As for me, I see everywhere that the evils [*maux*] to which nature subjects us are far less cruel than those we add to them" (109–11). Again, despite his flippant tone, Rousseau's point is that most physical evils are our own fault and are therefore effectively moral evils.

The most striking physical evil is death, but Rousseau disposes of it quickly. As he argues in the *Discourse*, natural man does not foresee death, "and the knowledge of death and its terrors is one of the first acquisitions man has made in moving away from the animal condition" (*Inequality*, 73). Since he does not know death, natural man makes no painful preparations for it: "They eventually expire without anyone perceiving that they cease to exist and almost without perceiving it themselves" (68). Perfected and therefore corrupted man, in turn, exercises his foresight to his detriment. "Is there a sadder end than that of a dying man who is burdened with useless cares, whose solicitor and heirs do not permit him to breathe, whose physicians leisurely assassinate him in his bed, and whom barbarous priests artfully make savor death? As for me, I see everywhere that the ills to which nature subjects us are far less cruel than those we add to them" (110–11). The remark about doctors, a favorite subject, is a barb intended for Voltaire, who, after reading the *Discourse*, protested his need for Dr. Tronchin when he quipped to Rousseau that he was no longer able to walk on all fours (in *CW*, 3:102). Although Rousseau might seem to argue in these various statements that death and dying are not evils, he actually always acknowledges that they are: death "is *almost* not an evil," natural men die "*almost* without perceiving it themselves," and man naturally knows how to "suffer," meaning that he does in fact suffer. Rather, the point is the contrast he draws between the physical evils he admits are suffered by natural man and the greater evils experienced by perfected man, which are exacerbated by the very remedies applied to them.

The argument concerning the goodness of nature is based less on Rousseau's denial of physical evil than a case for the goodness of existence. Having dispatched the evil of death and the pains associated with it, he therefore turns to his core claim concerning the sweetness of existence. "But if it is better for us to be than not to be, this would be enough to justify our existence, even if we were to have no other compensation to expect for the evils [*maux*] that we have to suffer, and even if these evils [*maux*] were as great as you depict them." In weighing the goods and evils of life, developed human beings—and especially philosophers—tend to exaggerate the evils and, more importantly, forget about the "the sweet sentiment of existence" (111). The sweet sentiment of existence *alone* suffices "to justify our existence," and therefore to justify nature. Philosophers prior to Rousseau had spoken of the sweetness of existence itself—Aristotle, for example,[20] but Rousseau makes the sentiment of existence the root of all true happiness and the foundation of his system of the natural goodness of man. As with his justification of nature in the *Discourse on Inequality*, his initial argument in the *Letter* remains on the plane of physical man existing under the physical laws of nature.

A good judge of existence must be sought far from men, far from the places frequented by philosophers, among country or mountain people, who, after all, constitute the majority of mankind. "In fact, I dare to state that perhaps there is in the upper Valais not a single mountain dweller discontented with his almost automatic life, and who would not willingly accept, even in the place of Paradise, the bargain of being reborn over and over again in order to vegetate thus in perpetuity." Speaking of the differing assessments of the value of life by philosophers and mountain dwellers, Rousseau writes: "These differences cause me to believe that it is often the abuse we make of life which renders it a burden to us; and I have a far less favorable opinion of those who are vexed at having lived than those who can say with Cato: *Nec me vixisse paenitet, quoniam ita vexi, ut frustra me natum non existimem*"—"I do not regret having lived, since I have lived in such a fashion that I do not think I was born in vain" (111–12).[21] The irony, of course, is that rustic mountain folk are far less likely to quote Cicero, especially in Latin, than philosophers. I include Rousseau's citation of Cicero in part because, as we shall see, it is an example of his use of echoing and doubling structures in presenting his twofold teaching concerning providence, in this case by citing the continuation of the passage from Cicero later in the letter. For the present, however, he offers a purely naturalistic justification of our existence based on the sweet sentiment of existence.

The sentiment of existence promotes the preservation and well-being of individual human beings, but more importantly the continuation of the species: "We have not been able, up to the present, to perfect ourselves to the point of generally rendering life a burden to ourselves and to prefer nothingness to our existence; without which preference, discouragement and despair would soon take hold of the greatest number, and the human race could not long subsist" (111). In a defense of the *Discourse on Inequality* addressed to the naturalist Charles-Georges Le Roy and written shortly after the *Letter to Voltaire*, Rousseau also points to the survival of the species as part of his argument about the order of nature: "The proof that all is well organized is taken from a general and incontestable fact, which is that all the species continue to exist" (*CW*, 3:134). His justification of our existence is not a justification of the existence of any particular individual, but of the species. Cast in the terms of the teaching concerning natural providence to which he now turns, the providence of nature is general.

The strictly naturalistic justification of nature and of our natural existence Rousseau first advances in the *Discourse* and then repeats in the *Letter* is carried through to the end of his life and writings. In the *Reveries of the Solitary Walker*, he underscores the strictly natural basis of his argument for the goodness of existence:

> The sentiment of existence, stripped of any other emotion, is in itself a precious sentiment of contentment and of peace *which alone would suffice* to make this existence dear and sweet to anyone able to spurn

all the sensual and earthly impressions which incessantly come to distract us from it and to trouble its sweetness here-below. But most men, agitated by continual passions, are little acquainted with this state. (*Reveries*, 46; emphasis added)

As in the *Letter to Voltaire*, Rousseau states that the sweet sentiment of existence "alone would suffice" to justify our existence, without any further compensation being necessary. If this is true, we have to ask why he feels it is necessary later in the *Letter* to supplement the argument concerning the natural goodness of man with a teaching concerning particular divine providence.

THE GENERAL PROVIDENCE OF NATURE

Up to this point, Rousseau has argued that the forgotten sweet sentiment of our existence itself justifies our existence, and he does so without any reference to the general order of nature or what might be termed natural providence. The subject of the order of nature as a whole arises when he replies to Voltaire's claim concerning the disorder of nature. Voltaire's claim is a response to Pope, who writes near the beginning of the "Essay on Man" of witnessing the spectacle of an ordered system of nature, including the regular orbits of the planets, with God upholding the "great chain of being" ordering the whole.[22] Voltaire refuses the supposed consolation that comes from viewing the spectacle of nature:

> No, no longer bring forward to my agitated heart
> Those immutable laws of necessity,
> That chain of bodies, spirits [*esprits*], and worlds.
> O dreams of the learned! O profound chimeras!
> God holds the chain by his hand, and is not himself enchained;
> Everything [*tout*] is determined by his beneficent choice:
> He is free, he is just, he is not implacable.
> Why then do we suffer under an equitable master?[23]

The theological thrust of Voltaire's questioning is clear: God in his omnipotence could have willed to spare us evil, but he chooses not to do so. Despite his claim that he has not penned a poem against providence, he in fact has.

Rousseau has already queried Voltaire as to why he chooses to emphasize the omnipotence of the deity over his goodness, but this is not the object of his attention at this point. Rather, he responds to a lengthy note Voltaire adds to the passage quoted, specifically to the verse concerning the chain of being. In the note, Voltaire first objects to Pope's image of "The strong connections, nice dependencies, / Gradations precise . . ." of this chain, stating that there is in fact an immense gap between man and the animals. Likewise, he denies that every being, down to every atom, is necessary and is necessarily in its proper place within the system of nature. He does so by bringing forward as an expert witness a critic of Pope, the "learned geometer" Jean-Pierre Crousaz, whose *Examen de l'essai de M. Pope sur l'homme* was published in 1737. Finally, and most importantly, Voltaire claims that "nature is subjugated neither to any precise quantity nor precise form" and "nature never acts rigorously."[24]

In response, Rousseau first protests his ignorance of Crousaz: "I have not read his writing against Pope, and perhaps I am in no position to understand it" (*Voltaire*, 112). This ignorance is in fact feigned. First, in a draft of the letter Rousseau reveals his familiarity: "A mediocre geometer, poor reasoner, obdurate and pedantic mind, obscure and cowardly writer" (cited at *Voltaire*, 193n12). Second, in a letter from 1742, Rousseau analyzes at length the very work by Crousaz of which he claims to be ignorant, exhibiting not only his familiarity with it but also his keen understanding.[25] Third, in *Julie* he makes a point that is highly relevant for understanding the substance and aims of the *Letter to Voltaire*, having Julie write to St. Preux about her reading:

> Monsieur de Crouzas has just given us a refutation of Pope's epistles which I have read with displeasure. I do not know, in truth, which of the two authors is right; but I know well that Monsieur de Crouzas' book will never inspire a good deed, and that there is nothing good one is not tempted to do after reading Pope's. I for one have no other manner of judging my readings than to sound the dispositions in which they leave my soul, and I scarcely imagine what sort of goodness a book can possess when it does not lead its reader to do good. (*Julie*, 2.18, *CW*, 6:214)

To this passage Rousseau adds a note in his role as the supposed editor of the correspondence: "If the reader approves this rule, and uses it to judge this collection, the editor will not appeal his judgment" (214n). As with his response to Voltaire's and Pope's poem, then, the emphasis is on the emotive and moral effects of reading them. We should expect that Rousseau has this aim in mind in the *Letter to Voltaire*. This expectation may help explain why Rousseau feigns ignorance of Crousaz, for, as Gourevitch persuasively argues, he presents himself in the *Letter to Voltaire* less as a philosopher than as a common man viewing the world through commonsense experience.[26] I would add that Rousseau presents himself as responding to nature—and to poems about nature—in a phenomenological and emotional rather than a scientific and rational manner.

The more important claim made by Voltaire that nature does not operate in a rigorous lawlike fashion attracts Rousseau's scrutiny. "Far from thinking that nature is not subject to the precision of quantities and of forms," in the sense of mathematically regular ratios and motions, "I believe quite to the contrary that she alone strictly follows this precision, because she alone knows how to compare exactly the ends and the means." To illustrate this principle, he uses an example that is of little interest in itself, but that nonetheless becomes quite important when he uses it again in a very different context later in the letter in another instance of echoing and doubling. "Let us assume two weights in equilibrium, and nevertheless unequal; to the smallest let the quantity be added which is the difference between them: either the two weights will still remain in equilibrium, and we shall have a cause without effect; or the equilibrium will be broken, and we shall have an effect without cause." But he objects that this is impossible, and suggests that there must be a natural explanation such as a hidden grain of magnet (112–13). The image is drawn from Voltaire's poem, where he states: "Scale in his hand, Bayle teaches us to doubt."[27]

In the same vein Rousseau counters Voltaire's claim that physical phenomena do not follow precise mathematical forms, using as one of his examples the apparently irregular motions of celestial bodies and explaining that these anomalous motions occur because the movements of natural bodies are modified by other natural bodies (112–13). This example is actually a pregnant one. In Newton, one of Voltaire's great heroes, there remains a role for God in celestial mechanics to intervene occasionally to keep the planets and other celestial bodies in their orbits, but in post-Newtonian mechanics these and other motions were conceived in dynamic terms, as Rousseau does here, whereby the apparently irregularities in motions were explained in terms of the system of bodies in motion without recourse to exterior causes, including divine intervention. In fact, in adducing this example, Rousseau is in fact throwing it in Voltaire's face, for Voltaire himself played a role in popularizing the dynamic revision of Newtonian physics, devoting a chapter of his *Éléments de la philosophie de Newton* (1738) to explaining that the apparently irregular motion of the moon was due to the laws of attraction acting on it by other celestial bodies.[28]

"Every event seems to me necessarily to have some effect, whether moral or physical, or composed of the two, but which are not always perceived." For Rousseau, nature—including man's place in it—is a system of causes and effects operating through general laws. The Lisbon earthquake would be one such example, and therefore Voltaire's complaint against the deity is to adopt the wrong perspective. He asks Voltaire whether "the most bizarre curve is not as regular to the eyes of nature as a perfect circle to ours" (113). "Our eyes" may prefer regular shapes and motions such as circles, but we must look at phenomena through "the eyes of nature." This seemingly innocuous phrase is another instance of an element of his discussion of natural providence that will soon be echoed within the teaching concerning divine providence, when Rousseau remarks on how through our pride we wish to matter more "in the eyes of God." In matters of physics we ought not let our pride make us dogmatic about our supposed demonstrations, as he insinuates Voltaire has done. Instead, he appeals to his and Voltaire's shared admiration for Bayle's "wisdom and caution in matters of opinion" (114).

The Teaching Concerning Divine Providence

The turn to the parallel teaching concerning divine providence is signaled by an abrupt change in subject when Rousseau introduces the divinity into his discussion. "As for the rest, you have made a very fitting correction in Pope's system, by observing that there is no proportional gradation between the creatures and the Creator, and that, if the chain of created beings leads to God, it is because he holds it, and not because he terminates it." Rousseau effects another arm's-length embrace of Pope, in this case a correction to the idea of the "chain of beings," which he introduces with a qualifying "if" and does not himself affirm. Rousseau has not spoken of Pope since the beginning of his letter, and by referring again to the poet he recalls the occasional cause for his discussion of theology: Voltaire's objection to Pope's maxim "All is well." He also recalls the importance of the issue of the emotive effect of Pope's and Voltaire's poems about nature when he imagines, as he did earlier, a speech in reaction to Voltaire's poem: "On the good of the whole, preferable to that of its parts, you have man say: 'I ought to be as dear to my master, I, a thinking and feeling being, as the planets, which probably do not feel at all.'" Up to this point, it was a question of knowing how things, including human things, appear "in the eyes of nature," but now we have the demand of the individual for recognition from on high: "I believe, I hope, I am worth more *in the eyes of God* than the land of a planet." What, then, of the probable inhabitants of Saturn or other planets? The individual still hopes to be worth more. In the end, Rousseau admits that "it is only human pride [*orgueil*]" that underlies this belief or hope

(114–15; emphasis added). When we imagine how things appear "in the eyes of God," pride enters the stage, and the scene changes. One reason I am emphasizing the fact that Rousseau's turn to a teaching concerning divine providence coincides with a consideration of human pride is that we will see the same pairing of pride and providence in the "Profession of Faith."

In claiming that the human desire to be worthy, even the worthiest, in the eyes of the divinity is owing to pride, Rousseau alludes to two passages in Voltaire's poem. The explicit reference is to a note Voltaire adds to the Preface in which he first quotes Shaftesbury on misplaced complaints of apparent irregularities in nature given the general order and then states: "This does not prevent man from being able to say: 'I ought to be as dear to my master, me being thinking and sentient, than the planets.'"[29] Second, the issue of whether it is prideful to lodge such complaints against a seemingly uncaring divinity arises near the beginning of his poem.

> It is pride [*l'orgueil*], you say, seditious pride,
> Which claims that being evil [*mal*], we could be better,

and then tells his imagined interlocutor to go ask the survivors of the earthquake:

> Whether it is pride which cries out: "O heaven, help me!"
> "O heaven, have pity on human misery!"[30]

Rather, according to Voltaire somewhat later in the poem, when he rejects the supposed consolation that comes from contemplating how our corpses nourish worms and insects, those who discount the particular evils we suffer in light of the general goodness of an ordered nature are the ones guilty of pride: "And I do see in you only the ineffectual effort / Of a hapless pride [*fier*] which feigns being content."[31] It is this part of Voltaire's poem to which Rousseau is responding when he alleges that our desire for particular attention from the divinity stems from pride.

Rousseau effectively admits that the doctrine of natural providence he has hitherto advanced is insufficient for perfected humans: "That the corpse of a man nourishes some worms, some wolves, or some plants is not, I admit, a compensation for the death of this man." In one last attempt to advance a theory of divine general providence consistent with his earlier doctrine of natural providence, he suggests that the death of the individual is necessary for the preservation of the human species and to the system of the universe, and thus "the particular evil [*mal*] of an individual contributes to the general good. I die, I am eaten by worms; but my children, my brothers will live as I have lived, and I do, by the order of nature, for all men" what the great Roman heroes "did voluntarily for a small part of men" (115). As in his first, naturalistic teaching concerning providence, the emphasis is not on the particular individual but rather on the species ("my children, my brothers will live as I have lived . . . for all men"), or even the whole of nature.

In developing a teaching regarding divine general providence, Rousseau nuances his defense of the "system" Voltaire attacks—that is, Pope's version of optimism—and we should remind ourselves that he does not fully embrace that system. One must distinguish "particular evil, whose existence no philosopher has ever doubted, from the general evil that the optimist denies. . . . Thus the addition of an article would render, it seems the proposition more exact: and in place of 'Everything is good' [*Tout est bien*], it would perhaps be better to say, 'The whole is good,' or 'Everything is good for the whole' [*Le tout est bien, ou Tout est bien pour le tout*]" (115). This system of optimism is drawn from the structure and regularity of the universe, according to Rousseau, but the devout, the philosophers, and others find this system insufficient and "they always have divine justice intervene into purely natural events." He counters: "It is to be believed that particular events here below are nothing *in the eyes of the Master of the universe*, that his Providence is only universal, that he is content to preserve the genera and the species, and to preside over the whole without being disturbed by the manner in which each individual spends this brief life" (116; emphasis added). Natural providence does not seem to be distinguished from divine providence here; looking at things "in the eyes of nature," as earlier, is equivalent to doing so "in the eyes of the Master of the universe," as here. All events seem to be purely natural, and God is equivalent to nature, or at least he has no particular relationship with any individual being.

Nonetheless, Rousseau can no longer maintain a purely natural analysis when the subject of death arises again. When he spoke of death in his natural teaching concerning providence, he cited Cicero, and I mentioned at that point Rousseau splits the quotation in two, and now in the divine discussion of providence he provides the continuation. First the portion quoted earlier: "*Nec me vixisse paenitet, quoniam ita vixi, ut frustrà me natum non existimem*" (112). And now the continuation: "*Commorandi enim Natura diversorium nobis, non habitandi dedit*"—"Nature has ordained that we be on earth as guests in passage, not as inhabitants" (116). The second part of the quotation, unlike the first, suggests a life after death. The continuation of the passage in Cicero is telling. Cicero has the speaker, Laelius, continue: "And if I err in my belief that the souls of men are immortal, I gladly err, nor do I wish this error which gives me pleasure to be wrested from me while I live.... Again, if we are not going to be immortal, nevertheless, it is desirable for a man to be blotted out at his proper time. For as Nature has marked the bounds of everything else, so she has marked the bounds of life."[32] Does Rousseau also gladly err in suggesting a life after death?

Rousseau now ties the question of providence to the question of the immortality of the soul as a recompense for the evils we suffer in this life, including death.

> To think rightly in this respect, it seems that things ought to be considered relatively in the physical order, and absolutely in the moral order: with the result that the greatest idea I can give myself of Providence is that each material being be disposed the best way possible in relation to the whole, and each intelligent and sensitive being the best way possible in relation to itself; which signifies in other terms that for whomever feels his existence, it is worth more to exist than not to exist. But it is necessary to apply this rule to the total duration of each sensitive being, and not to several particular instances of this duration, such as human life; which shows how much the question of Providence depends on that of the immortality of the soul in which I have the good fortune to believe, without being unaware that reason can doubt it. (116–17)

Let me consider this important passage in some detail.

We have here the familiar distinction between the "physical" and the "moral." As for the physical order, Rousseau effectively repeats what he has already argued: that particular beings, including human beings considered as physical beings, are ordered in terms of the whole—*le tout*. Particular evils must be considered in terms of the general order of nature, as entailed by the general providence of nature or, if one likes, nature's God. As for the moral order, he makes the question of providence depend on the goodness of existence for "each sensitive being," that is, for each human being taken individually. This opens the door to particular divine providence, but does Rousseau actually enter? Note that he frames his argument in terms of questions, not answers: "The *question* of Providence depends on [the *question*] of the immortality of the soul." The question of the immortality of the soul in relation to a particular divine providence, in turn, depends upon the answer to the question about the goodness of existence. In fact, Rousseau has already answered that question earlier in the letter with reference to the sweet sentiment of existence: "But if it is better for us to be than not to be, this would be enough to justify our existence" (111). In other words, we do not need to suppose the immortality of the soul to justify our existence and thus justify providence. The appeal to a particular moral providence of the deity and the belief in the immortality of the soul are necessary for us when we consider ourselves as moral beings: "man free, perfected, and thereby corrupted" (109), as Rousseau stated earlier when he identifies the source of moral evils. In other words, we demand recompense for the evils we suffer, including death, from the deity because of human pride.

Rousseau claims that he has the "good fortune" to believe in the immortality of the soul, and contrary to the generally a posteriori character of his arguments in the *Letter to Voltaire* (and elsewhere), he attempts to prove this fortunate belief, if a belief can even be proved, through a deduction from the divine attributes. "If God exists, he is perfect; if he is perfect, he is wise, powerful, and just; if he is wise and powerful, all is good; if he is just and powerful, my soul is immortal" (117). First, since he has just admitted of the divine perfections that "this knowledge is incontestably above human intelligence" (115), we have to take seriously the "If" at the head of the deduction. Second, while he speaks of three traditional attributes of God— wisdom, power, and justice, he does not relate all three to one another, nor does he relate wisdom and justice.[33] God could be wise and powerful, but not just from the perspective of the individual desiring immortality, in which case the conclusion "all is good" would still hold. This is the choice Rousseau has made in the natural discussion of providence, where he argues that God does not contravene the general laws of nature to care for particular individuals. This form of divine justice is equivalent to the general order of the universe. But the individual concerned for his own soul demands a different kind of divine justice and power. Third, and to this point, he does not claim that the divine attributes are superlative: God is wise, powerful, and just, but not omniscient, omnipotent, and omnibenevolent. God's power and justice may not extend to particular individuals; it is *our* demand for justice that demands God's solicitude. We will see a similar argument in the "Profession of Faith."

Rousseau admits that his proof of the immortality of the soul is doubtful. "As for me, I naively admit to you that neither the pro nor the con seems to me demonstrated on this point by the lights of reason, and that if the theist bases his sentiments only on probabilities, the atheist, even less precise, seems to me only to base his contrary probabilities. Moreover, the objections, on both sides, are always insoluble because they take in some things of which men have no genuine idea at all" (117). He chooses the side of the theist, the side of belief. And it is quite explicitly *belief*, and not reason, that tips the scales. To explain his choice, he compares his soul to a scale in equilibrium. This is the same analogy he used earlier in his letter when he imagined two unequal weights in equilibrium and furnished an explanation for this seeming impossibility, a bit of hidden magnet in one of the weights, which maintains the regularity of the laws of nature (113). Now he furnishes an explanation of his theological decision in the same fashion. Admitting the pros and cons in the debate, he says: "And yet I believe in God quite as strongly as I believe in any other truth, because to believe and not to believe are the things which depend the least on me, because the state of doubt is too violent for my soul, because when my reason wavers, my faith cannot for long remain in suspense, and is determined without it, because, finally, a thousand subjects of preferences entice me from the most consoling side and join the weight of hope to the equilibrium of reason" (117). Of course, one does not "believe" in a truth, one knows it. As Shklar comments, "Without that hope he would be too miserable, but to say that one believes something because one would despair otherwise, is not what is usually meant by an affirmation of faith."[34] Rousseau's belief, even if sincere, is by his own admission a belief founded on a hope that inclines to the more consoling side.

In a paragraph in a draft of his letter that follows the one just discussed, a paragraph he decided to delete from the version he sent and therefore the version originally published, Rousseau reveals that his doubts run even deeper. "I remember that what has struck me the most forcefully in my whole life, on the fortuitous arrangement of the universe, is the twenty-first philosophical thought"—that is, the *Pensées philosophiques* by his then-friend Diderot.[35] In fact, Rousseau was haunted by this example and returns to it on a number of occasions in his writings, including in the "Profession of Faith" and his 1769 letter to Franquières.[36] As he explains to Voltaire, Diderot argues there that the improbability of an event is "more than sufficiently compensated" by the number of throws of the dice, especially if the throws are infinite, therefore suggesting that the order of the universe could eventually arise out of chaos by chance alone. Rousseau admits the force of the argument, and also admits that he knows no way to counter it. Weighing this materialist explanation of the order of nature against the alternative of order by design of the divinity, he writes: "While both the one and the other seem equally convincing to me, the last alone persuades me" (117–18). He uses the language of persuading versus convincing familiar to us from the later discussion in the *Social Contract* of the lawgiver, who cannot reason with the people he is founding and must instead appeal to their passions by attributing his laws to the gods. To illustrate his incredulity at the option that fails to "persuade" him, Rousseau imagines someone telling him that the *Henriade* was composed by a fortuitous throw of letters, a claim he says he would reject out of hand, interestingly because the chances of persuading him are even smaller than the composition of the poem by chance. In other words, he implies that the infinity of throws could both compose the poem and ultimately persuade him. But he refuses to count the throws: "My incredulity, quite as little philosophical as one will like, will triumph thereon over the very demonstration itself. I do not deny that what I call on that matter a *proof of sentiment* might be called *prejudice*; and I do not give this obstinacy of belief as a model; but with a good faith perhaps without example, I give it as an invincible disposition of my soul" (118).[37] As Gourevitch concludes, "In short, the God of the *Letter to Voltaire* may be a premise, and the Providence of the *Letter* a 'great and consoling dogma.' They are not conclusions."[38] Finally, and perhaps revealingly, in the *Discourse on Inequality* Rousseau appeals to the same logic of the laws of probability accounting for a highly unlikely event when he states of his account of human development: "This will excuse me from expanding my reflections about how the lapse of time compensates for the slight probability of events" (*Inequality*, 90). Couldn't the same logic apply to the order of the universe?

Although he claims not to offer his obstinate unphilosophical belief as a model, Rousseau in fact does so, for belief in a divinity with care for his soul has precisely the consoling effect he has complained Voltaire's poem lacks. He will no longer dispute with Voltaire or the philosophers over these matters, and the philosophers should remain silent because "there is inhumanity in troubling peaceful souls, and in afflicting men to no purpose, when what one wishes to teach them is neither certain nor useful" (118). Once again, we have the question of the relationship between truth and utility. The belief in a caring divinity is useful in providing men hope and consolation, whether or not it is true.

Rousseau concludes with some remarks concerning the value of skepticism in theology, just as he ended the teaching concerning natural providence earlier in the *Letter* with remarks concerning healthy skepticism in philosophy and science. He affirms with Voltaire "the most perfect liberty" in faith, but he also recognizes "a sort of profession of faith that the laws can impose," a limited and negative profession, including a prohibition against intolerance, which helps assure the peace of the state. "Done carefully, this work would, it seems to me, be the most useful book ever composed, and perhaps the only one necessary for men." Rousseau speaks only of the utility of such a work, not of its veracity. Voltaire himself should lend his hand to the work, he suggests (119). It suffices to say that Voltaire never wrote such a profession, and that Rousseau did so in the chapter "On Civil Religion" in the *Social Contract*.

CHAPTER 4

Psychic Unity and Disunity and the Need for Religion

When examining how Rousseau's account of natural man in the pure state of nature constitutes a theodicy, I argued that his justification of nature through the natural goodness of man is restricted to physical man in physical nature, and therefore added the caveat that this theodicy is more accurately a physiodicy. In the present chapter I turn to Rousseau's account of human development in the *Discourse on Inequality* and *Emile* and the question of the psychological need for religion, and in doing so I add a further caveat to my argument about the theodicy or physiodicy of the *Discourse*. Namely, I examine how according to Rousseau human beings might develop from purely physical beings into moral beings in such a way that their development is in accord with their original nature, thereby retaining their natural goodness in some sense and creating psychic unity. The theodicy or physiodicy of the natural goodness of man would therefore be extended to developed humans insofar as this is possible.

A principal aim of this chapter is to argue that Rousseau's theory of human nature and development as it is found in both the *Discourse* and *Emile* is nondualist in terms of its metaphysical commitments. This argument prepares my analyses in the following two chapters of the "Profession of Faith," which does advance a dualist metaphysics. To forecast the main point: for Rousseau human beings are naturally unified beings whose divisions or contradictions come from without and are not intrinsic aspects of our being, whereas for the Vicar we are naturally divided beings, consisting of two "principles" associated with body and soul. In terms of metaphysical commitments, Rousseau's account in *Emile*, as in the *Discourse*, is monist or naturalistic, but certainly not dualist. Indeed, one might characterize his project in *Emile* as an attempt to prevent dualism in the human soul, or, alternatively, as meant to avert any temptation to appeal to a dualist theory to account for our experience of psychic division. In the conclusion to this chapter, I offer some reflections on how our psychic condition of unity or disunity leads to different psychological needs for religion.

Human Nature and Development in the *Discourse on Inequality*

In my analysis in chapter 2 of the *Discourse on Inequality* I restricted my focus to Rousseau's account of natural man in the pure state of nature, only touching on the question of the development of our passions and faculties made possible by the distinctively human attribute of perfectibility and doing so only in relation to Rousseau's justification of nature in the work. In this section I return to his theory of human nature and development as presented in the *Discourse*. I do not give a full account of this theory, but instead concentrate on the subjects he raises when he turns from "physical man" to man viewed "from the metaphysical and moral side": freedom, perfectibility, and the dynamic theory of human nature.

MAN FROM THE METAPHYSICAL AND MORAL SIDE

In the first part of the *Discourse on Inequality* Rousseau portrays natural man in the pure state of nature as a physical being in physical nature, but he interrupts his account midway to look at man "from the metaphysical and moral side" (71).[1] Before examining this digression, the first task at hand is terminological: What does Rousseau mean by "metaphysical" and "moral"? The short answer is that in both cases these terms have a much broader and somewhat different meaning in Rousseau's own time and in his own usage than we would today ordinarily attribute to them. Failing to recognize the meaning of the terms has, I believe, led to considerable misunderstanding of Rousseau's argument concerning the two attributes he identifies as distinguishing human beings from the other animals, freedom and perfectibility, and their metaphysical entailments. Let me therefore address his terminology.

As for the term "metaphysical," in the broad sense it is nearly synonymous with what we would mean by "psychological." As far as I am aware, Rousseau uses neither *psychologie* or *psychologique* in any of his writings. The words were recently available in his time—for example, in the *Essai de psychologie* (1754) by Charles Bonnet, incidentally the author who would shortly later write a critical response to the *Discourse on Inequality* under the pseudonym "Philopolis." Yet the term *métaphysique* was more common for discussions that we would call "psychological." Two examples will suffice, both familiar to Rousseau. First, in the *Essai sur l'origine des connaissances humaines* (1746), his friend Condillac explains:

> Two sorts of metaphysics must be distinguished. The first, an ambitious one, seeks to pierce every mystery—nature, the essence of beings, the most hidden causes—this is what it flatters itself to do and what it promises to discover. The second, more restrained, proportions its researches to the weakness of the human mind, and, as uneasy about what must escape it as eager about what it can grasp, it knows how to limit itself within the limits that are marked out for it.... The philosophers have been particularly exercised about the first sort, and have regarded the second as an accessory part which hardly merits the name of metaphysics. Locke is the sole whom I believe must be excepted; he limited himself to the study of the human mind, and he has fulfilled this object with success.[2]

As a follower of Locke, Condillac will limit himself to the study of the operations of the mind. The second example is d'Alembert, who writes in the "Preliminary Discourse" to the *Encyclopédie* (1751): "In a word, [Locke] reduced metaphysics to what it in fact ought to be: the experimental physics of the soul."[3] This meaning of "metaphysical" as the study of how sensations give rise to ideas explains why Rousseau's exposition of man from the "metaphysical and moral side" continues with a discussion of language and reason. Consider his inaugural remark in that discussion: "The more one meditates on this subject, the more the distance from pure sensations to the simplest knowledge increases in our eyes" (*Inequality*, 74). Nonetheless, for Rousseau the term *métaphysique* in this context encompasses not only the broad sense of the psychological attributes of human beings such as mental and emotional processes and states, but also questions concerning free will and the metaphysical status of the soul that consideration of these processes and states raise, or metaphysical issues in the narrow sense of the term.

As for the term "moral," I already noted in chapter 2 that for Rousseau it is not restricted to what we would call "morality," but is nearly synonymous with "social." We have seen that in the *Discourse on Inequality* and elsewhere Rousseau uses the term "moral" in opposition to "physical." The "moral" attributes of human beings are those that are not strictly "physical" in character, which in the developmental framework of the *Discourse* means those attributes that are not natural in the sense of original. As with the term "metaphysical," the examination of man from the "moral side" includes broad matters concerning moral or social relations of all sorts and questions of morality in the narrower sense. With these terminological matters addressed, we can better understand Rousseau's investigation of man "from the metaphysical and moral side."

FREEDOM AND PERFECTIBILITY

Rousseau commences his investigation by attempting to determine what distinguishes human beings from the other animals—that is, what makes man more than a simply physical being. He first claims that it is "his capacity as a free agent" that distinguishes man only to then put aside this claim, given that there are "difficulties" concerning free will, and instead argues that the "faculty of self-perfection," or "perfectibility," is the distinctive attribute of humans (71–72). His argument is the subject of ongoing scholarly debate, including the question of the relationship between freedom and perfectibility, including whether he abandons his claim about freedom. Without wading into these debates, let me stake out my own position insofar as is necessary for my purpose of arguing that Rousseau does not advance a dualist metaphysics.

To illustrate his claim that man is distinguished from the animals by being a "free agent," Rousseau asserts that a pigeon would die of hunger near a basin of meats and a cat would perish atop a heap of fruits or grain whereas a human could elect to eat either food, perhaps to his detriment, because "the will still speaks when nature is silent" (71). Does this example prove human freedom? Or limited instinct? The reader of the *Discourse* has already seen intimations of man's distinctive attribute in the initial description of how human beings find plenty of sustenance in nature because they "perhaps" have no instinct and can "appropriate" the instincts of other beasts (66). The question of instinct in fact frames Rousseau's discussion of freedom and perfectibility, for he returns to instinct when he concludes his discussion of perfectibility and before he launches into his digression on language: "Savage man, left by nature to instinct alone, or rather compensated for that instinct he perhaps lacks by faculties capable of substituting for it at first and then of raising him far above nature, will therefore begin with purely animal functions" (73). At minimum, man's limited instinct seems to be the ground for being able to choose (freedom) as well as his ability to change (perfectibility).

After providing the example of the lack of a fixed dietary instinct in man, Rousseau turns to the operations of the mind, in keeping with the broad sense of "metaphysical" discussed above. "Every animal has ideas since it has senses, it even combines its ideas up to a certain point, and man differs in this regard from beast only by degree.... It is therefore not so much understanding that constitutes the specific difference of man among the animals as it is his capacity as a free agent." Note that Rousseau actually leaves open the possibility that "understanding" may also constitute a qualitative difference: "It is therefore *not so much* understanding..." (*Ce n'est donc pas tant l'entendement*...). I note this because I believe it clarifies his claim about freedom. "Nature commands every animal, and the beast obeys. Man feels the same impetus, but he recognizes that he is free to acquiesce or resist, and it is above all in the consciousness [*conscience*] of this freedom that the spirituality of his soul is shown." A few observations. First, if man (almost) lacks instinct, he does not feel the same "impetus" from nature that commands the beast, so this is less a positive claim about freedom than a way of keeping the door open for freedom. Second, then, it is the "recognition" that he is free to act and especially the "consciousness" of this freedom that distinguishes man from beast, or rather that will come to distinguish them. In other words, it is a cognitive feature of the developed understanding, or mind, that is involved: self-consciousness. "For physics in a way explains the mechanism of the senses and the formation of ideas," Rousseau states in good Lockean and Condillacian fashion, "but in the power of willing, or rather of choosing, and in the feeling [*sentiment*] of this power are found only purely spiritual acts, about which nothing is explained by the laws of mechanics" (71–72). Note again that the mental state of a "feeling" or "sentiment" is at play. Also note that Rousseau already backs away from a strong claim about free will by calling it the power of "choosing." The consciousness of the ability to choose will come to distinguish humans.

Let us now consider what metaphysical stance is implied in his argument concerning freedom. Rousseau's language about the "spirituality" of the soul, and especially his assertion that the acts of willing or choosing cannot be explained by the laws of mechanics, have led a number of interpreters to argue that he embraces some form of metaphysical dualism. Further, to rebut those who maintain that Rousseau abandons his initial argument concerning freedom for a metaphysically neutral claim about perfectibility, these interpreters argue that freedom and perfectibility are effectively synonymous, and that he therefore does not in fact abandon that position. Finally, they also adduce evidence elsewhere in his writings for the argument concerning freedom as well as metaphysical dualism, principally from the "Profession of Faith."[4] However, as these interpreters sometimes acknowledge, such a dualist metaphysics sits rather uneasily in the otherwise naturalistic or even materialist framework in the *Discourse*, and some even argue that Rousseau evolves through his writings from the largely naturalistic account of the *Discourse* to a more dualist position exemplified most clearly in the "Profession of Faith."[5] I postpone the question of the relationship between what Rousseau writes in his own name from what he puts into the mouth of the Savoyard Vicar until chapter 6.

Here I limit myself to suggesting that Rousseau does not in fact embrace a dualist metaphysics in the *Discourse*, but instead offers what one might call a phenomenological account of freedom. We experience the "consciousness" or the "feeling" of being free to choose, whatever the ontological status of that experience. Goldschmidt seems to have in mind a similar interpretation, calling dualism "a moral experience" for Rousseau, and he therefore writes of his supposed "'dualism'" in scare quotes.[6] Finally, Rousseau adopts a similar position in the "Fragment on Freedom": "I have no idea if the acts of my will are in my own power or if they follow an outside impetus, and I care very little about knowing that, since this knowledge could not influence my behavior in this life. . . . Therefore, I have no wish at all to speak here about this metaphysical and moral freedom" (*CW*, 4:12).

My suggestion of a phenomenological reading has several advantages. First, it resonates with the prevailing naturalism of the *Discourse*. Second, it also harmonizes with Rousseau's argument concerning perfectibility, including its apparent status as a metaphysically neutral attribute. Third, and more generally, it accords with Rousseau's frequently voiced suspicion of metaphysical arguments as being beyond the limits of the human mind. For example, in the "Moral Letters" he speaks of "the obscure question of the two substances" and, straight to the case at hand, states that "simple physics [*la simple physique*] is no less obscure to us than metaphysics and morality [*la métaphysique et la morale*]" (*CW*, 12:186–87).

When Rousseau puts aside his argument concerning human freedom to claim that perfectibility distinguishes man from the animals, he does not so much abandon freedom as reframe it in terms of perfectibility. If the argument that freedom distinguishes human beings is disputable, Rousseau has identified an indisputable difference: "There is another very specific quality that distinguishes them and about which there can be no argument: that is, the faculty of perfecting himself [*faculté de se perfectionner*]," or, as he immediately renames it, "perfectibility" (*perfectibilité*). His contemporaries must have been surprised by his claim, in large measure because they had never heard the word. "Perfectibility" was Rousseau's neologism.[7] As Victor Goldschmidt suggests, Rousseau appears to pattern *perfectibilité* after Pufendorf's coinage of *sociabilité* (in Barbeyrac's translation).[8] According to Pufendorf, humans are by nature "sociable," or possess "sociability," without being naturally political animals in Aristotle's strong sense and also without being asocial or even anti-social as in Hobbes.[9] Rousseau takes the same route and goes further, explicitly rejecting Pufendorf's claim about natural sociability (55), and instead regrounding sociability, along with the other attributes previously considered natural to humans—reason, speech, and also freedom—on his own newly minted "perfectibility." As Céline Spector nicely puts it, perfectibility is "the faculty of faculties."[10]

The psychological dynamics that make the development of our passions and faculties possible are described by Rousseau right after his claim concerning perfectibility being the distinctive human attribute, and indeed this dynamic process might be characterized as a way of redescribing perfectibility itself. The passage is worth quoting at length.

> Whatever the moralists may say about it, human understanding owes much to the passions which, as is generally acknowledged, owe much to it as well. It is by their activity that our reason is perfected. We seek to know only because we desire to have pleasure, and it is not possible to conceive why someone who had neither desires nor fears would go to the trouble of reasoning. The passions, in turn, derive their origin from our needs and their progress from our knowledge. For one can desire or fear things only through the ideas one can have of them or by the simple impulsion of nature; and savage man, deprived of every kind of enlightenment, experiences only the passions of this latter type. His desires do not exceed his physical needs. (73)

This account of the basic structure of the human mind follows the logic of the epistemological and psychological theories of Hobbes, Locke, Condillac, and others, but Rousseau goes further by making this process more explicitly dynamic and developmental in character. He begins by arguing against the "moralists," referring foremost to the natural law theorists such as Pufendorf, as well as more traditional authorities, who argue that reason is and ought to be the master of the passions.[11] Following Hobbes and others, Rousseau reverses the priority: reason works on behalf of the passions. For example, Hobbes writes: "For the thoughts are to the desires as scouts and spies, to range abroad and find the way to the things desired."[12] Or as Hume, admittedly not a source for Rousseau, bluntly states, "Reason is and only ought to be the slave of the passions, and can never pretend to any other office than to serve and obey them."[13] Rousseau writes that "human understanding owes much to the passions which, as is generally acknowledged, owe much to it as well." The "general acknowledgment" would be those who challenge the primacy of reason. More importantly, he takes up the hint of a dynamic relationship between human understanding and the passions. "The passions, in turn, derive their origin from our needs and their progress from our knowledge." Thus, there is a dynamic feedback loop among needs, passions, and reason: increases in needs lead to more active passions, which in turn require the development of reason, which then further increases needs, etc. This dynamic psychology is what enables Rousseau to meditate on the human soul to identify its "first and simplest operations" by analytically stripping away those needs, passions, and faculties that are artificial or acquired, ending up with the physical man living in the pure state of nature as portrayed in the first part of the *Discourse*. In turn, the dynamic psychology underlies the synthetic account of human development he will describe in the second part of the work.

HUMAN DEVELOPMENT AND PSYCHIC DIVISION IN THE *DISCOURSE ON INEQUALITY*

If the fundamental principle of Rousseau's works is the natural goodness of man and his corruption in society, then the second part of the *Discourse* is devoted in large measure to the second prong of the principle: man's corruption in society. Of course, the activation of the distinctive human faculty of perfectibility also carries with it positive developments as they become recognizably human. As Rousseau says of perfectibility, "It is this faculty which, over the centuries, by causing his enlightenment and his errors, his vices and his virtues, to bloom, makes him in the long run the tyrant of himself and of nature" (72–73). Errors and vices, yes, but also enlightenment and virtues. As a notable example, he will state that the inhabitants of primitive societies come to experience "the sweetest feelings known to men: conjugal love and paternal love" (94), feelings unknown to natural man, and he terms this stage of human development as "occupying a golden mean between the indolence of the primitive state and the petulant activity of our pride" and as "the best for man" (97). Nonetheless, despite these gains, or perhaps because of them, the seeds of psychic division are sown in the process of human development. Since the account of the tragic course of development Rousseau sketches in the *Discourse* is familiar and beyond my purview here, I restrict myself to some remarks about the emergence of psychic division. I do so to prepare my discussion in the next section of this chapter of how Rousseau attempts to prevent such psychic division and its corrupting effects through the educational program of *Emile*.

Natural man in the pure state of nature might with little exaggeration be said to lack the psychic division experienced by developed humans because he does not have a psyche in any meaningful sense. Rousseau characterizes natural man: "His soul, which nothing agitates, gives itself over to the sole feeling of its present existence, without any idea of the future, however near it may be" (74). In other words, natural man lacks the self-consciousness of an "I" that exists through time, and self-consciousness itself is an acquisition made in the course of the development of the passions and faculties. As Rousseau writes in *Emile*, "We are born capable of learning but able to do nothing, knowing nothing. The soul, enchained in imperfect and half-formed organs, does not even have the sentiment of its own existence" (61). The initial lack of self-consciousness is relevant for what Rousseau says about freedom in the *Discourse*—namely, that the "consciousness" of our freedom shows the "spirituality" of the soul (72). Namely, the necessary condition for the "consciousness" (*conscience*) of our freedom is self-consciousness (*conscience*), meaning that this "consciousness" only comes to distinguish human beings as they develop.[14] This insight once again suggests a phenomenological reading.

The dawning of the development of self-consciousness is described by Rousseau near the outset of the second part of the *Discourse* when he describes how developing humans become conscious of their superiority over the animals. "This is how the first glance he directed upon himself produced in him the first movements of pride. This is how, as yet scarcely knowing how to distinguish ranks and looking upon himself as in the first rank as a species, he prepared himself from afar to claim the first rank as an individual." Related, he perceives "conformities" among his fellow human beings that lead him to conclude "that their way of thinking and feeling was entirely in conformity with his own" (92–93). Self-consciousness emerges through observations and sentiments of identity and difference.

These observations and sentiments ultimately produce hitherto unknown social relations and needs. Rousseau writes of the gathering of members of different families in nascent society, particularly members of the different sexes: "They grow accustomed to consider different objects and to make comparisons. They imperceptibly acquire ideas of merit and beauty that produce sentiments of preference" (95). Thus, moral love develops out of what was previously physical love.

> Each began to look at the others and to want to be looked at himself, and public esteem had a value. The one who sang or danced the best, the most beautiful, the strongest, the most clever, or the most eloquent became the most highly considered—and this, then, was the first step toward inequality and at the same time toward vice. From these first preferences arose vanity and contempt, on the one hand, and shame and envy, on the other. And the fermentation caused by

these new leavens eventually produced compounds fatal to happiness and innocence. (96)

The Fall, if perhaps a happy one. The gains of human development come at the cost of psychic unity, here in budding form and eventually in burgeoning ways.

Rousseau's account of further development through the invention of agriculture and metallurgy, the establishment of property, the ersatz social contract perpetrated by the rich, and so on tends to proceed on the level of society. Nonetheless, he allows us to see the psychic cost. Speaking of how one needed either to possess the qualities necessary for success or to affect having them, he writes: "To be and to appear to be became two entirely different things, and from this distinction came ostentatious display, deceitful cunning, and all the vices that follow in their wake" (100). Although he does not use the language of psychic unity or disunity in this context, its existence and effects are clearly present. We can conclude our brief tour with Rousseau's own conclusion, where he turns to a comparison of natural man and civilized man. Imagining the representative of natural man, a Carib, trying to understand civilized man, he writes: "He would have to learn there are men of a sort who count the esteem of the rest of the universe for something, who know how to be happy and satisfied with themselves based on the testimony of others rather than on their own. Such, indeed, is the genuine cause of all these differences: the savage lives within himself; sociable man, always outside himself, knows how to live only in the opinion of others, and it is from their judgment alone that he, so to speak, derives the feeling of his own existence" (116–17). If this is the result of human development as Rousseau sketches it in the *Discourse*, then one purpose of the educational project of *Emile* is to produce "a savage made to inhabit cities" (205) whose development is in accord with the natural goodness of man in such a way as to avert psychic disunity.

The Natural Goodness of Man and Psychic Unity in *Emile*

In this section I continue to address Rousseau's theory of human nature and development, here as seen in his educational treatise, *Emile*. I do so with two narrowly tailored aims. First, I examine the educational program in *Emile* designed to form a human being in whom the development of his passions and faculties is, unlike the course sketched in the *Discourse*, somehow in accord with the natural goodness of man by maintaining psychic unity. In this way, then, I am addressing the caveat mentioned at the outset of this chapter regarding how his theodicy or physiodicy may extend beyond physical man living in physical nature. Second, I analyze the metaphysical commitments of Rousseau's theory of human nature and development as they come to light in *Emile*, arguing that his theory is thoroughly nondualist, including his account of conscience.

THE NATURAL GOODNESS OF MAN AND PSYCHIC UNITY

The opening sentence of book 1 of *Emile* relates directly to Rousseau's justification of nature through the doctrine of the natural goodness of man and his corruption in society: "Everything is good, as it leaves the hands of the Author of things, everything degenerates in the hands of man" (37).[15] The first phrase—"Everything is good," *Tout est bien*—is an echo of the version of philosophical optimism he articulated in the *Letter to Voltaire*. We therefore have a direct line from the *Discourse on Inequality* to the *Letter to Voltaire* to *Emile*. Yet, despite the opening pronouncement, "the Author of things" immediately exits the scene in *Emile*, and man is left alone in his garden, where "he forces one soil to nourish the products of another, one tree to bear the fruit of another," and otherwise subverts everything as it was made by nature (37). Indeed, the opening passage is, by my reckoning, one of only two times Rousseau uses the phrase "the Author of things" in the entire work, and he rarely employs similar phrases such as "the Author of nature." To be sure, he sometimes writes of God or nature as giving us certain faculties and the like, for example: "Our passions are the principal instruments of our preservation. It is, therefore, an enterprise as vain as it is ridiculous to want to destroy them—it is to control nature, it is to reform the work of God" (*Emile*, 212). Nonetheless, as this passage illustrates, such references are not presented in terms of a systematic theological or philosophical view and are instead best viewed as rhetorical devices. The exception to this rule is the "Profession," but of course my ultimate aim is to understand the relationship between the "Profession" and *Emile*. In short, even though he commences *Emile* with a statement concerning everything being good as it leaves the hands of "the Author of things," man is left to his own devices.

Rousseau is more emphatic in *Emile* than in perhaps any of his works concerning the fundamental principle of the natural goodness of man. Indeed, in reply to a correspondent who voiced skepticism about its pedagogical methods, he denied the book was even a treatise on education and instead stated: "It is a philosophic enough work on the principle put forward by the author in his other works that man is naturally good."[16] Likewise, in the *Dialogues*, he explains that it is "nothing but a treatise on the original goodness of man, destined to show how vice and error, foreign to his constitution, enter it from outside and imperceptibly change him" (*Dialogues*, *CW*, 1:213). As his characterizations of the work suggest, the demonstration of this principle in *Emile* consists largely in the *via negativa* of showing that all vices are extrinsic to human nature.

The way in which Rousseau proceeds in *Emile* to demonstrate the principle that man is naturally good is evident when he puts forward this principle as an "incontestable maxim." The context for this statement occurs when he criticizes current educational methods. "With each lesson that one wants to put into their heads before its proper time, a vice is planted in the depths of their hearts. Senseless teachers think they work wonders when they make children wicked in order to teach them what goodness is. And then they solemnly tell us, 'Such is man.' Yes, such is the man you have made." Having illustrated how vices enter from without, he pronounces: "Let us set down as an incontestable maxim that the first movements of nature are always right. There is no original perversity in the human heart. There is not a single vice to be found in it of which it cannot be said how and whence it entered" (92). His argument is explicitly directed against philosophers such as Hobbes: "When Hobbes called the wicked man a robust child, he said something absolutely contradictory. All wickedness comes from weakness. The child is wicked only because he is weak. Make him strong; he will be good." Confronted with the appearance of vice, "philosophy will explain it as being a result of natural vices: pride the spirit of domination, *amour-propre*, the wickedness of man" (67). "Philosophy," not to mention theology with its doctrine of original sin, is decidedly wrong about human nature. Interestingly, his confrontation with Hobbes is the context in which he makes the sole reference in the main text of *Emile* to the "Profession," when he claims that "goodness" is the attribute most necessary for conceiving of an "all-powerful divinity," to which he adds: "See hereafter the Profession of Faith of the Savoyard Vicar" (67). We will have to wait until chapter 6 to see what the Savoyard Vicar has to say about the goodness of the divinity. For the present we can say that Rousseau's emphasis in the main text of *Emile* is on the natural goodness of man independent of any consideration of God, consistent with the *Discourse on Inequality*.

In order to prevent the introduction of vices and contradictions in man as he develops in society that development must be guided. "In the present state of things a man abandoned to himself in the midst of other men from birth would be the most disfigured of all. Prejudices, authority, necessity, example, all the social institutions in which we find ourselves submerged would stifle nature in him and put nothing in its place" (37). In short, we require education. The fundamental flaw of the current education is that it produces individuals who are at odds with themselves. "Each of us is thus formed by three kinds of master"—

namely, nature, men, and things: "The disciple in whom their various lessons are at odds with one another is badly raised and will never be in accord with himself. He alone in whom they all coincide at the same points and tend to the same ends reaches his goal and lives consistently" (38). Most importantly, the way in which we are educated makes us divided against ourselves because of the inconsistent demands of nature and society. Such dividedness is most clearly seen when compared to two models of a unified soul. "Forced to combat nature or social institutions, one must choose between making a man or a citizen, for one cannot make both at the same time." A "man" is raised strictly according to nature: "Natural man is entirely for himself. He is a numerical unity, the absolute whole which is relative only to itself or its kind." By contrast, a "citizen" is raised strictly in accordance with his political society: civil man's "value is determined by his relation to the whole, which is to the social body" (39–40).[17] We can view the "man" and the "citizen" as described here as "ideal types." What both types have in common is that they produce a unified soul, and Rousseau's presentation of them offers a contrast to the disunified beings we have before our eyes. "He who in the civil order wants to preserve the primacy of the sentiments of nature does not know what he wants. Always in contradiction with himself, always floating between his inclinations and his duties, he will never be either man or citizen. He will be good neither for himself nor for others. He will be one of these men of our days: a Frenchman, and Englishman, a bourgeois. He will be nothing" (40). Or, slightly later when discussing the present education: "Nor do I count the education of society, because this education, tending to two contrary ends, fails to attain either. It is fit only for making double men, always appearing to relate everything to others and never relating anything except to themselves alone" (41). He explains the source of our contradictions:

> From these contradictions is born the one we constantly experience within ourselves. Swept along by contrary routes by nature and by men, forced to divide ourselves between these different impulses, we follow a composite impulse which leads us to neither one goal nor the other. Thus, in conflict and floating during the whole course of our life, we end it without having been able to put ourselves in harmony with ourselves and without having been good either for ourselves or for others. (41)

The aim of *Emile* is therefore to show how a developed human being could be educated in such a way that he is not in contradiction with himself, so that he retains a harmonized or unified soul.[18]

THE NATURE OF HUMAN DEVELOPMENT

If natural man in the pure state of nature is a purely physical being, although a being with potential, Emile will actualize this potential by developing into a moral being. How can that development be guided in such a way to preserve his natural goodness and psychic unity, even if on a different plane, so to speak, than that of natural man? The central goal of *Emile* is to demonstrate that our faculties and passions can, at least by hypothesis, develop without becoming corrupted, even if there are steep challenges to doing so in practice. A full examination of the educational strategies Rousseau employs to achieve this aim is beyond the scope of my present inquiry. What I want to focus on here is what I would term the "nature" of this developmental process—that is, on the metaphysical commitments of Rousseau's educational project in the main text of *Emile*. As I noted at the conclusion to chapter 2 when discussing the distinctive human attribute of perfectibility, if I were to elaborate I would argue that Rousseau is attempting to articulate a nonreductionist materialist theory of human development, a theory he intended to develop in his abandoned project, *La morale sensitive, ou le matérialisme du sage*. Indeed, I would argue that *Emile* is as close as any of his writings to being a stand-in for the abandoned treatise on metaphysics.[19] For the present, however, I restrict myself to arguing that his theory of human development as expressed in *Emile* is nondualist, and I do so in part to prepare the contrast with the dualism of the "Profession of Faith."

Since Rousseau's pupil will be a developed human being, he is not strictly "natural" in the sense that the physical man in the pure state of nature of the *Discourse* is, but he is nonetheless meant to be "natural" in some sense, especially in contrast to the "artificial" and self-divided men we have before our eyes. Rousseau tackles the polyvalent meaning of the term at the outset of the work. "If the name *nature* were limited to habits conformable to nature, we would spare ourselves this garble" concerning the relationship between nature and education (39). In other words, although Emile's passions, faculties, and other acquisitions are not strictly "natural," they will *conform* with nature or will not be contradiction with it, making him a unified being. He then offers a summary of this course of development:

> As soon as we have, so to speak, consciousness [*conscience*] of our sensations, we are disposed to seek or avoid the objects which produce them, at first according to whether they are pleasant or unpleasant to us, then according to the conformity or lack of it that we find between us and these objects, and finally according to the judgments we make

about them on the basis of the idea of happiness or perfection given us by reason. These dispositions are extended and strengthened as we become more capable of using our senses and more enlightened; but constrained by our habits, they are more or less corrupted by our opinions. Before this corruption they are what I call in us *nature*. (39)

Rousseau offers what I have been calling a phenomenological account of human development, here beginning with the individual's "consciousness" (*conscience*), which is a form of self-consciousness (*conscience*), a development that culminates in the "consciousness" (*conscience*, once again) of our freedom that he states in the *Discourse* is unique to human beings. In the passage quoted above, he describes a progress from purely physical phenomena, pleasure and pain, to moral phenomena, including judgments about conformity, happiness, and perfection, and therefore about virtue and vice. Ryan Hanley nicely terms this theory a "virtue epistemology."[20] There is no metaphysical discontinuity in this progress from the physical to the moral. Similarly, when discussing the development of sensations into "perceptions or ideas" (the main subject of what Condillac and d'Alembert mean by "metaphysics"), he distinguishes between the "sensual reason" of the child and the "intellectual reason" of the adult, which is a developed version of the primitive form (157–58). As Timothy O'Hagan states concerning this argument, "There is no trace of dualism here."[21] In other words, moral phenomena develop from physical phenomena without being reducible to them.

A guiding tenet of Rousseau's educational program is his argument that happiness consists in a proportion between our desires and the faculties necessary for fulfilling them. "Our unhappiness consists, therefore, in the disproportion between our desires and our faculties.... In what, then, consists human wisdom or the road of true happiness? It is not precisely in diminishing our desires, for if they were beneath our power, a part of our faculties would remain idle, and we would not enjoy our whole being. Neither is it in extending our faculties.... But it is in diminishing the excess of the desires over the faculties and putting power and will in perfect equality" (80; see also 165). This model of psychic equilibrium is patterned after natural man in the pure state of nature as described in the first part of the *Discourse*, a being whose limited needs and passions are readily satisfied by his endowments. Emile's education follows the model of natural man only in a formal way by maintaining a proportion between his desires and his faculties as he actualizes his whole being.[22] "It is thus that nature, which does everything for the best, constituted him in the beginning. It gives him with immediacy only the desires necessary to his preservation and the faculties sufficient to satisfy them. It puts all the others, as it were, in reserve in the depth of his soul, to be developed there when needed." Nonetheless, once these faculties develop there is ever the danger of disequilibrium. The intrinsic difficulty in putting his educational program into effect is signaled by Rousseau in this context when he writes: "All the animals have exactly the faculties necessary to preserve themselves. Man alone has superfluous faculties. Is it not very strange that this superfluity should be the instrument of his unhappiness?" (80–81). We should not however let the practical difficulties in guiding human development obscure Rousseau's more important point that the disproportion between desires and faculties, and thus our experience of unhappiness and evil, are not intrinsic to human nature or inevitable.

The greatest threat to maintaining our psychic unity and happiness is *amour-propre*, the "relative" form of self-love, and the other relative passions that come with it. As we saw in chapter 2, in the *Discourse on Inequality* Rousseau distinguishes between two forms of self-love, *amour de soi-même* and *amour-propre*, which he characterizes as "two passions very different in their nature and their effects" (*Inequality*, note XV, 147). His account in *Emile* is somewhat different, with *amour-propre* being a developed form of the natural passion of *amour de soi*. Indeed, he argues that all the passions have their origin in the "principle" of natural self-love, and here we should recall his language in the *Discourse* about self-love and pity being "principles" of the psyche. "In this sense, if you wish, all passions are natural," he explains. "But most of these modifications have alien causes without which they would never have come to pass; and these same modifications, far from being advantageous for us, are harmful. They alter the primary goal and are at odds with their own principle. It is then that man finds himself outside of nature and sets himself in contradiction with himself." When he states that these modifications "are at odds with their own principle," Rousseau alludes to the principle of the natural goodness of man. Namely, whereas our primitive passions lead to our self-preservation and well-being, making us "good" in his sense of the term, the developed passions nearly always work against our self-preservation and well-being, making us "evil" or, as he says here, putting us in "contradiction" with ourselves by creating psychic disunity. After elaborating on how natural self-love "regards only ourselves" whereas *amour-propre* is based on comparisons we make to others, Rousseau explains how the development of our passions and faculties makes us either good or evil: "Thus what makes man essentially good is to have few needs and to compare himself little to others; what makes him essentially wicked is to have many needs and to depend very much on opinion." As he writes immediately after this passage, so long as the child remains a "physical being" he should study his relations with things, but as he "begins to sense his moral being" he must consider his relations with his fellow human beings (212–14). The challenge is to develop his moral being and relations in such a way that does not lead to psychic disunity.

MORAL RELATIONS AND THE CONSCIENCE

As mentioned above, Rousseau argues in *Emile* that "all" the passions are developments of the primary "principle" of self-love (212–13), presumably including pity, considered as our tendency to identify with our fellows through "expansive force" of the heart by which we extend our self-love to others (223). Without entering into the complications of his account, what matters for the present purpose is that Rousseau's project of developing Emile's moral relations, including as it relates to conscience, involves extending self-love and pity through careful regulation of the imagination, reason, and other faculties. The main point I want to make in my brief consideration of this project is that Rousseau's account of moral development remains nondualist in nature, including with regard to the conscience, once again by contrast to the Savoyard Vicar's teaching, especially the conscience.

The emergence of Emile as a moral being comes in book IV of the work, which is also importantly the context in which we encounter the "Profession of Faith," and Rousseau's account of this emergence involves the wakening of all the passions that extend beyond the child's hitherto physical being, including *amour-propre*, pity, and the budding sexual passion. "So long as his sensibility [*sensibilité*] remains limited to his own individuality," he explains of his pupil, "there is nothing moral in his actions. It is only when he begins to extend outside of himself that it takes on, first, the sentiments and, then, the notions of good and evil which truly constitute him as a man and an integral part of his species" (219–20).[23] In keeping with his description at the outset of the work of how our moral notions develop out of an initially physical consideration of pain and pleasure once we gain "consciousness" of our sensations, as discussed above, here our "sensibility" extends in such a way that produces moral sentiments and ideas. How this works with regard to pity is perhaps more obvious, and Rousseau provides several "maxims" about how to develop pity in ways that cooperate rather than compete with self-love (222–26). As he states, his pupil will direct "his nascent sensibility" to his fellows (*semblables*), to those "whose nature has a more manifest identity with his own and thus makes himself more disposed to love himself" (233). The case of self-love itself is less obvious and more perilous: "*Amour-propre* is a useful but dangerous instrument" (244). Rousseau's project is to manage the development of natural self-love into the "relative" sentiment of *amour-propre* in such a way that it is turned toward virtue rather than vice. "Let us extend *amour-propre* to other beings. We shall transform it into a virtue, and there is no man's heart in which this virtue does not have its root" (252).

The directed development of *amour-propre* and the other passions has both psychological and moral aspects, meaning "moral" in both the broad and narrow senses of the term. In a critical passage for my purposes, Rousseau outlines his theory of this development and then retreats from elaborating it.

> If this were the place for it, I would try to show how the first voices of conscience arise out of the first movement of the heart, and how the first notions of good and bad are born of the sentiments of love and hate. I would show that *justice* and *goodness* are not merely abstract words—pure moral beings formed by the understanding—but are true affections of the soul enlightened by reason, and hence only an ordered development of our primitive affections; that by reason alone, independent of conscience, no natural law can be established; and the entire right of nature is only a chimera if it is not founded on a natural need of the human heart.* But I am reminded that my business here is not producing treatises on metaphysics and morals. (235)

In the note to this passage, indicated by the asterisk, Rousseau writes: "Even the precept of doing unto others as we would have them do unto us has no true foundation other than conscience and sentiment," and "Love of men derived from love of self is the principle of justice" (235n).

A few remarks. First, the "first voices of conscience" arise out of the "first movement of the heart": self-love. In this regard it is worth noting that "conscience" translates *conscience*, which is the same word translated as "consciousness."[24] Recall once again, then, Rousseau's argument that moral judgments involve a psychological development once we become "conscious" of our primitive affections, which all relate to self-love. Second, likewise, the moral notions of justice and goodness are "true affections of the soul" that emerge through "an ordered development of our primitive affections"—namely, self-love and pity.[25] In short, the main point is that moral attributes and phenomena, including the conscience, are ordered developments of initially merely physical principles.

Since one of my principal purposes here is to prepare the contrast I will draw between Rousseau's account of the conscience and that of the Savoyard Vicar, let me dwell for a moment on what Rousseau writes about the subject outside of the "Profession of Faith." Beginning with *Emile* itself, there are a few brief mentions of the conscience. First, at the point where Rousseau argues for the natural goodness of man against Hobbes, he writes: "Reason alone teaches us to know the good and bad. Conscience, which makes us love the former and hate the latter, although independent of reason, cannot therefore be developed without it. Before the age of reason we do good and bad without knowing it, and there is no morality in our actions" (67). Second, when discussing promises and contracts in the episode with Robert the gardener, he writes in a note: "Moreover, if this duty to keep commitments were not consolidated in the child's mind by the weight of its utility, soon the inner sentiment, beginning to sprout, would impose it on him like a law of conscience, like an innate principle which awaits in order to bloom only the kinds of knowledge to which it applies. This first sketch is not drawn by the hand of man but is graven in our hearts by the Author of all justice" (100n). The question is the identity of this "inner sentiment": Is it a separate sentiment than self-love or a developed form of self-love? In any case, Rousseau hedges his claim, stating that the "inner sentiment" is "*like* a law of conscience" and that it is "*like* an innate principle." I therefore suggest that this passage should be read as more metaphorical than programmatic. In short, insofar as Rousseau evokes the conscience at all in *Emile*, it is a development of self-love and pity guided by reason and not, as the Vicar would have it, an innate principle opposed to the passions and in tension with reason.

Outside of *Emile* Rousseau only occasionally speaks of the conscience, and he does not extensively develop the concept. At the very end of the *Discourse on the Sciences and the Arts* he famously concludes with a paean to virtue: "O virtue! Sublime science of simple souls, are then so many efforts and preparations needed to know you? Are not your principles engraved in all hearts, and is it not enough to learn your laws to return into oneself and to listen to the voice of one's conscience in the silence of the passions?" (*Sciences*, 36). Several scholars have made the connection between Rousseau's mention of the conscience here and the "Profession."[26] Nonetheless, his evocation of conscience in the *Discourse* remains that: an evocation. The *Discourse on Inequality* contains no mention of the conscience beyond a few passing uses of the term in a nontechnical sense. The *Letter to d'Alembert* includes one substantive remark on conscience. Speaking of how spectators have an aesthetic appreciation of moral virtue displayed on the stage, Rousseau explains in a note: "We have to do with the morally beautiful here. Whatever the philosophers may say of it, this love is innate to man and serves as principle to his conscience" (*CW*, 10:267n). As for *Julie*, the novel includes about thirty references to the conscience, all of them nontechnical references to the "voice of conscience," a "troubled conscience," and so on, and does not contain a substantive discussion.[27] In turn, the *Social Contract* has no mention of conscience.

In defense of *Emile* against Archbishop Beaumont, Rousseau takes up the conscience at one point. After summarizing the natural goodness of man as the "fundamental principle of all morality," he explains: "Man is not a simple being. He is composed of two substances.... Once this is proved, the love of self is no longer a simple passion. But it has two principles, namely the intelligent being and the sensitive being, the well-being of which is not the same. The appetite of the senses conduces to the well-being of the body, and the love of order to that of soul. The latter love, developed and made active, bears the name of conscience" (*Beaumont*, 28). As we can see, Rousseau claims to agree with the archbishop concerning the existence of two substances, and therefore might also agree with the Vicar, although he in fact declines to do so. Nonetheless, the two "substances" are for Rousseau here intellect and sensitivity, or mind and body, which one might characterize as a "naturalistic" dualism compared to a full-fledged metaphysical dualism. The naturalist turn is signaled by Rousseau by relating these two "substances" to the two "principles" of self-love, or what he elsewhere terms *amour de soi* and *amour-propre*. Although this is not the occasion to pursue the argument any further, the two "substances" and "principles" Rousseau posits ultimately seem to be congruent with his argument in *Emile* concerning conscience as an "ordered development of our primitive affections."[28]

Finally, Rousseau's most elaborate discussion of conscience is found in an unpublished writing that served as a sort of quarry from which he mined material for the "Profession," including passages on the conscience repeated almost verbatim—namely, the "Moral Letters." Since these letters are often characterized as personal correspondence and since Rousseau claims to propound "my profession of faith" there (*CW*, 12:178), interpreters have understandably taken these letters as evidence that the "Profession" is congruent with Rousseau's own views, including on the conscience.[29] Predictably, I am more cautious about such an assumption, in part because of the occasion and aim of the writing. The "Moral Letters" were written in about 1757 for the object of Rousseau's infatuation, Sophie d'Houdetot, but were not published for more than a century. The erotic charge of the letters can be seen at the outset: "In recalling the circumstances in which you asked me for rules of morality for your use, I cannot doubt that at that time you were putting into practice one of the most sublime ones, and that, in the danger to which a blind passion was exposing me, you were giving thought to my instruction even more than to your own" (*CW*, 12:175).[30] Put bluntly, Rousseau did not succeed in seducing her. The entirety of the "Moral Letters" might be characterized as a sublimation of erotic desire, and in this light as similar to the *New Heloise*, for which Sophie d'Houdetot provided the model for Julie.[31] Rousseau states that these letters to his beloved "were not written to be made public," but he also offers her the opportunity to publish them (179). Even if we were to take these letters to be "private," insofar as any correspondence during this period can be considered to be private, a subject I discussed in the introduction, Rousseau's invitation suggests that he wrote the "Moral Letters" with possible publication in mind. We therefore cannot take them as the unalloyed expression of his beliefs.

The "Moral Letters" contain much material familiar to the reader of the "Profession," including having the main purpose of discovering rules for moral conduct and voicing distrust of philosophic speculation (*CW*, 12:175, 179–83). However, the metaphysical elements of Rousseau's account are even more tentative than those of the Vicar, for he writes of "the obscure question of the two substances," states that the relationship between the body and soul "was always the despair of metaphysics," and leaves all this "puerile labor to those children who are called philosophers" (186, 188–89).[32] The discussion of conscience is occasioned by Rousseau's claim that he overcame himself—that is, he overcame his illicit love for the recipient—by listening to "that interior voice that judges me in secret," and he urges her to do the same (192–93). He appeals to the cries of remorse we feel at our "hidden crimes" and calls as witness the universal accord among peoples everywhere on the same ideas of justice and decency, the same principles of good and evil. "There is then in the depths of all souls an innate principle of justice and moral truth anterior to all national prejudices, to all maxims of education. The principle is the involuntary rule based on which we judge our actions and those of others as good or bad in spite of our own maxims, and it is to this principle that I give the name of conscience." Unlike the Vicar, however, Rousseau does not treat the conscience in terms of metaphysical dualism, and quite to the contrary he states: "I do not have the intention of entering here into metaphysical discussions which do not lead to anything" (194–97).[33] In sum, without denying the unmistakable similarities between the "Moral Letters" and the "Profession," his account of the conscience in the former falls short of the Vicar's metaphysical dualism and the attendant appeal to an immaterial soul necessary to rectify the injustices we experience in his life.

Conclusion

How does the project of directing the development of our passions and faculties in such a way as to preserve psychic unity and retain the natural goodness of man, even if on a different plane than natural man himself, relate to theology and religion? In chapter 3 we saw in the *Letter to Voltaire* that a strictly natural account of general providence consistent with the *Discourse on Inequality* does not suffice for developed human beings because of their pride and their psychological need for the consolation and hope provided by the doctrine of particular divine providence. We will see in the next two chapters that the Savoyard Vicar and the auditor of his speech, a youth who is Emile's age but not Emile himself, also require certain theological teachings that reflect the psychic division they experience and that offer hope and consolation. In other words, developed human beings who do experience psychic division and evil have a psychological need for religion. What about Emile?

Rousseau addresses this question in the main text of *Emile* and does so immediately before he presents the "Profession of Faith." "I foresee how many readers will be surprised at seeing me trace the whole first age of my pupil without speaking to him of religion" (*Emile*, 257). Children ought to be raised in their father's religion, Rousseau states in a concession to society. But what about Emile? "To what sect shall we join the man of nature?" We shall put him in a position to choose the one that he finds most in accord with his reason, he answers (260). Yet, rather than following Emile in this pursuit, as he has done throughout the work, Rousseau instead introduces the "Profession." And after the "Profession" ends, when the Vicar ceases to speak, Rousseau resumes his authorial voice and states: "I have transcribed this writing not as a rule for the sentiments that one ought to follow in religious matters, but as an example of the way one can reason with one's pupil in order not to diverge from the method I have tried to establish. So long as one concedes nothing to the authority of men or to the prejudices of the country in which one was born, the light of reason alone cannot, in the education founded by nature, lead us any farther than natural religion. That is what I limit myself to with my Emile." We get no further information on what religious instruction his pupil might receive. Instead, tellingly I think, Rousseau repeats the purpose of his educational project: "in order that man may as much as possible be one." Whatever natural religion Emile receives seems to consist in a love of the deity that makes him do his duty and love virtue, a love of "the Author of his being," which Rousseau states "is confounded [*se confonde*] with that same love of self" (313–14). Now we have an extension of the natural principle of self-love to the conscience all the way to love of the divinity as the creator of the being we love so much—that is, ourselves.

Let me therefore conclude with a speculation. I suggest that, insofar as the educational program of producing an individual who retains psychic unity and preserves his natural goodness succeeds, Emile does not require a religion that goes beyond a teaching concerning the general providence of nature such as Rousseau outlines in the first part of the *Letter to Voltaire*, if even that. By contrast, those individuals who do not have the benefit of being educated by a seemingly omniscient tutor in accordance with the philosophy of the natural goodness of man—that is to say, almost everyone else—have a psychological need for a religion that goes further.

CHAPTER 5

Introduction to the "Profession of Faith"

The most extended treatment of theology and religion in Rousseau's corpus is the "Profession of Faith of the Savoyard Vicar." Rousseau's own estimation of the writing was high indeed. In the *Letter to Beaumont* he declares: "I will always consider it the best and most useful writing in the century during which I published it" (47). Similarly, writing a little more than a decade later in the *Dialogues*, he characterized *Emile* as his "greatest and best book" (*Dialogues*, CW, 1:23, 209–13). Finally, in the *Reveries* he characterizes the "Profession" as "a work unwarrantedly prostituted and profaned among the present generation but which may one day make a revolution among men, if good sense and good faith are ever reborn among them" (23).

The "Profession" is included within *Emile* and yet presented as an explicitly separate section of the work and moreover as supposedly written by an unidentified author. Neither of the personages in the writing, the Savoyard Vicar and the youth to whom he delivers his speech, plays any role in the main narrative of *Emile*. Further, putting aside Rousseau's remarks immediately before and after the "Profession," there is only one reference in the main text to the writing. Finally, although scholars long assumed that it was composed separately and only included at a late point of composition, we now know from analyses of the drafts of the work that Rousseau intended from perhaps the outset to include the "Profession" in *Emile*.[1] In other words, the "Profession" is somehow integral to *Emile* and yet separate from it.

The anomalous character of the "Profession" poses a number of interpretive challenges. Most important is the question of the extent to which the pedagogical aims and audience of the "Profession" and the philosophical commitments expressed there (i.e., the metaphysical, epistemological, and other philosophical claims) cohere with what Rousseau argues in his own name in *Emile* and elsewhere. In the previous chapter, I examined the main text of *Emile* in order to begin to address this question, and I suggested that the audience, aim, and substance of the educational program of managing the development of an individual in accordance with the natural goodness of man differ from the audience, aim, and substance of the "Profession." In this chapter I further this argument through an analysis of the placement of the "Profession" within *Emile* and especially the narrative elements of the "Profession," including the dramatis personae, dramatic setting, and indications of the intended audience. Doing so will prepare my examination of the theological and religious teaching of the "Profession" itself in the two subsequent chapters.

To highlight my contribution, let me now review how previous interpreters have approached the "Profession." Most scholars have assumed there is a relatively seamless continuity between the theological and religious views articulated by Rousseau in his own name in *Emile* and his other writings and the arguments contained in the "Profession." Thus, they quote the "Profession" alongside what Rousseau himself writes on both philosophical and theological matters. Further, they almost always do so on the further assumption that what he writes on theological issues in particular, in his own name or otherwise, is a full and sincere expression of his views. To be fair, Rousseau encourages us to associate his own views with those of the Vicar—for example, stating in the *Reveries* that the results of his own self-examination were "more or less" the same as those contained in the "Profession" (*Reveries*, 22–23), as I discussed in chapter 1. Similarly, he elsewhere claims that the Vicar's profession and Julie's profession of faith in the *New Heloise* are "sufficiently in accord that one can explain one of them by the other, and from this agreement it can be presumed with some likelihood that if the author who published the books that contain them does not adopt both of them in their entirety, he at last favors them greatly" (*Mountain*, 39).[2] Yet how close are they? And in what regard ought we to presume that the author "favors" them? And why does he maintain the fiction that he "published" these books as opposed to wrote them? Likewise, and in my view more problematically, many scholars reference the "Profession" on more strictly philosophical issues—for example, referring to the Vicar's arguments concerning metaphysical dualism, freedom, conscience, and sociability as the expression of Rousseau's own position on these matters, and indeed even his fullest and most developed views. For example, Henri Gouhier asserts that the "Profession" "represents the purest and most fully realized form" of Rousseau's philosophy, and states that "what is certain, is that Jean-Jacques saw in it the perfect expression of what he believed to be true."[3]

Insofar as these scholars do acknowledge the interpretive difficulties posed by the separate textual status of the "Profession" and by the distance Rousseau puts between himself and the "Profession," they usually assume that in both cases he did so because he was attempting to avoid the critical attention of the secular and religious authorities.[4] Under this interpretation, the Vicar is a "mouthpiece" for Rousseau, as, for example, the archbishop of Paris assumed.[5] If this is correct, his strategy was tragically mistaken. Even so, as I asked in chapter 1 when examining the *Letter to Beaumont*, why would Rousseau consistently persist in insisting that the views expressed in the "Profession" were those of the Savoyard Vicar, and not his own, and continue to present himself as the editor of the "Profession" and not its author, after the work was condemned and he had no reason to dissimulate? We need an alternative interpretation of *why* Rousseau distances himself from the Savoyard Vicar and his profession, both within *Emile* itself and in defense of the work.

Probably the second largest group of scholars is those who do acknowledge the interpretive difficulties, but nonetheless continue to cite the "Profession" when investigating Rousseau's theological and religious thought and its relationship to his philosophy, but with some caution in doing so. For example, whereas many in the first group of scholars simply attribute what the Vicar says to Rousseau ("Rousseau argues X..."), this second group generally distinguishes between what Rousseau writes in his own name and what the Vicar says ("The Vicar says Y...").[6] Further, they commonly account for tensions between what Rousseau writes and what the Vicar says by pointing to Rousseau's oft-stated caution regarding these obscure questions concerning metaphysics and the like and by following him in his epistemological modesty. For example, Roger Masters refers to the Vicar's argument for dualism as a "detachable metaphysics," which Rousseau advances tentatively but does not fully embrace because he wishes to make his thought as metaphysically neutral as possible.[7] Still others acknowledge the tensions but allege a development in his thought to explain them—for instance, claiming he moves from the early "Epicureanism" of the *Discourse on Inequality* to the "Stoicism" of *Emile* and especially of the "Profession."[8]

Finally, a relatively small number of interpreters argue that the discrepancies between Rousseau's own stated views and those advanced in the "Profession" are in fact intentional, with Rousseau having different aims and audiences in mind.[9] In this light, it is revealing that these interpreters are almost without exception the only ones who attend to the narrative elements of the "Profession," such as the framing narrative, dramatis personae, and so on. As the reader may have already ascertained, I join this minority group of scholars in my interpretation.

As the reader of this book knows well by now, I am not concerned here to ascertain Rousseau's personal theological and religious views. Thus, the scholarly debates over the relationship between the sentiments expressed in the "Profession" and Rousseau's personal views do not interest me, except insofar as those sentiments are in tension with the philosophical positions Rousseau expresses, foremost the doctrine of the natural goodness of man. The question with respect to the theological and religious views expressed by the Vicar—or by Julie or other characters in the *New Heloise*, or even by Rousseau himself in the *Letter to Voltaire* or elsewhere—is *why* Rousseau chose to present these views when they are in tension with his own express philosophical position. In brief, my answer is that, unlike with the philosophical system of the natural goodness of man, the truth of which Rousseau seeks to convince his reader is authoritative, in the "Profession" he leaves to his reader the authority to judge the truth or persuasiveness of the doctrines advanced and, in addition, offers those doctrines as less true than useful.[10]

The Context of the "Profession of Faith"

The "Profession of Faith of the Savoyard Vicar" comes as something of a surprise. About one-third the way through book IV, with almost no preparation, Rousseau inserts the "Profession" as an explicitly separate section of the work whose relationship to what comes before and after it within the main text is unclear. This separate section comprises fully a third of book IV. Unlike the other two explicitly separate sections within *Emile* ("Sophie, or the Woman" and "On Travel"), both in book V—the "Profession" as a whole—that is, the narrative frame and the speech by the Savoyard Vicar—is presented by Rousseau as having been written by another, unidentified author. He even goes so far as to put the entirety in quotation marks and to give the "Profession" proper—that is, the speech itself—a subtitle to set it off from the main text.

The context within *Emile* in which the "Profession" is inserted provides us with some clues about Rousseau's intention in including it. Book IV marks a kind of "second birth" of the pupil as the passions are enflamed with the dawning of adolescence. "We are, so to speak, born twice: once to exist and once to live; once for our species and once for our sex" (211). The book is devoted to managing the development of the passions of self-love, pity, and especially the sexual passion, along with the imagination and other faculties related to these passions. The entire strategy might be characterized as prophylactic in nature, we may suspect that the "Profession" has a similar purpose.

Shortly after having spoken of extending *amour-propre* to other beings in order to transform it into a virtue (252), a passage I quoted in the preceding chapter, Rousseau engages in a dialogue with an imagined reader who finds his project incredible, perhaps because the reader supposes that *amour-propre* and the other passions are signs of our natural wickedness. He answers: "But consider, in the first place, although I want to form the man of nature, the object is not, for all that, to make him a savage and to relegate him to the depths of the woods. It suffices that, enclosed in the social whirlpool, he not let himself get carried away by either the passions or the opinions of men." Having written this, he makes an unexpected transition to discussing the limitations of our intellectual faculties and specifically the difficulties in conceiving of the "incomprehensible Being who embraces everything, who gives motion to the world and forms the whole system of beings." Over the next few pages Rousseau, in his own voice, elaborates this epistemological modesty—for example, warning that the precipitous ascent from material to immaterial substances produces either materialism or superstition. He presents a brief natural history of religion, telling of how primitive humans animated the entire universe with beings whose action they believed they felt, how they slowly came to recognize a single deity by generalizing their ideas and ascending to a first cause of the universe and to the obscure idea of a "substance," how there arose the notion of two substances, one material and another immaterial, hence metaphysical dualism. Nonetheless, the mode of his explanation is that of conjectural history, a kind of natural history of religion à la Hume, and Rousseau does not make any substantive claims on these subjects in his own name. Rather, his emphasis is, first, on the difficulty of conceiving these substances, the divine nature, ideas of creation and annihilation, eternity, omnipotence, and so on, and the pervasive tendency of children as well as adults to anthropomorphism and, second and related, on the psychological need for religion that gives rise to these doctrines (255–57).

Then suddenly: "I foresee how many readers will be surprised at seeing me trace the whole first age of my pupil without speaking to him of religion" (257). Indeed, such a delay would of course be very surprising given the universal practice of his time, not to mention our own. If most children become fanatics or unbelievers because of the "deformed images of the divinity" with which they are presented since infancy, we need not fear anything of the kind for Emile, who has been tutored in epistemological modesty (259). Children ought to be raised in their father's religion, Rousseau states in a concession to society. But: "To what sect shall we join the man of nature?" We shall put him in a position to choose the one that he finds most in accord with his reason (260). Yet, rather than following Emile in this pursuit, as he has done throughout the work, Rousseau instead introduces the "Profession."

The introduction begins with an address to the readers that immediately complicates the question of the status of the "Profession" in relation to what Rousseau writes in his own name. "Readers, do not fear from me precautions unworthy of a friend of the truth. I shall never forget my motto"—namely, *Vitam impendere vero*, "To consecrate one's life to the truth."[11] The initial complication is that our truthful author will not speak in his own name.

> Instead of telling you here what I think for my own part [*de mon chef*], I shall tell you what a man worthier than I thought. I guarantee the truth of the facts which are going to be reported. They really happened to the author of the paper I am going to transcribe. It is up to you to see if useful reflections can be drawn from it about the subject with which it deals. I am not propounding to you the sentiment of another or my own as a rule. I am offering it to you for examination. (260)

With this said, Rousseau begins to transcribe this "paper." Of course, few readers will likely be persuaded that someone other than Rousseau is the actual author. If he is not being truthful in this regard, his evocation of his motto amounts to a deliberate provocation. This distancing is usually taken as his attempt to evade responsibility for the unorthodox content of the "Profession." As we have seen in chapter 1, Rousseau denied this was his aim in defense of his work against the Archbishop of Paris, all the while insisting that one must maintain the distinction between what the author writes in his own name and what the Savoyard Vicar says. Moreover, he confessed even graver sins to his critic, notably his denial of the doctrine of original sin, and that in his own name. Why not fess up to his authorship?

But let us stay closer to home and focus on what he actually states in the passage introducing this mysterious "paper." First, he only guarantees the "facts" contained in the paper as having really happened to its supposed "author." How can he make this guarantee if he is not in fact the author? I have argued elsewhere that the paradox may be resolved if we consider his both being and not being the author of the paper as an instance of Rousseau doubling himself in the text, parallel to the way in which he is both Rousseau author of *Emile* and Jean-Jacques the imaginary tutor.[12] At any rate, he does not guarantee the truth of the theological and religious sentiments expressed by the Vicar. Second, he states that he leaves it to the reader to judge the contents: "It is up to you to see if *useful* reflections can be drawn from it.... I am offering it to you for examination." Rousseau cedes authority to the reader to examine and judge. In this light, he distances himself not so much from the content of the writing as from *judging* it in his own name.[13] His abstention from exercising his authority as the author and his investiture of the reader with the authority to judge parallels the "Profession" itself, for the Vicar repeatedly asks his auditor to judge the contents of his speech for himself (e.g., 266, 294–95). Further, when Rousseau returns to the main narrative, he states that the "Profession" is meant as an example for examination and not as an authority (313–14). In sum, far from guaranteeing the truth of the theological and religious views expressed in the "Profession," Rousseau asks the reader to examine the writing in terms of its truth and especially its utility.

The Narrative Frame of the "Profession"

"'Thirty years ago in an Italian city a young expatriate found himself reduced to utter destitution'" (260). So begins the transcription of the supposed paper containing the "Profession." The narrative introduction provides the setting and characters of the drama. Very few scholars who examine the "Profession" pay more than cursory attention to its narrative frame. In fact, many interpreters not only assume that the Vicar is Rousseau's "mouthpiece," but also suppose that Emile is the audience of the "Profession," either taking the unnamed youth who does listen to the speech to be Emile or assuming that Emile hears or reads the Vicar's speech secondhand, as though he is reading *Emile*.[14] Other interpreters, and for better reasons to which I will return, take the auditor to be the young Jean-Jacques, with the "Profession" being essentially autobiographical, providing further warrant for taking the views expressed in the writing to be Rousseau's own.[15] As a representative example of these interpretive assumptions we can take Stephen Ellenburg, who suggests that the "Profession" is equivalent to Rousseau's own theological views, maintains that the auditor of the Vicar's speech is the young Jean-Jacques, and assumes that Emile is presented with the "Profession." As for the narrative frame, Ellenburg states: "The details... need not detain us."[16] At any rate, in making these assumptions, interpreters close the distance Rousseau establishes between the "Profession" and the main text of *Emile*.

What the narrative frame given to the Vicar's speech establishes, among other things, is that the characters of the Savoyard Vicar and the young proselyte are in fact very different from those of the tutor

Jean-Jacques and Emile. As Céline Spector states, "The Vicar belongs to fiction," and she goes on to explain that "the rhetorical status of the 'Profession of Faith' also matters," noting that it is a speech directed at an audience with specific needs and suggesting that its teaching "may in some respects be influenced by the requirements of the speech situation."[17] If a speech should be tailored to the character of the auditor, as Rousseau insists just after the "Profession" when he imagines himself as tutor making a speech to Emile (321ff.), then the information supplied about the characters and history of the Savoyard Vicar and the young proselyte should inform us about the rhetorical nature, intended audience, and aims of the writing. As Heinrich Meier, the scholar who has devoted the most attention to the narrative frame, explains, "The framing narrative is no ornamental add-on, but the part of the writing that puts the speech about religion in perspective and determines its task."[18] In short, we should presume that Rousseau—and for simplicity's sake I will refer to him as the author—presents information in this narrative frame necessary for interpreting the intended audience and aim of the "Profession."

THE DRAMATIS PERSONAE

There are two characters in our drama: the unnamed young proselyte and the Savoyard Vicar. The story is told three decades after the events narrated, initially in the third person and then later in the first person, a shift in narrative voice that further complicates matters. I will address this change in narrative voice in due course.

We learn a number of things about the youth from his narrative. First, he has left his homeland for another country, was born a Calvinist, and changed religion to have bread. He finds himself in an almshouse for proselytes and, in addition to being instructed in the religious controversies in such a way as to unsettle what little faith he had before, he is introduced to "morals that were still newer to him" and of which he nearly became the victim. His reaction was rage and indignation. He would have been lost if it had not been for a decent ecclesiastic who assisted the youth's escape and took him in. We are further told that the boy's early reading of novels (*romans*) had spoiled his ability to live in the world in which he found himself, and further hints suggest that the youth been prematurely sexually awakened (260–63). Finally, the young man's experience has made him cynical and suspicious. We are told that the Vicar observed that "'ill fortune had already dried up the young man's heart, that opprobrium and contempt had beaten down his courage, and that his pride [*fierté*], changed into bitter spite, took men's injustice and hardness only as proof of the viciousness of nature and the chimerical character of virtue. He had seen that religion served only as the mask of interest and sacred worship only as the safeguard of hypocrisy'" (262). Having seen through appearances, the youth thought he glimpsed the corruption hiding beneath—a sort of obverse version of the "Illumination of Vincennes," in which Rousseau saw our natural goodness lying beyond the appearance of corruption. In short, the young proselyte is corrupt, if not yet irremediably so.

The comparison of the young proselyte to Emile, who has reached the same age, is instructive. The young proselyte is proud, cynical, indignant, and sexually precocious—all qualities notably absent in Emile. Most importantly, the gap the young man glimpses between reality and appearance in others creates a similar breach within himself and in relation to others, and if he is not already psychically divided, he is on the verge of becoming so. The Vicar's theological and religious teaching is appropriate and necessary for the young proselyte, who requires an explanation for his psychic division and who needs the teaching as a brake on his corrupted passions and salve for his unhappiness. In turn, such a teaching is unnecessary for Emile.[19] We are told that Emile will use his reason to arrive at some sort of natural religion, that is, religion limited to reason alone (260, 313–14), but that is all we are told. At any rate, Emile does not receive the Vicar's profession or anything like it.

The narrative frame also introduces us to the Savoyard Vicar, initially from the young proselyte's perspective and then with additional material provided in the "Profession" proper from the Vicar himself. From the narrative we learn that the Vicar had an unspecified "youthful adventure" that earned disfavor from his bishop and that he, like the youth, became an expatriate. Although his upright character could have enabled the disgraced Vicar to find a prestigious post, he preferred his independence. He cherished the hope that he would regain his bishop's favor and find a little parish in the mountains (262). (NB: a vicar is an ecclesiastic without a permanent position, and who will take the place of a prelate in his absence, hence the etymological relationship between "vicar" and "vicarious."[20]) We are told that the Vicar takes in the young proselyte and gains his trust. "The ecclesiastic saw the danger and the resources" within the young man to effect a cure. "The degradation of the young man was in progress but had not proceeded too far. To protect the unfortunate young man from this moral death to which he was so near, the priest began by awakening *amour-propre* and self-esteem in him" (263–64). Or, as he later puts it, his mentor tried to awaken *amour-propre* to lead him to "pride" (*fierté*) (265). In other words, like the tutor with Emile, the Vicar will direct *amour-propre* in the young man to transform it into a virtue (252), but unlike Emile he is working with an already corrupted passion. Meier notes the importance of Rousseau's references to *amour-propre* in the framing narrative for understanding the purpose of the "Profession": "The two passages in the framing narrative in which *amour-propre* is spoken of leave no doubt as to the central importance it has for moral education."[21] The narrator relates a little story, a bagatelle, to illustrate the Vicar's methods that concludes in a way that suggests that the method might be applied to others: "Lessons of this kind are rarely lost on the hearts of young people who are not completely corrupt" (264). Perhaps an indication of the intended audience of the "Profession"?

What we learn next about the Vicar occurs with the shift in the narrative voice mentioned above and concerns the central theme in Rousseau's works of reality and appearance, a theme we just saw arise in relation to the young proselyte. Having just related the bagatelle illustrating the Vicar's proceedings in awakening the youth's *amour-propre* in a healthy direction, the supposed author of this paper interjects himself in the first person. "'I am tired of speaking in the third person. And the effort is quite superfluous, for you are well aware, dear fellow citizen, that this unhappy fugitive is myself. I believe myself far enough from the disorders of my youth to dare to admit them, and the hand which drew me away from these disorders deserves, at the expense of a bit of shame, that I render at least some honor to his benefaction'" (264).

Most interpreters have assumed that Rousseau is here acknowledging that the youth is himself and therefore that he is in fact the author of this "paper."[22] Certainly the similarity of the biographical details concerning the young proselyte and Jean-Jacques encourages such a view, although these details were not available to the contemporary reader of *Emile*, since Rousseau only revealed them a decade later in the *Confessions* (and they were only published yet another decade later). Further, in the *Confessions* Rousseau states that he modeled the Savoyard Vicar on two prelates he met around the same biographical point in his own life, although he does not mention hearing anything like the Vicar's profession of faith (*Confessions*, CW, 5:50–58, 100). Nonetheless, we have some reason for rejecting this hypothesis, at least in its most straightforward version. First, if Rousseau is the author, then who is the "'dear fellow citizen'" to whom this admission is directed? The most obvious candidate is the "Citizen of Geneva" himself, author of *Emile*. If Rousseau were simply admitting his authorship such an address would be superfluous. Second, after concluding the "Profession" and returning to the main text, Rousseau still maintains the stance that he has transcribed the "paper" (313), which would be odd if he had acknowledged he was the author. Third, and similarly, if he had admitted his authorship, why would he continue to distinguish between this "paper" and the "body of the work" when later defending it? As I mentioned above, elsewhere I have suggested that one way to resolve the question is to take this as an instance of Rousseau doubling himself, here as author of *Emile* and author of the paper containing the "Profession," all the while insisting on distinguishing the two authorial personae.

The authorial interjection by the narrator, who may or may not be Rousseau, disrupts the reader's own experience of who is who, of reality and appearance, and this narrative disruption parallels a similar disruption in the young proselyte's view of the Savoyard Vicar as he takes up the narrative again. "'What struck me most was seeing in my worthy master's private life virtue without hypocrisy, humanity without weakness, speech that was always straight and simple, and conduct always in conformity with this speech.'" Curiously, however, the youth soon learns that appearance and reality are not, in fact, always the same for the Vicar. For although his behavior was always consistent in private and public, with a notable exception, the opinions he expressed were not. "'But what was I to think when I heard him sometimes approve dogmas contrary to those of the Roman Church and show little esteem for all its ceremonies? I would have believed him a disguised Protestant if I had observed him to be less faithful to these very practices by which he seemed to set little store'" (264–65). Indeed, when he concludes his speech, the Vicar will urge the youth to return to the faith of his fathers, which he—a Catholic priest, no less—calls "of all the religions on earth . . . the one which has the purest morality and which is the most satisfactory to reason" (311). Yet the youth reports that the Vicar was punctilious in fulfilling his priestly duties, "when there were no witnesses as when in the public eye." The young man did not know how to judge these "contradictions." Finally, the youth testifies that the Vicar's private behavior was irreproachable, with one exception: "'the failing which had formerly brought on his disgrace, and of which he was not too well corrected'" (265). The reader will soon learn from the Vicar himself what this failing is. The youth reports that he was curious to learn "the principle on which [the Vicar] founded the uniformity of so singular a life" (265). The question again concerns whether there is "uniformity" beneath the seeming divergence between what the Vicar is and what he appears to be.

The narrative introduction to the "Profession" concludes with a description of the setting for the Vicar's speech, to which I will return in the next section, but the further autobiographical information provided by the Vicar within his speech is, I think, crucial for assessing the aims and substance of the "Profession." Let me begin by noting that this information could have been presented in the narrative introduction in the voice of the supposed author of the writing. In fact, that is precisely what Rousseau originally did, for the earlier drafts of the passage where the Vicar relates his own history originally had the third-person *il* and *lui*, with the narrator relating the information, instead of the final draft employing the first-person *je* and *moi*.[23] By putting this information in the Vicar's mouth, Rousseau makes it a revelation about the Vicar's self-understanding.

There are two related bits of autobiographical information provided by the Vicar. First, he explains that his parents determined that he would earn his bread in "the priest's trade" (*le métier de Prêtre*), a phrasing that reveals the attitude with which he approached the career chosen for him. He relates that in preparing for his trade he was concerned solely with what he needed to know and say to be ordained. Second, and more importantly, he states that having become a priest, he sensed that "in obligating myself not to be a man I had promised more than I could keep." After an intervening paragraph concerning the conscience, the Vicar returns to himself and explains that his reverence for marriage as "the first and the holiest institution of nature" led him to satisfy his human all too human passions by pursuing sexual relations with only unmarried women. He explains that this resolve is what destroyed him, for other priests had more safely lain with married women and even reproached him for not aggravating his fault to escape punishment (266–67). Since the youth remarks in the narrative introduction that the Vicar was "not too well corrected" of what he there characterizes as his unnamed "failing," we know that the Vicar still engages in these sexual exploits at the point he delivers his profession.

Tellingly, this autobiographical information is the occasion for the Vicar's reflections on the conscience. He will later take up this subject at length in a more philosophical vein, which I will investigate in the following chapter, but he here first broaches it in highly personal terms. The Vicar states that in taking the vow of celibacy and thereby "obligating" himself to be celibate he had "promised" too much. Note that he admits the obligation and acknowledges the promise. Yet in the following paragraphs he will admit that he did not honor the obligation or keep his promise. In the intervening paragraph the Vicar departs from his particular case in order to interject some general reflections on the conscience.

> We are told that conscience is the work of prejudices. Nevertheless, I know by my experience that conscience persists in following the

order of nature against all the laws of men. We may very well be forbidden this or that, but remorse always reproaches us feebly for what well-ordered nature permits us, and all the more so for what it prescribes to us. Oh, good young man, nature has as yet said nothing to your senses! May you live a long time in the happy state in which its voice is that of innocence. (267)

In following "well-ordered nature," the Vicar's conscience reproaches him "feebly" for breaking the law. That is, his conscience does bother him, but not enough to desist. His "senses," his bodily urges, press the Vicar to sleep with women despite his vows.

Now, we have good reason to believe that Rousseau himself holds celibacy to be unnatural, based on his understanding of the natural sexual passion, and also perhaps based on what he writes elsewhere—for example, what he has Julie state in the *New Heloise*: "Man is not made for celibacy, and it is very unlikely that a state so contrary to nature will fail to lead to some public or hidden disorder. How can one forever escape from the enemy one constantly carries within? Look at those rash men in other countries who take a vow not to be men" (*Julie*, VI.6, *CW*, 6:549). Rousseau would seem to condone this view, but given my insistence that the views expressed by the Vicar cannot simply be assumed to be those held by Rousseau, I hasten to acknowledge that this statement is voiced by a character in his novel. At any rate, the Vicar's belief that marriage is "the first and the holiest institution of nature" is at minimum in some tension with Rousseau's own views. According to Rousseau, human beings are by nature limited to "physical love," the indiscriminate sexual desire for mating: "Once the appetite is satisfied, the man no longer needs a given woman nor the woman a given man" (*Inequality*, 85–87, note XI, 145).[24] If the Vicar discriminates between the unnatural act of defiling the marriage bed and the "voice of nature" which dictates that he lie with unmarried women, nature is not so fastidious.[25]

The Vicar will later characterize the conscience as the "voice of nature," but here the "voice of nature" is the voice of the body, which tells him to engage in sexual relations. The voice of nature is no longer a voice of innocence for the Vicar, as it allegedly is for the youth. For the Vicar, nature is in conflict with the law or society; he has two "voices" speaking to him, and he struggles to reconcile them. In short, the Vicar's soul is divided against itself. Recall it was precisely the youth's observations of the Vicar's conduct, including sexual conduct, which perplexed him and aroused his curiosity to learn "the principle on which he founded the uniformity of so singular a life" (265–66). Of course, "singular" (*singulière*) has the primary sense of something being remarkable or extraordinary, but Rousseau's use of the term to describe the Vicar's seemingly contradictory life evokes the alternative sense of the word relating to whether something is singular or plural, many or one. Now we learn that the Vicar's soul is not entirely "one," is not entirely unified.[26] Johanna Lenne-Cornuez points to the Vicar's experience of disunity as the "rhetorical situation" evidenced by the Vicar's initial remarks about the conscience as "the key element, in our eyes, for its interpretation," and argues that the order the Vicar seeks in himself and in the moral world is a "projection" meant to overcome the contradictions he experiences.[27]

When we reach the Vicar's thematic discussion of conscience in the following chapter we will have several questions to ask based on this initial evocation. On the autobiographical plane, we may ask whether the Vicar's appeal to conscience is not rather too convenient a justification for his actions. Why, for example, does he break his vow of chastity, but not the marital vows of potential sexual partners, as do his fellow clergymen? The Vicar holds marriage to be natural and the interdict against sleeping with unmarried women to be conventional, yet his allocation of what is natural and conventional seems somewhat expedient. Is the Vicar's conscience casuistic? How reliable a guide is the conscience? On the philosophical plane, we can further explore the connection between the appeal to conscience and the experience of a divided soul. More generally, we might wonder whether the theological doctrines of the "Profession" are the reflection of the Vicar's psychic dividedness and whether such doctrines are appropriate for or useful to the corrupted and unhappy youth to whom they are addressed.

THE DRAMATIC SETTING

Let us return to the conclusion of the dramatic introduction to the "Profession" to examine the setting the Vicar chooses for his speech to the youth. The setting is a summer sunrise looking over the Po with the Alps crowning the landscape. The language used to describe the scene is highly emotive:

> "The rays of the rising sun already grazed the plains and, projecting on the fields long shadows of the trees, the vineyards, and the houses, enriched with countless irregularities of light the most beautiful scene [*tableau*] which can strike the human eye. One would have said that nature displayed all its magnificence to our eyes in order to present them with the text for our conversation [*entretiens*]. It was there that after having contemplated these objects in silence for some time, the man of peace spoke to me as follows." (266)

In examining the *Letter to Voltaire*, I termed attempts to interpret the spectacle of nature as the "rhetoric of nature": What does the spectacle *say* to us, and what do we *wish* it would say to us? The spectacle of nature serves not only as the dramatic setting of the Vicar's speech, but also as the text to be interpreted by him with respect to the order of nature and its author. In the next chapter I take up the Vicar's theological teaching with the book of nature as its backdrop, so for now I will ask about the intended rhetorical effect of the dramatic setting of the "Profession" on its auditor, the young proselyte, and on the reader of *Emile*.

We can glean something of the intended effect of the sunrise scene of the "Profession" from a strikingly similar scene earlier in *Emile*, in this case of a sunset. At the beginning of book III the tutor wishes to teach his pupil a lesson in cosmography and takes him to witness a sunset. Interestingly, just before the attempted lesson Rousseau offers a caution about the difficulties of ascending from sensations to abstract ideas, a warning resembling the cautionary note on the same subject he sounds just before the "Profession." "Let us transform our sensations into ideas, but not leap all of a sudden from objects of sense to intellectual objects.... No other book than the world, no instruction other than the facts." With that said, the tutor then bungles his lesson in cosmography. "One fine evening we go for a walk in a suitable place where a broad, open horizon permits the setting sun to be fully seen," he begins the story. The next day they return to the same spot to witness the rising sun, but the tutor-narrator temporarily forgets the strictly utilitarian purposes of these observations and lapses into emotive prose:

> We see it announcing itself from afar by the fiery arrows it launches ahead of it. The blaze grows; the east appears to be wholly in flames. By their glow one expects the star for a long time before it reveals itself. At every instant one believes that he sees it appear. Finally one sees it. A shining point shoots out like lightning and immediately fills all of space. The veil of darkness is drawn back and falls. Man recognizes his habitat and finds it embellished.... The birds in chorus join together in concert to greet the father of life.... There is here a half-hour of enchantment which no man can resist. So great, so fair, so delicious a spectacle leaves no one cold. (168)

Then Rousseau in his role as author steps in to save the impassioned tutor-narrator.

> Full of the enthusiasm he feels, the master wants to communicate it to the child. He believes he moves the child by making him attentive

to the sensations by which he, the master, is himself moved. Pure stupidity! It is in man's heart that the life of nature's spectacle exists. To see it, one must feel it. The child perceives the objects, but he cannot persuade the relations linking them; he cannot hear the sweet harmony of their concord. For that is needed experience he has not acquired. (168–69).

Most importantly, the child does not have the emotional experience required for such associations. He does not know the "accents of love and pleasure." Nor does he know the divinity: "Finally, how can he be touched by the beauty of nature's spectacle, if he does not know the hand responsible for adorning it?" (169). Whose hand adorns the spectacle? God? The aesthetic, emotional, or even erotic response of the observer? Lenne-Cornuez suggests: "The contemplation of the order is founded on a desirous perception: the truth of the *spectacle* of nature is in *the heart of man*, who projects on to it a harmonious order."[28]

The dramatic setting and poetic language used to describe this scene are remarkably similar to the dramatic setting of the "Profession."[29] Here it is the tutor who would communicate his enthusiasm to his pupil, approximately age twelve, who is not capable of feeling or understanding the emotions and thoughts inspired by the scene. In the case of the "Profession," it is the youth, approximately age fifteen, who describes the sunrise in highly emotional language and, although he is recalling the scene thirty years later, it seems that he was capable of feeling the emotions he describes. We know from the biographical details that he is prematurely sexually awakened. Likewise, unlike Emile, he has had religious instruction and so knows something, if confusedly or superstitiously, about the "hand" responsible for adorning nature's spectacle. If the tutor's desire to communicate what he feels to his pupil is "pure stupidity," the dramatic setting of the "Profession" is designed to provoke an emotional response in the auditor to aid in persuading him of the speech's content. The dramatic setting would not be appropriate for persuading Emile; it is suitable for the young proselyte.

Finally, before turning to the question of the intended audience(s) of the "Profession," I want to note that Rousseau writes elsewhere of how the spectacle of nature speaks differently to different individuals. In the *Letter to Beaumont*, responding to the archbishop's claim that "the great spectacle of nature" obviously proclaims the creator and governor of the world, Rousseau writes: "The order of the universe, admirable as it is, does not strike all eyes equally" (40). In *Julie* he illustrates the different responses to the spectacle of nature of the pious Julie and the unbeliever Wolmar: "Imagine Julie out walking with her husband; she admiring, in the rich and brilliant adornment which the earth displays, the work and gifts of the Author of the creation; he seeing nothing in all this but a fortuitous combination in which nothing is linked to anything except by blind force. . . . Alas! She says affectedly; the wonders of nature, so alive, so animate for us, are dead in the eyes of the unfortunate Wolmar, and in this great harmony of beings, where everything speaks of God in so sweet a voice, he perceives nothing but an eternal silence" (V.5; *CW*, 6:484). Finally, in a letter Rousseau explains: "This picture [*tableau*], although always the same, depicts itself in as many ways as there are different dispositions in the hearts of the spectators."[30] In short, these different responses, emotional and intellectual, to the spectacle of nature by individuals with different characters and capacities make nature an ambiguous witness for the prosecution of natural religion, including the version presented by the Vicar.

THE AUDIENCE

The description of the sunrise scene concludes the dramatic introduction, and the Vicar's speech immediately follows, headed by a subtitle: "Profession of Faith of the Savoyard Vicar" (266). Hitherto we have heard the Vicar a few times, in indirect speech as retrospectively reported by the young proselyte, but now the prelate will do all the talking (also retrospectively reported) with a couple exceptions. One of the exceptions is an aborted attempt by the youth to interrupt the Vicar in the only instance in the speech in which the first-person voice of the Vicar is disrupted by a brief first-person interjection by the youth (or, rather, the author writing in the past tense three decades later). I will examine this interesting, and I think illuminating, exception in the following chapter. The other exception occurs in a brief intermission in the Vicar's speech that divides the "Profession" into two parts. The intermission begins: "The good priest had spoken with vehemence. He was moved, and so was I. I believed I was hearing the divine Orpheus sing the first hymns and teaching men the worship of the gods." The Vicar's song, aided by the beautiful sunrise setting, succeeded in moving his auditor. But it did not entirely win him over: "Nevertheless I saw a multitude of objections to make to him. I did not make any of them, because they were less solid than disconcerting, and persuasiveness was on his side" (294). The narrator does not reveal what objections he had to the Vicar's theological reasonings, but at any rate the emphasis in the dramatic interlude is on the persuasiveness of the speech, on emotional appeals rather than rational argumentation.

The young proselyte is the sole audience of the Vicar's speech, but of course Rousseau elects to include this writing in *Emile*, and so we can enlarge our concern with the intended audience and effect of the "Profession" to the readers of the book. We can get some light on this question by attending to what the Vicar states about the intended effect of his speech and what Rousseau adds in his own name as the supposed editor of the "Profession." When he agrees to deliver his profession to the young proselyte, the Vicar states that he will unburden his heart and mind to show him why he esteems himself happy in responses to the incredulity on the boy's part that a poor, persecuted clergyman could not possibly be happy (265–66). During the dramatic intermission between the two parts of the "Profession," the youth admits to the Vicar that, whatever his lingering doubts, in his current state he would have to "ascend rather than descend in order to adopt your opinions" (294). When he recommences his speech, the Vicar agrees: "But in your present condition you will profit from thinking as I do." To this last statement quoted, Rousseau in his role as editor adds a note: "This is, I believe, what the good vicar could say to the public at present" (295 and n). Rousseau thereby indicates the intended audience, or at least an intended audience, of the "Profession": the public. Like the young proselyte, who unlike Emile has not been educated according to the principle of the natural goodness of man, ordinary readers have been corrupted by society, whether they know it or not. The Vicar's profession, and the "Profession" itself, are therefore appropriate for this audience, and their persuasive force is directed at making them useful for their audience.[31]

Finally, the aim and intended audience of the "Profession" is further indicated by Rousseau immediately after the transcription of the "paper" ceases. The Vicar's speech comes to an end without any commentary by the young proselyte or by Rousseau, who then resumes his authorial voice. "I have transcribed this writing not as a rule for the sentiments that one ought to follow in religious matters, but as an example of the way one can reason with one's pupil in order not to diverge from the method I have tried to establish" (313–14). Rousseau does not judge the "example" he has provided through the "Profession," leaving it to the reader to do so in accordance with his invitation when introducing the writing.

CHAPTER 6

The Theological Teaching of the "Profession of Faith"

The "Profession of Faith of the Savoyard Vicar" is divided into two parts, separated by the dramatic interlude in which the youth states that he refrained from raising any of the "multitude of objections" he had to the Vicar's speech (*Emile*, 294).[1] In the *Letter to Beaumont* Rousseau explains the content and aims of the two parts:

> The Profession of the Savoyard Vicar is composed of two parts. The first part, which is the longer, the more important, the more filled with striking and new truths, is intended to combat modern materialism, to establish the existence of God and natural religion with all the force of which the author is capable.... The second part, very much shorter, less regular, and less thorough raises doubts and difficulties about revelation in general, ascribing to others, however, its true certitude in the purity and sanctity of its doctrine, and in the wholly divine sublimity of the person who was its author. The object of this second part is to make each more circumspect from within his own religion about accusing others of bad faith within theirs, and to show that the proofs of each are not so conclusive to all eyes that those who do not see them with all the same clarity as we do must be treated as guilty people. (75)

As elsewhere in defense of the "Profession," Rousseau here maintains the fiction that it is the Vicar who speaks for himself. Finally, he also notes that it is the second part of the speech that almost exclusively attracted the censure of the archbishop and others, with the first part going almost without comment because, he suggests, it did not touch their self-interest (75).

The present chapter is the first of two chapters devoted to the "Profession" proper, that is, the Vicar's speech. In this chapter I present an analysis of the substance and aims of the theological teaching of the first part of the "Profession," and the following chapter will examine the critique of religion found in the second part. In keeping with Rousseau's statement that the first part is the "more important," most interpreters focus their attention on the theological teaching contained in that part, and conversely scant the second part as being of more historical than philosophical interest.[2] Since I focus throughout this book on Rousseau's concern with both the truth and the utility of the theological and religious teachings he offers, I will attend to both parts of the "Profession" with an eye to Rousseau's somewhat different aims of each of these parts as revealed in his defense of publishing them. As for the present chapter, my analysis is confined to the theological views expressed by the Vicar, while remaining agnostic on the question of how similar they may be to Rousseau's own personal views on the subject. I do, however, explore how the Vicar's arguments compare with what Rousseau writes in his own name, especially within *Emile*, concerning philosophical issues such as human nature and epistemology, to ascertain how and why the Vicar's views differ from those of Rousseau on these subjects.

Autobiographical Prelude to the "Profession"

Perhaps it is helpful to begin by remarking on something obvious yet worth stating: the Vicar's speech is autobiographical. This autobiographical character is first signaled by the title Rousseau gives it: "Profession of Faith of the Savoyard Vicar." Given that the Vicar is a Catholic priest, one might expect that "profession of faith" would refer to the Tridentine profession of faith first promulgated by the Church in 1564 in the face of Protestantism or to the recitation of the Nicene creed required of those converting to Catholicism, such as the young proselyte who hears his speech. Yet that is far from what we get. The Vicar's "profession of faith" is a personal profession of *his* faith: "My young friend, I have just recited to you with my own mouth *my* profession of faith such as God reads it in my heart. You are the first to whom I have told it. You are perhaps the only one to whom I shall ever tell it" (310; emphasis added). Indeed, far from having the youth recite the Catholic credo, the Vicar concludes his speech by counseling the youth to return to his country and to "the religion of your fathers," Calvinism, a religion that he even characterizes as "the one which has the purest morality and which is most satisfactory to reason" (311). In short, the Vicar's "profession of faith" is far from being the profession required by the Church.

From the very outset of his speech, the Vicar cedes authority to judge to his auditor just as Rousseau cedes authority to the reader of *Emile* to judge the "Profession," an authorial strategy I discussed in the previous chapter and have explored elsewhere.[3] As for the auditor, the "Profession" begins: "My child, do not expect either learned speeches or profound reasonings from me. I am not a great philosopher, and I care little to be one. . . . I do not want to argue with you or even attempt to convince you. It is enough for me to reveal to you what I think in the simplicity of my heart. Consult yours during my speech. This is all I ask of you" (266). During his speech, the Vicar repeatedly insists that what he offers are his own beliefs and states that is up to the youth to judge them himself. For example, toward the end: "Now it is for you to judge" (310). The Vicar's profession is not catechismal, but as a speech its rhetoric and substance are instead tailored to be appropriate for its audience.

The theological ruminations of the Vicar may also be tailored to his own psychic needs. In the previous chapter in my examination of the narrative frame of the "Profession" I referred to the "Profession" proper only to highlight some autobiographical details provided there by the Vicar, information I suggested may be important for understanding the substance and aim of his teaching. Let me briefly recapitulate the points I made there. First, I noted that the Vicar's first appeal to the voice of the conscience occurs within his explanation of the failing that cost him his post—namely, sleeping with unmarried women—a fault for which his conscience reproached him only "feebly." I wondered whether the Vicar's appeal to what he terms the "voice of nature" in justifying his failing wasn't rather too convenient, even casuistic. We should keep this first appeal to the conscience in mind when we reach the Vicar's thematic discussion of the conscience. Second, and related, I noted the dividedness of the Vicar's soul as he struggled to balance the dictates of the "voice of nature" of the conscience, on the one hand, and the urges of the "voice of the body," on the other. I suggested that this psychic division might be related to the Vicar's appeal within the "Profession" to the conflict we experience between body and soul as part of his derivation of a doctrine of metaphysical dualism. In other words, the Vicar's theological teaching may be based on his own experience and needs, as well as those of the audience of the "Profession," whether the youth who hears it or the public who reads it as part of *Emile*. Let me now turn to the remainder of the autobiographical prelude with which the Vicar commences his speech.

If the Vicar's conscience is unperturbed by his sexual escapades with single women, or at least not sufficiently troubled to stop him, he relates that the scandal caused by the discovery of his crimes and especially the hypocrisy he witnessed in his brethren precipitated a moral crisis.

"Seeing the ideas that I had of the just, the decent, and all the duties of man overturned by gloomy observations, I lost each day one of the opinions I had received." He draws the parallel of his own case to that of the young proselyte: "And finally reduced to no longer knowing what to think, I reached the same point where you are, with the difference that my incredulity, the late fruit of a riper age, had been more painfully formed and ought to have been more difficult to destroy" (267). Recall the description in the narrative introduction of what the Vicar saw in the youth: "His pride, changed into bitter spite, took men's injustice and hardness only as proof of the viciousness of their nature and the chimerical character of virtue" (262–63). Both the youth and the Vicar have had the experience of seeing through appearances in such a way that challenged their view of reality, in both cases seeing self-interest and hypocrisy behind the veil of virtue and uprightness. As I remarked in the previous chapter regarding the young proselyte, they both experience something like the obverse of the "Illumination of Vincennes" in which Rousseau glimpsed the natural goodness of man beneath the corruption of society. These parallel but inverted discoveries could alternatively be framed as Rousseau glimpsing the unity of the soul beneath its apparent dividedness, and the youth and the Vicar experiencing the dividedness of the soul where there was once innocent unity.

The Vicar describes in Cartesian terms the doubts that arose concerning moral conduct when the scales fell from his eyes: "I was in that frame of mind of uncertainty and doubt that Descartes demands for the quest for truth. This state is hardly made to last, it is unsettling and painful, it is only the self-interest of vice or laziness of soul which leaves us in it" (267). How similar is the Vicar's state of doubt to that of Descartes? Other scholars have explored this question at length and have reached two main conclusions.[4] First, that, far from pursuing a Cartesian line of thought, Rousseau (or the Vicar) draws on multiple philosophic antecedents—for example, rationalists as diverse as Descartes, Malebranche, Leibniz, and Clarke along with empiricists such as Locke and Condillac—and, further, that he does so without attempting to reconcile the tensions among them. Second, with respect to Descartes in particular, that there is only a limited or superficial resemblance. Since my aim here is not to trace the genealogy of the Vicar's philosophical and theological reflections, let me endorse these conclusions and build on them.

As for the relationship between Descartes and the Vicar, while it is true that the Vicar's account of his doubt and his attempts to overcome it takes an autobiographical form that evokes Descartes's story of his intellectual journey,[5] there is a vast difference between the occasions for their doubt and especially their aims. Descartes's methodological doubt is in the service of attaining metaphysical and epistemological certainty and is occasioned by the doubts he entertained concerning what he had been taught about philosophy or science. The quest for such certainty, and its guarantee in the existence of the deity, is in the service of making humans "like masters and owners of nature."[6] Further, when entering into the state of radical doubt necessary for discovering the Archimedean point for attaining true science, Descartes adopts a "provisional morality" that consists in outwardly following the laws and customs of those around him, including with regard to religion, without inwardly affirming their truth or falsity.[7]

The contrast to the Vicar is clear. First, the Vicar's doubt is occasioned by moral uncertainty and is then directed by an ethical imperative: What are the rules by which I should direct my conduct? The Vicar secures nothing like the metaphysical and epistemological certainty of Descartes, nor does he aim to do so. Indeed, far from identifying "clear and distinct ideas," throughout his reasonings he emphasizes the limits of his knowledge and the uncertainty of his conclusions. For example, after postulating his "first article of faith" concerning the existence of a will moving the universe, he admits: "It is true that the dogma I have just established is obscure" (274). Second, the differing durations of their doubt further underscores the dissimilarity. Descartes reports that he spent nine years in his state of doubt, and seemingly happily and productively so. Tellingly, he offers this report within his discussion of adopting his "provisional morality," thus calling attention to the fact that he left his opinions on morals intentionally unsettled, and he never reveals whether he ever replaced this provisional morality with anything more certain, and if so by what.[8] By contrast, the Vicar finds doubt "unsettling and painful," especially with regard to moral conduct: "Although I have often experienced greater evils, I have never led a life so constantly disagreeable as during those times of perplexity and anxiety, when I ceaselessly wandered from doubt to doubt and brought back from my long meditations only uncertainty, obscurity, and contradiction about the cause of my being and the principle of my duties" (268). Unlike Descartes, the Vicar is paralyzed by doubt and hastens to be released from it. "How can one systematically and in good faith be a skeptic?" he asks. "These skeptic philosophers either do not exist or are the unhappiest of men. Doubt about the things it is important for us to know is too violent a state for the human mind; it does not hold out in this state for long; it decides in spite of itself one way or the other and prefers to be deceived rather than to believe nothing" (268). The allusion to being "systematically" a skeptic recalls Descartes's systematic doubt. Yet the purpose of

Cartesian doubt is precisely to overcome skepticism and secure certain knowledge. Cartesian doubt is also methodical in the sense of slowly advancing through reason to identify clear and distinct ideas. In turn, the Vicar's remarks about our mind's proclivity to decide one way or the other without good reason to escape this violent state might make us wonder about the basis on which he adopts the positions he does in his inquiry. We might recall in this light the image Rousseau uses in the *Letter to Voltaire* of a scale that inclines to one side for reasons that have nothing to do with reason: "A thousand subjects of preferences entice me from the most consoling side and join the weight of hope to the equilibrium of reason" (*Voltaire*, 117).

One way in which the Vicar does follow Descartes is in his rejection of the philosophers as sources of the knowledge he seeks. When Descartes relates his growing dissatisfaction with the philosophers, he emphasizes that his doubts were raised by the uncertainty of their doctrines and the fact that everything among them was disputable and therefore doubtful.[9] In turn, the Vicar stresses less the epistemological problem of the uncertainty of reasoning not guided by a proper method than the psychological motives that lead to the disputes among the philosophers. "I consulted the philosophers, I leafed through their books, I examined their various opinions. I found them all to be proud, assertive, dogmatic, even in their pretended skepticism, ignorant of nothing, proving nothing, mocking one another, and this last point, which was common to all, appeared to me the only one about which they are all right." The Vicar diagnoses this philosophical farrago in both epistemological and psychological terms: "I comprehended that the insufficiency of the human mind is the first cause of this prodigious diversity of sentiments and that pride is the second." If the limit of the human mind is one source of the diversity of philosophical systems, pride is what actuates their proponents. "If the philosophers were in a position to discover the truth, who among them would take an interest in it? Each knows well that his system is no better founded than the others. But he maintains it because it is his.... The essential thing is to think differently from others. Among believers, he is an atheist; among atheists he would be a believer" (268–69). Rousseau does not disagree. In the *Discourse on the Sciences and the Arts* he traces the root of "all" the sciences to "human pride" (23), and in defense of the prize essay he writes: "Philosophy will always defy reason, truth, and even time, because it has its source in human pride, stronger than all those things" (*Observations, CW*, 1:45–46n). Many other examples could be adduced. As for the Vicar, throughout his speculations he exhibits a keen and constant awareness of the limits of the human mind, but what I am more interested in exploring is how at certain critical junctures the Vicar's argument is infected by pride.

Man: Who Am I?

Having abandoned the philosophers because of the doubts they multiply and the assertive but uncertain doctrines they haughtily propound, the Vicar rejects all exterior authorities and instead seeks the criterion of truth within himself. "Therefore, I took another guide; and I said to myself, 'Let us consult the inner light; it will lead me astray less than they lead me astray; or at least my errors will be my own.'" The Vicar's inward turn and examination of his self are in part epistemological matters, designed to identify the source and limits of knowledge and the instrument for judging it. "But who am I?" he will soon ask concerning the "instrument" he will use to examine himself and the world (269–70). His inward turn therefore serves as a preparation for turning to the outside to ascertain what he can know about nature and nature's god. Nonetheless, as we shall see, the Vicar's conclusions about his self and its relationship to the external world prepare the dualistic metaphysics he will embrace, and also serve as an analogue for his reasonings concerning the divinity and its relationship to nature.

What the Vicar means by the "inner light" he will consult to guide him is unclear, and nowhere else in the "Profession" does he use the phrase, much less explain it. He does use the term "interior sentiment" at various points, perhaps as an equivalent for "inner light," although he does not explain that term either. As Robert Derathé states, "Truth be told, in this writing Rousseau hardly clarifies for the reader the nature of this sentiment to which he so often appeals."[10] Arthur Melzer is more pointed: "In the end, it would seem to be left unclear how, or even whether, the Vicar distinguishes between the inner sentiment and mere wishful thinking of some kind."[11] In the following paragraph the Vicar speaks of "inner assent," which is not so much a "light" that illuminates truth as the mind's probabilistic nod after having weighed the available evidence. "Then, going over in my mind the various opinions which had one by one drawn me along since my birth, I saw that, although none of them was evident enough to produce conviction immediately, they had various degrees of verisimilitude, and inner assent was given to or refused to them in differing measures." He weighs the claims on each side to ascertain which seems more likely "in the silence of the prejudices," without explaining how he identified or silenced these prejudices. Finally, he notes that we have a tendency when entertaining various ideas to give consent to the last one, presumably because of exhaustion due to weighing all the uncertainties (269).

Given that he is about to embark upon an inquiry which proceeds step-by-step from the sensations he experiences, to the world of bodies in motion he senses, and so on, the Vicar's initial illustration of his method of assaying opinions in the scale of verisimilitude is surprising. He asks his auditor to imagine surveying the "bizarre systems" of the ancient and modern philosophers, and specifically the various materialist theories, and then to picture the "illustrious Clarke" stepping forward to enlighten the world and proclaim "Being of beings and the Dispenser of things." "With what universal admiration, with what unanimous applause would this new system have been received—this new system so great, so consoling, so sublime, so fit to lift up the soul and to give a foundation to virtue, and at the same time so striking, so luminous, so simple, and, it seems to me, presenting fewer incomprehensible things to the human mind than the absurdities it finds in any other system!" (269).[12] I note that Clarke is the last speaker to appear.

The Vicar's encomium has led interpreters to claim that Samuel Clarke, the defender of Newton against Leibniz and the author of *A Demonstration of the Being and Attributes of God* (1705), is the Vicar's— and Rousseau's—principal inspiration in his theological reasonings. Indeed, Ronald Grimsley characterizes Clarke as "Rousseau's metaphysician."[13] While Rousseau may invite this conclusion by having the Vicar reserve his sole positive praise of a philosopher for Clarke, it turns out to be largely a red herring. The main attribute that the Vicar's theological investigation shares with Clarke's is that they are both versions of natural religion—that is, investigations that rely solely on human reason. They otherwise largely diverge, especially in terms of method.

Without entering into a detailed comparison, Clarke's argument in the *Demonstration* is principally an a priori proof: first, that something has existed from eternity; second, that one immutable and independent being has existed from eternity; third, that this immutable and independent being necessarily exists; and so on. In turn, the Vicar's argument is almost entirely a posteriori in form, appealing to the argument from design based on observation of the order of the universe, but even more so building on our inner experience. Clarke does employ a posteriori arguments when he admits that the a priori argument he advances ultimately proves only the nonimpossibility of the truth of the propositions rather than their certitude, and he turns to an a posteriori argument concerning the perceived order of the universe because it provides alternative assurance for the existence of God.[14] In turn, on the rare occasion on which the Vicar turns to a priori arguments they concern the logical relationship among the divine attributes, the comprehension of which he admits is beyond human understanding. Unlike Clarke, the Vicar makes no attempt to buttress his argument by a priori or other proofs, and the doctrines he propounds do not exceed the level of verisimilitude. The main way in which the Vicar does follow Clarke is, I suggest, in arguing that the doctrines he establishes are nonimpossible rather than certain. For example, after establishing his first dogma concerning a will moving the universe, the Vicar admits that the dogma is "obscure," but maintains that it "contains nothing repugnant to reason" (274). An indication that nonimpossibility is what the Vicar shares with Clarke comes from what he states to himself just after his praise of the metaphysician: "'Insoluble objections are common to all systems because man's mind is too limited to resolve them. They do not therefore constitute a proof against any one in particular. But what a difference in direct proofs! Must not the only one which explains everything be preferred, if it contains no more difficulties than the others?'" (269).

Why does the Vicar appeal to Clarke if his own inquiry is so different? Let me begin by noting that he characterizes Clarke's system as "striking," "luminous," and "simple"; he does not claim it is true. He asserts only that his system presents fewer absurdities than the other "bizarre systems" he imagines surveying; he does not build on Clarke's system. Instead, the Vicar's praise of Clarke's system has less to do with its truth value than how it affects him: "this new system so great, so consoling, so sublime, so fit to lift up the soul and to give a foundation to virtue." Given that the addressee of his speech, the young proselyte, requires consolation and a foundation for his virtue, the Vicar's praise of Clarke's system appears to owe as much or more to its utility as its truth. Such an interpretation is suggested by what the Vicar states immediately after the praise of Clarke. He explains that he will accept as "evident" all knowledge to which he cannot refuse consent "in the sincerity of my heart," and that he will leave everything else in uncertainty "if it leads to nothing useful for practice" (269–70). The "heart" is judge; utility the criterion.[15]

"But who am I? What right have I to judge things, and what determines my judgments?" The Vicar frames his inquiry in epistemological terms concerning the instability of his judgments amid the sense impressions he receives. "Thus my glance must be turned toward myself in order to know the instrument I wish to use and how far I can trust its use." The way in which the Vicar casts his glance already seems to suppose the distinction between what is inner and what is outer, between an "I" that judges sense impressions and an exterior world of sensory phenomena. "I exist, and I have senses by which I am affected. This is the first truth that strikes me and to which I am forced to acquiesce. Do I have a particular sentiment of my existence, or do I sense it only through my sensations? This is my first doubt" (270). The Vicar does not doubt his senses, but instead questions whether he has a sentiment of his existence. The distance from Descartes is immense; the senses are the first thing Descartes doubts, considering them illusory, the stuff of dreams, or the playthings of an evil genius.[16] Likewise, the first proposition Descartes determines is certain, the *cogito* is more or less analogous to the distinct sentiment of existence that the Vicar doubts, so whereas Descartes is because he thinks, the Vicar senses because he is. Or as Melzer remarks, "by the 'indubitable,' Descartes meant what cannot be doubted logically; the Vicar means what cannot be doubted psychologically."[17]

Despite his first doubt, the Vicar quickly concludes that sensations take place within him, since they make him sense his existence, but their cause is external to him, since they affect him without him having anything to do with it. He therefore reasons that he exists and that there exist other beings outside of him, whatever their ontological status. Finally, although he does not explicitly resolve his first doubt concerning whether he has a distinct sentiment of existence, he does conclude that he has a faculty of judging distinct from sensing, an "active force" that compares passively received sensations. "To perceive is to sense; to compare is to judge. Judging and sensing are not the same thing." He develops this point against unnamed thinkers who claim that "the sensitive being distinguishes the sensations from one another by the differences among these very sensations"—that is without a separate faculty of judgment. The Vicar insists that judgment is active and cannot be reduced to sensation, which for him is passive. "Therefore, I am not simply a sensitive and passive being but an active and intelligent being; and whatever philosophy may say about it, I shall dare to pretend to the honor of thinking" (271–72). The distinction between the passive and active aspects of his being sets the stage for the dualist metaphysics he will soon embrace.[18]

Let us compare the Vicar's argument concerning the self as a sensing and judging being to what Rousseau writes in his own name. There are indeed similarities, but, as we saw in the previous chapter, Rousseau's account of the formation of the self is a developmental one that explains the emergence of the sentiment or idea of a separate self without a hint of dualism. To begin, whereas the Vicar's first doubt concerns whether he has a sentiment of his own existence independent of the sensory flux, Rousseau argues that an infant lacks a sentiment of his own existence. "We are born capable of learning but able to do nothing, knowing nothing. The soul, enchained in imperfect and half-formed organs, does not even have the sentiment of its own existence" (61). The separate sentiment of one's own existence comes through the experiences derived from the senses and bodily motion as the child learns to distinguish what is interior from what is exterior. He concludes his discussion of infancy: "The first developments of childhood occur almost all at once. . . . Before it he is nothing more than he was in his mother's womb. He has no sentiment, no idea; hardly does he have sensations. He does not even sense his own existence" (74). In short, while for Rousseau there is a phenomenologically distinct "self," it is not metaphysically distinct.

Where Rousseau does agree with the Vicar concerns the distinction between sensing and judging, but once again in the Vicar's hands the distinction leads to a dualist metaphysics. We know that Rousseau agrees with the Vicar on this point based on what he writes in his own name. The unnamed philosopher whom the Vicar combats is Helvétius in *De l'esprit* (1758), along with the article "Evidence" in the *Encyclopédie* (1756).[19] Rousseau added marginal notes to his copy of *De l'esprit* critical of Helvétius's argument that mental faculties, principally memory and judgment, are reducible to the faculty of sensation. As for judging, like the Vicar, Rousseau distinguishes between a passive faculty of sensation and an active faculty of judging. "In the first operation the mind is purely passive, but in the other it is active" ("Notes on Helvétius's On the Mind," *CW*, 12:204–5). Toward the end of his notes, he repeats his main objection: "The principle from which the author deduces the natural equality of minds in the following chapters, and which he tried to establish at the beginning of the work, is that human judgments are purely passive. This principle has been established and discussed with much philosophy and profundity in the Encyclopedia article *Evidence*." And, after (incorrectly) guessing at the author's identity, he writes: "I have tried to attack it and to establish the activity of our judgments, both in the notes that I have written at the beginning of this book, and above all in the first part of the profession of faith of the Savoyard Vicar" (211). Rousseau embraces the Vicar's argument concerning the activity of judgment, which is incidentally the only occasion on which he does so unambiguously with regard to the first part of the "Profession." Nonetheless, in his notes he does not derive a dualist metaphysics from the distinction between passive sensation and active judgment. Since the notes on Helvétius are rather fragmentary and were also never intended for publication, it is difficult to go any further than I just have to distinguish Rousseau's own views from those of the Vicar. Thankfully, we have Rousseau's account of judgment in the main text of *Emile*.

Rousseau's account is ultimately quite different from the Vicar's assertion of a seemingly firm distinction between passivity and activity.

"Before the age of reason the child receives not ideas but images. . . . Our sensations are purely passive, while all our perceptions or ideas are born out of an active principle which judges. This will be demonstrated hereafter" (107). The "active principle" appears to be part of a process connected to the development of a distinct sentiment of one's own existence through sensory experience and bodily movement that produces a sense of "inside" and "outside." A passage later in the work where he returns to the distinction between sensation and ideas sheds some light on this. When an individual reaches the age of reason, he explains, he "has become aware of himself as an individual"—that is, he has a distinct sentiment or idea of his existence. Rousseau suggests in this context that this awareness emerges "by exercising his body and his senses" which in turn "exercised his mind and his judgment." "We have made an active and thinking being," he proclaims, implying a rather literal reading of "active"—that is, relating to movement in which the "self" interacts with the surrounding world. "At first our pupil had only sensations. Now he has ideas. He only felt; now he judges; for from the comparison of several successive or simultaneous sensations and the judgment made of them is born a sort of mixed or complex sensation which I call an 'idea'" (203). To illustrate this process, he employs the example of a stick half submerged in water. The stick appears to be broken, but the well-educated child will not immediately judge the sensation and will instead conduct a series of experiments consisting in looking at the stick from different angles, ultimately judging that it is not actually broken (206). In other words, the "active principle" is not a metaphysically separate "self" in Rousseau's account; instead, the activity consists in a series of comparisons of sensory experiences that form ideas. Indeed, in the *Discourse on Inequality*, Rousseau explains that "every animal has senses since it has ideas, it even combines its ideas up to a certain point, and man differs in this regard from beast only by degree" (71). For Rousseau the progression from sensations to ideas to judgment can be explained purely naturalistically. Even if the Vicar only slightly diverges from Rousseau on this matter at his point, his divergence will ultimately prove pregnant.

God: The First Two Articles of Faith

After having concluded that he is "an active and intelligent being" as well as a "sensitive and passive being," the Vicar is done with his self-examination. "Having, so to speak, made certain of myself, I begin to look outside of myself," and he finds himself initially drowned in the immensity of beings (272). His method is to compare these beings with himself—that is, to the "active and intelligent being" he has discovered. The Vicar's approach would seem to be suffused with the very anthropomorphism against which Rousseau warned the reader of *Emile* just before the "Profession," writing in his natural history of religion: "The sentiment of our action on other bodies must at first have made us believe that when they acted on us they did so in a manner similar to the way we acted on them. Thus man began by animating all the beings whose actions he felt" (256).

As he looks out at the world, the Vicar perceives matter in motion. He derives the essential properties of matter from what his senses inform him about them. "I see it now in motion and now at rest, from which I infer that neither rest nor motion is essential to it." So far the Vicar is a good Newtonian. "But motion, since it is an action," he continues, "is the effect of a cause of which rest is only the absence. Therefore, when nothing acts on matter, it does not move; and by the very fact that it is neutral to rest and to motion, its natural state is to be at rest" (272). No longer is the Vicar a good Newtonian, having effectively denied the principle of inertia, according to which neither rest nor motion is the natural state of matter.[20] Indeed, we are prompted to think of Newton when the Vicar names him a page later regarding the law of attraction (273). What do we make of the Vicar's departure from Newton?

Now, we know that Rousseau was quite familiar with Newton, and we can presume with the first law of motion. For example, in his autobiographical poem concerning his self-education while living at Les Charmettes, he writes: "Sometimes with Leibniz, Malebranche, and Newton / I raise my reason upon a sublime tone, / I examine the laws of bodies and of thoughts" ("The Orchard of Madame de Warens," *CW*, 12:8). In the *Discourse on the Sciences and the Arts* he names Newton as one of the "preceptors of the human race," and at one point he draws on his theory of the ebb and flow of the tides due to the gravitational force of the moon (34–35, 15). He would have likewise been familiar with Newton's theory from his former friends the Encyclopedists, especially d'Alembert. Most importantly, he displays his familiarity in a footnote he adds in his role as "editor" of the "Profession" to the passage in question in which he undercuts the Vicar's argument. "This rest is, if you wish, only relative," he begins the note, and argues that we conceive of rest by way of abstraction from the opposition to the motion we observe, concluding: "Now, it is not true that motion is of the essence of matter if it can be conceived at rest" (272n). In other words, Rousseau himself does not subscribe to the Vicar's claim that matter is at (absolute) rest, much less argue that rest is the natural state of matter.[21]

What, then, is the effect of the Vicar's argument that rest is the natural state of matter? The Vicar's argument concerning motion will lead him to deduce his first "article of faith" concerning a will that moves the universe, given his claim that rest is the natural state of matter. He begins by distinguishing between communicated and voluntary motion. He appeals to the analogy of a watch familiar to deistic arguments from design to argue that its motion cannot be spontaneous and must therefore be communicated. How does he know there is spontaneous motion? "I shall tell you that I know it because I sense it. I want to move my arm, and I move it without this movement's having another immediate cause than my will." He argues that nonanimate bodies are incapable of voluntary motion and therefore their motion must be communicated. "My mind rejects all acquiescence to the idea of unorganized matter moving itself or producing some action." As for the visible universe, the Vicar argues that it is composed of unorganized matter and moreover contends that its very lawlike character demonstrates that it does not have the liberty characteristic of voluntary motion. "Therefore there is some cause of its motions external to it, one which I do not perceive. But inner persuasion makes this cause so evident to my senses that I cannot see the sun rotate without imagining a force that pushes it; or if the earth turns, I believe I sense a hand that makes it turn." After arguing that the general laws of motion he observes must have a cause outside of the motion itself, the Vicar deduces that there must be a "first cause, for to suppose an infinite regress of causes is to suppose no cause at all." Finally, he concludes with his first article of faith: "In a word, every motion not produced by another can come only from a spontaneous, voluntary action. Inanimate bodies act only by motion, and there is no true action without will. This is my first principle. I believe therefore that a will moves the universe and animates nature. This is my first dogma, or my first article of faith" (272–73).

Several features of the Vicar's derivation of his first article of faith deserve notice. First, his argument remains on the level of belief: it is, as he says, an "article of faith." Second, his argument is anthropomorphic. At the outset of his reasoning, he appeals to his own experience of moving his arm as evidence for spontaneous or voluntary motion with its source in his will. This then becomes the analogue for attributing the motion of the universe to a will external to the universe itself, or what he will soon term God. The anthropomorphic character of his argument is underscored by the language he employs: "I cannot see the sun rotate without imagining a force that pushes it; or if the earth turns, I believe I sense a hand that makes it turn." Rousseau could, of course, have had the priest present a more traditional argument from design, but the Vicar's emphasis is his own experience as a voluntary agent, an experience that he does not attempt to explain beyond citing "this sentiment in me." Indeed, after presenting his first article of faith, he addresses this very question: "How does a will produce a physical and corporeal action? I do not know, but I experience within myself that it does so" (273). He restates the will moving the body as a fact of experience, a phenomenological matter.

The Vicar does not attempt to explain how the will relates to the body, or how sense impressions affect his soul, but his unresolved ruminations on the subject are the occasion for his first explicit adoption of a dualist metaphysics. "As for me, whether it is when I am passive or when I am active, the means of uniting the two substances appears absolutely incomprehensible." He admits that the dogma he has just established, apparently the dogma of two substances, is "obscure." Nonetheless, eschewing an appeal to Occam's razor that would reduce the two substances to a single one, he claims that materialism is even more repugnant to reason or observation. "Is it not clear that if motion were essential to matter, it would be inseparable from it and would always be in it in the same degree?" But the materialist would argue that neither motion nor rest is an essential attribute of matter. The Vicar entertains conceiving matter as naturally in motion, which he finds does not explain the phenomena, including rest. Then he considers the alternative of conceiving it as naturally at rest and therefore only put into motion by a spontaneous or voluntary will outside of matter, which is the position he adopts.

At this point, the Vicar addresses the young proselyte for the first time in the "Profession" proper, something he will do several times, and I suggest as a preliminary approach to these dramatic moments that they are meant to spur the reader to entertain precisely the option the Vicar does not. "Tell me, my friend," he asks, "whether someone who talks to you about a blind force spread throughout the whole of nature brings any veritable idea to you mind? . . . Far from being able to imagine any order in the fortuitous concurrence of elements, I am not even able to imagine their conflict, and the chaos of the universe is more inconceivable to me than its harmony" (274–75). The Vicar cannot "imagine" the spontaneous ordering of the universe, although he also admits that the workings of the universe are not "intelligible to the human mind." As we shall see momentarily, he comes back to the issue as if he cannot shake his unease at the possibility.

The posited harmony of the universe leads the Vicar to his second article of faith: "If moved matter shows me a will, matter moved according to certain laws shows me an intelligence." The actions of this intelligence suggest "an active and thinking being. Therefore this being exists." Just like the Vicar himself, this being has an active principle. The anthropomorphic character of his argument for the second article of faith is, as with the first, underscored by the language he uses. "'Where do you see him existing?' you are going to say to me," he addresses the youth again, and replies: "Not only in the heavens which turn, not only in the star which gives us light, not only in myself, but in the ewe which grazes, in the bird which flies, in the stone which falls, in the leaf carried by the wind" (275). Although he thus far makes only claims about the general order or lawlike character of the universe, his language here evokes the biblical verse claiming God's particular providence: "Are not two sparrows sold for a penny? And not one of them will fall to the ground without your Father's will. But even the hairs of your head are all numbered. Fear not, therefore; you are of more value than many sparrows" (Matthew 10:29–31). As we shall see, the Vicar will later appeal to the need for particular providence to rectify the disorder of the moral realm of mankind.

The Vicar judges that there is order in the world. Employing a deist trope, he compares the universe to a watch and admires the workman. Yet his principal strategy is not the argument from design, but rather the appeal to sentiment. "Let us compare the particular ends, the means, and the ordered relations of every kind. Then let us listen to our inner sentiment." The "inner sentiment" moves him to believe in an intelligence that has set the world in motion according to certain laws. But the Vicar cannot shake the materialists who argue that this apparent order is the work of chance; they can silence him with their arguments but they cannot "persuade" him. "I should not, I agree, be surprised that a thing happens, if it is possible and the difficulty of its occurrence is compensated for by the number of throws of the dice," he admits. Nonetheless, despite admitting the hypothetical, he cannot bring himself to believe it could be true. The Vicar employs a comparison that Rousseau himself draws. The priest cannot believe that the *Aeneid* could have been composed by chance, just as Rousseau claimed in the *Letter to Voltaire* that the *Henriade* could not be the result of chance (but instead the product of a supreme intelligence—Voltaire himself!). "'You forget,' I shall be told, 'the number of throws'" (276). Now, as I noted in chapter 3 when discussing the *Letter to Voltaire*, in a draft passage that he excised from the final version, Rousseau remarks on how struck he was with Diderot's argument in the *Pensées philosophiques* concerning how an ordered whole could result from chance with a sufficient number of throws of the dice, with the *Iliad* along with the *Henriade* serving as the example. And I also earlier remarked that Rousseau uses the same logic in the *Discourse on Inequality* when defending the course of human development he traces, saying "the lapse of time compensates for the slight probability of events" (90).

In his concluding reflections on the divinity the Vicar emphasizes the limits of our reason concerning the intelligence that ordered the universe, but he also speaks to the danger of *amour-propre* in pursuing such reasonings. I earlier emphasized the Vicar's initial diagnosis of the limits of philosophy due to both epistemological and psychological reasons, notably in the pride of the philosophers. We ought to be alert to the role *amour-propre* is about to play in the Vicar's inquiry. Having rejected the argument that order is the result of chance, he draws toward a conclusion to his discussion of the being he finally calls "God." "I believe therefore that the world is governed by a powerful and wise will. I see it or, rather, I sense it; and that is something important for me to know." Note again that while the Vicar does refer to the traditional deistic argument from design, from what he can "see" about the universe, his emphasis is once again on his interior sentiment, what he senses or feels. Note also that he describes the "will" governing the world as "powerful" and "wise," not omnipotent and omniscient. Such claims of superlative attributes of the divinity are, it seems, beyond his ken. "But is this same world eternal or created? Is there a single principle of things? Or, are there two or many of them, and what is their nature? I know nothing about all this, and what does it matter to me? As soon as this knowledge has something to do with my interests, I shall make an effort to acquire it. Until then I renounce idle questions which may agitate my *amour-propre* but are useless for my conduct and are beyond my reason" (276–77).

Several things are notable about this passage. First, the priest's avowal of ignorance about the divine attributes, the creation of the world, and the number of "principles" of things is obviously heterodox. After all, though, the Vicar restricts himself to natural reason in his inquiries and does not appeal to revelation. In the following paragraph he elaborates on what he professes to deduce through reason concerning the deity: "This Being which wills and is powerful, this Being active in itself, this Being whatever it may be, which moves the universe and orders all things, I call *God*. I join to this name the ideas of intelligence, power, and will which I have brought together, and that of goodness which is their necessary consequence" (277). The conclusion that goodness is the necessary consequence of the other attributes is explained by the sole reference within the main text of *Emile* to the "Profession," in a passage I discussed in chapter 2. Positing the natural goodness of man against Hobbes in particular, Rousseau explains that evil is the result of weakness, and therefore counsels his reader to make his child strong, that is, relative to his needs and passions. "Of all the attributes of the all-powerful divinity, goodness is the one without which one can least conceive it. . . . See hereafter the Profession of Faith of the Savoyard Vicar" (67). If Rousseau attributes goodness to the "all-powerful divinity," or more accurately our *conception* of such a being, the Vicar only claims that God is potent, not omnipotent. Thus, the goodness of the divinity is in question as well, or more precisely the question arises as to the extent of goodness as the ordering principle. If, as the Vicar will soon argue, goodness is defined as the "love of order which produces order" (282), is this order limited to the general laws of nature or general providence? Or does it extend to particular beings through particular providence?

Second, the fact that the Vicar entertains the possibility of there being more than one "principle" of things caught the eye of the archbishop of Paris. Indeed, this is the sole passage in the first part of the "Profession" to draw his attention. What is meant by "principles" in the passage is not clear. That is, what the Vicar means: for Rousseau takes the opportunity in replying to Beaumont to insist on the distinction between himself as author of the main text of *Emile* and the Vicar. Beaumont accuses him of Manicheaism. In reply, Rousseau admits that the Manichean's two principles, one good and one evil, would more easily explain the existence of evil than the assumption of a single one. But he states that this was not what was meant by "principles" in the "Profession." Asserting that he admits only one first moving cause, Rousseau explains that the question is whether there is both an "active" and a "passive" principle in the universe—that is, whether the divine will and intelligence are the sole principle, with passive matter being created, or whether the active principle of the divinity acts on already existing matter. This is consistent with the Vicar's admission that he does not know whether the universe is eternal or created. As for Rousseau, apparently writing in his own name, he remarks to the archbishop that the claim of creation ex nihilo is the less comprehensible alternative. "For so many men and philosophers, who in all times have meditated on this subject, have all unanimously rejected the possibility of creation," except, that is, a few who bow to authority and keep silent out of caution (*Beaumont*, 42–43). Rousseau is silent about what he himself believes.

Third, and most important for my present purposes, is the Vicar's worry that speculations beyond his reason or those not useful for moral guidance, his chief aim, may "agitate my *amour-propre*." Why? One possibility is suggested by his earlier criticism of philosophers motivated by pride, meaning that pursuing such "idle questions" will pique his *amour-propre*. But why these particular questions? While I can only speculate, given the third dogma of faith he is about to propound concerning the immateriality of the soul, and therefore its continued existence after the death of the body, the question of the eternity or creation of the world, as well as the number of "principles" of things, involves the far from indifferent questions of being and time, finitude and essence. That is, what is the nature of our being, and are we mortal or immortal? Further, as I am about to suggest, the Vicar's reasonings about the place of mankind in the universe, and especially his own place in it, are animated by *amour-propre*.

God, Man, and Evil

Having assured himself about God, the Vicar turns to mankind to ascertain what place we—and he—have in the order of things. "After having discovered those attributes of the divinity by which I know its existence, I return to myself and I try to learn what rank I occupy in the order of things that the divinity governs and that I can examine. I find myself by my species incontestably in the first rank" (277). I have already noted the anthropomorphic aspects of the Vicar's arguments concerning the divinity, and I have signaled how pride may infect his argument—for example, just above when he voices worries that his *amour-propre* may be agitated by his reasonings. The anthropomorphism and pride now come into full view when the Vicar congratulates himself on being in the first rank. His explanation for this conclusion is likewise telling: his will and the power he possesses to execute it are unrivaled. In addition to power, he possesses intelligence: "By my intelligence I am the only one that has a view of the whole. What being here on earth besides man is able to observe all the others, to measure, calculate, and foresee their movements and their effects, and to join, so to speak, the sentiment of common existence to that of its individual existence?" (277–78). For a man whose first doubt was whether or not he possessed a separate sentiment of his existence, the Vicar has come a long way. Indeed, his description of himself and his kind—of his will, power, and intelligence—is reminiscent of what he says about the divinity. After further ruminating on his capacity to "appropriate" the stars he contemplates and his ability to wonder at the sun (with the rising sun providing the backdrop for his speech), the Vicar declares himself content with his place in the universe. "The effect of this reflection is less to make me proud than to touch me"—*Cette réflexion m'engorgueillit moins qu'elle me touche* (278). More touched than proud perhaps, but still proud.[22]

The Vicar's first glance at himself is reminiscent of Rousseau's depiction in the *Discourse on Inequality* of man emerging from the primitive condition as he becomes conscious of his superiority over the animals:

"This is how the first glance he directed upon himself produced in him the first movements of pride. This is how, as yet scarcely knowing how to distinguish ranks and looking upon himself as in the first rank as a species, he prepared himself from afar to claim the first rank as an individual" (92). In any case, let me note before proceeding that the reference to feeling pride voiced by the Vicar as he contemplates man's place in the order of things parallels the same structural feature I noted in chapter 3 when examining the *Letter to Voltaire*. There the mention of pride signaled a shift from the first, naturalistic teaching concerning a general providence of nature and nature's God to a second, divine teaching concerning particular providence. As we shall now see, the Vicar's reference to pride signals a similar shift.

THE DISORDER OF THE MORAL WORLD

Yet pride is promptly followed by a fall.

> But when next I seek to know my individual place in my species, and I consider its various ranks and the men who fill them, what happens to me? What a spectacle! Where is the order I had observed? The picture of nature had presented me with only harmony and proportion; that of mankind presents me with only confusion and disorder! Concert reigns among the elements, and men are in chaos! . . . O wisdom, where are your laws? O providence, is it thus that you rule the world? Beneficent Being, what has become of your power? I see evil on earth. (278)

Let me first point out that the Vicar discovers chaos and evil after seeking to know his individual place in the species. He might well have found this disorder just before when examining the species instead of congratulating himself on the power and intelligence he finds in mankind. Instead, he finds disorder when he considers his own place among "the various ranks and the men who fill them." Recall that the Vicar's search for moral guidance began when he lost his own rank in society with the discovery of his sexual escapades and beheld the hypocrisy of those who filled those ranks.

The Vicar's reflections lead him to the central problem of theodicy: how to reconcile the power and goodness of the divinity with the existence of evil. He poses three questions about the divinity before stating that he sees evil on earth: first, concerning the laws of nature, that is, the intelligence of the divinity; second, concerning providence, or divine goodness; third, concerning the extent of its power. The theological tradition poses the dilemma in terms of the superlative nature of the divine attributes—omniscience, omni-goodness, and omnipotence—but recall that the Vicar limits himself to identifying intelligence, goodness, and power in God. He thus potentially lowers the threshold of understanding the existence of evil—for example, by opening the possibility that divine power somehow does not extend to individual human beings qua individuals.

Turning to understand the existence of evil, the Vicar addresses the youth: "my good friend," a dramatic action, I suggested above, that invites us as readers to wonder about alternatives to the arguments he propounds. He states that, surprisingly enough, the "apparent contradictions" he had discovered when wondering about the existence of evil led him to "sublime ideas of the soul" he had not yet glimpsed. "In meditating on the nature of man, I believed I discovered in it two distinct principles," one of which raised him to truth, justice, and moral beauty and the other of which lowered him to the empire of the senses and passions. These two principles parallel the distinction he earlier drew between the "active principle" that judges and the "passive" one that senses. The incipient dualism of the Vicar's argument now flourishes in the face of explaining the origin of evil and will shortly blossom into a full-fledged metaphysical dualism so as to offer a solution to the problem of evil. For the present, though, the Vicar notes the combat between these two "principles" within himself, and he reports saying to himself, "'No, man is not one,'" for he wants and does not want, is both enslaved and free, loves the good and does the bad, is "active" when he listens to reason and "passive" when he succumbs to the passions. As I suggested above, the Vicar's own experience of disobeying his vows and heeding the supposed voice of nature, the point when he first appeals to the conscience, revealed a dividedness in his soul.[23] He now sees that "man is not one," and he will shortly return to the conscience.

Once again addressing the youth in the very next paragraph, the Vicar makes a surprising concession. "Young man, listen with confidence; I shall always be of good faith. If conscience is the work of the prejudices, I am doubtless wrong, and there is no demonstrable morality. But if to prefer oneself to everything is an inclination natural to man, and if nevertheless the first sentiment of justice is innate in the human heart, let him who regards man as a simple being overcome these contradictions, and I shall no longer acknowledge more than one substance" (279). In fact, it is this occasion of addressing the proselyte that first suggested to me that such addresses might be signals to the reader.

The Vicar opposes natural self-love to a sentiment of justice, or the conscience, as evidence that there must be "two distinct principles" in man, often in contradiction with one another, as he himself experiences. Yet we need look no further than the main text of *Emile* for an account of self-love and justice cohering with one another in an account of "man as a simple being," that is, naturally unified. Shortly before the "Profession," in a passage I quoted in chapter 4, he writes of Emile entering the moral world: "If this were the place for it, I would try to show how the first voices of conscience arise out of the first movement of the heart, and how the first notions of good and bad are born of the sentiments of love and hate. I would show that *justice* and *goodness* are not merely abstract words—pure moral beings formed by the understanding—but are true affections of the soul enlightened by reason, and hence only an ordered development of our primitive affections" (235). In short, it is Rousseau himself who would demonstrate to the Vicar that man is a "simple being," and there is therefore no need to subscribe to the existence of two "principles," much less two "substances." Perhaps the reader of *Emile* is signaled to recall this passage and related ones by the Vicar's repeated addresses to his auditor in this context.

The question of ontology is in fact where the Vicar turns next in an argument which culminates in his third article of faith concerning the immaterial soul. He begins by acknowledging that Occam's razor would require admitting only one substance if all essential attributes of a being can be explained by a single one, but he argues that extended and divisible matter cannot be reconciled with thought, which is neither extended nor divisible, and therefore that there must be two substances (279). He therefore rejects Locke's famous conjecture that matter may be capable of thought. Rousseau adds a note in his role as editor in which he appears to agree with the Vicar. "It seems to me that far from saying that rocks think, modern philosophy has discovered, on the contrary, that men do not think. It no longer recognizes anything but sensitive beings in nature.... But if it is true that all matter senses, where shall I conceive the sensitive unity of the individual *I* to be?" (279n). The target here is less Locke than Helvétius. As with his concurring opinion in support of the Vicar's argument concerning the distinction between judging and sensing, also directed at Helvétius, however, Rousseau does not appeal to two principles or substances when discussing thought or mental capacities generally. In the note he does not put forward a dualist position in his polemical confrontation with "modern philosophy." What his own understanding of thought and judgment may be is beyond the scope of the present examination, so I will leave it at saying that Rousseau's support of the Vicar's argument concerning two substances offers little support indeed.

The Vicar jousted uneasily with the materialists for some time before revealing his second article of faith. As before, when distinguishing between the "active principle" of judging and the "passive" one of sensing in his incipient dualism, the Vicar appeals to his own experience of willing to counter materialism. "No material being is active by itself, and I am." He states that he experiences the "sentiment of [his] freedom" in his soul, including when it conflicts with the desires of the body. "The principle of every action is in the will of a free being. One cannot go back beyond that." In this argument, again as before, he analogizes the initiation of motion by his own free will to the divine will, which orders the motion of the universe. From this freedom he now derives his third article of faith: "Man is therefore free in his actions and as such is animated by an immaterial substance. This is my third article of faith" (280–81). The Vicar's "sentiment" of his freedom recalls Rousseau's argument in the *Discourse on Inequality* that the "sentiment" or "consciousness" of our freedom is what distinguishes us from the animals, and I suggested in my examination of that passage that he offers what I termed a phenomenological as opposed to metaphysical argument concerning the consciousness of our freedom. The Vicar, in turn, begins with a phenomenological account, here of freedom of and contradiction in the will, but adopts metaphysical dualism.

PROVIDENCE

Although the Vicar posits an immaterial soul, the article of faith owes even more to the problem of evil, to which he now turns. The Vicar's ensuing argument concerning providence evinces an unresolved tension, if not downright contradiction, which revolves around the relationship between the general providence of ordered physical nature, on the one hand, and the question of a particular providence that extends to the disordered moral realm of human beings, on the other. As I hope to show, his argument concerning particular providence collapses into the argument for general providence. Or, differently put, particular providence turns out to be an unnecessary adjunct to the argument for general providence, with its justification consisting in the fact that it provides hope and consolation for those who experience the disorders of the moral world, such as the Vicar himself. Let me now turn to his arguments.

"If man is active and free, he acts on his own," the Vicar continues after positing the third article of faith: "All that he does freely does not enter into the ordered system of providence and cannot be imputed to it. Providence does not will the evil a man does in abusing the freedom it gives him; but it does not prevent him from doing it, whether because this evil, coming from a being so weak, is nothing in its eyes, or because it could not prevent it without hindering his freedom." He further explains that man's strength is so limited that "the abuse the freedom [providence] reserves for him cannot disturb the general order. The evil that man does falls back on him without changing anything in the system of the world, without preventing the human species from preserving itself in spite of itself" (281). Now, surely even if the free will of humans lies outside the realm of physical necessity, as the Vicar claims, the actions emanating from that will are part of the physical world of nature. How could these actions be so weak as not to disrupt the general order unless they are in fact part of that general order—that is, physical acts that conform to the general laws of nature?

The traditional distinction between physical and moral evils, which I also explored earlier with reference to the *Letter to Voltaire*, now comes into play in the Vicar's argument. "It is the abuse of our faculties which makes us unhappy and wicked. Our sorrows, our cares, and our sufferings come to us from ourselves. Moral evil is incontestably our own work, and physical evil would be nothing without our vice, which have made us sense it." Even the most conspicuous physical evil, death, is not necessary truly an evil. In an appeal to something like Rousseau's natural man, the Vicar explains: "How few ills [*maux*] there are to which the man living in primitive simplicity is subject! He lives almost without diseases as well as passions and neither foresees not senses death." In other words, to use Rousseau's terminology in the *Discourse on Inequality*, natural man is a purely physical being who experiences only physical evils, which are not in fact evils from the perspective of the general order of nature. "If we were satisfied *to be what we are*," the Vicar continues, "we would not have to lament our fate. But to seek an imaginary well-being, we give ourselves countless real ills [*maux*]" (281; emphasis added). The phrase "to be what we are" is susceptible to at least two interpretations. First, the Vicar may be offering moral counsel similar to the Stoics: that we should live according to nature, and thus not increase the evils we experience owing to imagination, foresight, and the passions. Second, the passage could alternatively or additionally mean that we are, in fact, fundamentally physical beings for whom there is no problem of evil within the general natural order or general providence. The latter alternative, I have argued, is Rousseau's own position.

The Vicar concludes this stage of his confrontation with evil as follows:

> Man, seek the author of evil no longer. It is yourself. No evil exists other than that which you do or suffer, and both come to you from yourself. General evil can exist only in disorder, and I see in the sys-

tem of the world an unfailing order. Particular evil exists only in the sentiment of the suffering being, and man did not receive this sentiment from nature: he gave it to himself.... Take away our fatal progress, take away our errors and vices, take away the work of man, and everything is good [*tout est bien*]. (282)

It is no wonder that many readers take the "Profession" to be Rousseau's own views on the subject, for this passage in particular sounds very much like what he writes in his own name. However, the Vicar does not stop there.

The general providence of nature and nature's god is traditionally associated with the attribute of goodness, as it is in Rousseau's own version of the argument in the *Discourse on Inequality* and the *Letter to Voltaire*, but the Vicar demands justice from God as well. "Where everything is good, nothing is unjust. Justice is inseparable from goodness," he argues. "Now, goodness is the necessary effect of a power without limit and of the self-love essential to every being aware of itself.... Therefore, the supreme good Being, because he is supremely powerful, ought also to be supremely just. Otherwise, He would contradict Himself; for the love of order which produces order is called *goodness*; and the love of order which preserves order is called *justice*" (282).[24] Recall that earlier the Vicar only claimed that the intelligent being who orders the universe is powerful and good. Now he attributes omnipotence to the "supremely good Being." The expansion of power and goodness allows him to extend the deity's brief from general to particular providence, to argue that divine providence must embrace justice as well as goodness.

This expansion from general to particular providence enables the Vicar to solve the problem of evil because justice, as he sees it, requires rectifying the disorder and evil he witnessed when he turned to examine his place in the ranks of society. "God, it is said, owes His creatures nothing; I believe he owes them everything [*tout*] He promises in giving them being." When the Vicar consults his soul, he hears the words: "*Be just and you will be happy.*" And yet experience belies that voice. "That is simply not so, however, considering the present state of things: the wicked man prospers, and the just man remains oppressed. Also, see what indignation is kindled in us when this expectation is frustrated! Conscience is aroused and complains about its Author. It cries out to Him, moaning: 'Thou hast deceived me!'" (282). God owes the Vicar justice.[25]

The rectification of the disorder of evil and good is made possible by the metaphysical dualism the Vicar just embraced as his third article of faith. "If the soul is immaterial, it can survive the body, and if it survives the body, providence is justified. If I had no proof of the immateriality of the soul other than the triumph of the wicked and the oppression of the just in this world, that alone would prevent me from doubting it." This is an astonishing statement. The conditional phrasing in the first sentence indicating doubt—"If the soul is immaterial . . . ," "if it survives the body . . ."—is rendered indicative, and assertively so, by the Vicar's insistence that justice be done. Now the immateriality of the soul is in fact proved by the disorder of good and evil that demands rectification. "But this question is no longer a difficulty for me as soon as I have acknowledged two substances," he states (283). The third article of faith holding that man is animated by an "immaterial substance" only implied a metaphysical dualism the Vicar now fully asserts. His assertion is justified by the very conflict he experiences between body and soul, the "violent condition" of their union, or rather lack of union. Once again, the Vicar's soul is divided, and he takes the experience of that division as evidence of two substances in uneasy coexistence.

Finally, the Vicar confesses that his knowledge of the immaterial soul is limited— for example, he does not know whether or not it is immortal. "I believe that the soul survives the body long enough for the maintenance of order," he avers, thus once again making the demand for justice the basis for what he attributes to the immaterial soul. "Since this presumption consoles me and contains nothing unreasonable, why would I be afraid of yielding to it?" (283). The doctrine of the immaterial soul *consoles* the Vicar as a salve for the injustice he witnesses and the dividedness he experiences. As Céline Spector writes, "Some of the Vicar's claims, in particular the mind-body dualistic approach of the 'Profession of Faith,' which is unusual in Rousseau, may in some respects be influenced by the requirements of the speech situation."[26] We hardly need remind ourselves that Rousseau argues that man is by nature unified and therefore naturally good, thus requiring no rectification of disorder and injustice.

The Vicar concludes his ruminations on evil and the soul before turning to the conscience with some reflections on the afterlife. If the soul is immaterial, then the "identity of the *I* [*moi*]" must persist, and so memory must endure as well. He argues that the recollections of the deeds and feelings would persist, with this recollection being the source of the felicity of the good and the remorse of the wicked once the chains of the bodily passions are released and the conscience regains its strength and empire. "Do not ask me, my good friend, whether there will be other sources of happiness and suffering. I do not know, and those I imagine are enough to console me for this life and to make me hope for another." If my suggestion holds that these addresses by the Vicar to the youth constitute signals to the reader to wonder about his argument, then perhaps we are meant to ask whether his entire sketch of the immaterial soul and the afterlife is a product of his imagination spurred by his need for consolation and hope.

The Vicar also asks the youth not to ask him whether the torments of the wicked are eternal, for he does not know, although he doubts that the divinity would take such retribution. "If supreme justice does take vengeance, it does so beginning in this life.... Supreme justice employs the evils that you do to yourselves to punish he crimes which brought on those evils.... What need is there to look for hell in the other life? It begins in this one in the hearts of the wicked" (284). If the Vicar is correct here, there would appear to be no reason to conceive of the afterlife. As Heinrich Meier writes, "This has the consequence that for him who experiences felicity in this life, no just recompense in a life beyond and, consequently, no future life has to be postulated."[27] Yet if there is eternal damnation on behalf of justice, the Vicar accepts it: "O clement and good Being, whatever Your decrees are, I worship them! If you punish the wicked, I annihilate my weak reason before Your justice" (284). Perhaps an alternative suggestion of what the Vicar's address to the youth in this context is meant to prompt us to consider is his hesitation over just how far he is willing to go in his demand for divine justice.

Conscience

The Vicar's inquiry was initiated principally to seek guidance for his moral conduct, and that is the subject to which he now turns. The centerpiece of his moral teaching is the conscience. Two preliminary remarks are in order before turning to the Vicar's account. First, recall that he first appealed to the conscience in the autobiographical prelude to his profession, adducing as evidence for its existence the fact that his conscience did not rise up against what "well-ordered nature" permitted, in his case having sexual relations with unmarried women (267). When discussing this passage, I wondered whether the Vicar's distinction between what the "voice of nature" permits as opposed to what the law forbids wasn't rather convenient and therefore whether his conscience wasn't casuistic. The Vicar's account of the conscience should be read in light of his own psychological experience and needs.

THE CONSCIENCE OF A VICAR

Echoing the beginning of his entire inquiry, the Vicar explains that he does not draw moral guidance from "high philosophy," but instead finds it "written by nature with ineffaceable characters in the depth of my heart." He approaches his account of the conscience through a series of binary oppositions that reflect the divisions he feels within his heart.[28] First, he poses a contrast between conscience and reasoning: "The best of all casuists is the conscience, and it is only when one haggles with it that one has recourse to all the subtleties of reasoning." What is meant by characterizing the conscience as "the best of all casuists"? Does the conscience become casuistic when the "subtleties of reasonings" are rationalizations, when we convince ourselves or others that we are heeding the voice of conscience when we are actually pursuing our passions? If so, this is arguably true of the Vicar's appeal to conscience in defense against the crimes of which he is accused. Second, he opposes the natural care one has for oneself to the experience we have of heeding the voice that tells us that we should not pursue our care for ourselves by harming others. Of course, Rousseau has his own explanation of this phenomenon in natural self-love and pity. Third, again echoing the beginning of the "Profession," he opposes the senses, the "passive being," to the heart, the "active being." "Conscience is the voice of the soul, the passions are the voice of the body. Is it surprising that these two languages often are in contradiction? ... But conscience never deceives, it is man's true guide; it is to the soul what instinct is to the body;* he who follows conscience obeys nature and does not fear being led astray" (286–87). (I will return momentarily to the note Rousseau adds to this passage at the point marked by an asterisk.) The Vicar's dualist metaphysics now extends to the moral realm.

I have conjectured that the Vicar's direct addresses to his auditor may be signals to the reader of *Emile* to raise questions about his argument, but now it is the youth who attempts to interrupt the priest. At the point where the Vicar just stated that following the conscience is to obey nature without fear of being led astray, the transcribed writing reads: "This point is important, continued my benefactor in seeing that I was going to interrupt him; allow me to tarry a bit to clarify it" (287). This is the sole occasion on which the youth tries to interject. Why this dramatic detail? Elsewhere I have suggested two possibilities that I now repeat.[29] First, especially given the curiosity he voices in the dramatic introduction concerning how the Vicar's seemingly contradictory conduct could be explained, perhaps the youth wishes to ask him whether having sexual relations with unmarried women is in fact following the conscience understood as the "voice of nature" or the "voice of the soul." Or is he instead following the voice of the body, his passions? Second, might the youth—especially if he is the future Jean-Jacques Rousseau—wish to propose an alternative explanation of the conflict the Vicar finds in his soul—for example, the tension between the natural goodness of man and his corruption in society?

The distance between the Vicar and Rousseau is signaled by a lengthy note Rousseau adds to the passage at the point where the Vicar claims that conscience "is to the soul what instinct is to the body." The note contains one of his characteristic diatribes against "modern philosophy," here in defense of instinct, which he claims his adversaries hold is an acquired habit. The principal target once again appears to be Helvétius. His example of observed instinctual behavior is his dog (the inimitable and irreplaceable Turc). He offers several examples of instincts displayed by his dog, most interestingly for the present purposes the alleged "moral ideas" that lead him to exhibit gratitude or clemency. Putting aside the anthropomorphism of the example, even if it does provide evidence of instinct, it hardly proves the existence of the conscience. In fact, it undercuts the Vicar's dualist account of the soul and conscience, for the animal behaviors he explains in terms of instinct offer no hint of dualism. This undercutting is deepened if we consult the discussion of pity in the *Discourse on Inequality*, where Rousseau claims that animals show "perceptible signs" of it, remarking that generosity and clemency, the very attributes he claims to see in his dog, are developed versions of pity, all without recourse to a dualist metaphysics (83–84). While it may be the case that the versions of materialism Rousseau attacks cannot explain instinct, he himself does not argue that dualism is required to explain it.[30]

Returning to the Vicar's speech, the question of the relationship between his argument and Rousseau's own views is immediately thrust to our attention by the Vicar's discussion of goodness. "If moral goodness is in conformity with our nature, man could be healthy of spirit or well-constituted only to the extent that he is good. If it is not and man is naturally wicked, he cannot cease to be so without being corrupted, and goodness in him is only a vice contrary to nature." The core principle of Rousseau's system is, of course, the natural goodness of man. His argument for our natural goodness is based principally on his account of our original wholeness or psychic unity due to the limited extent of our natural needs and passions and our ability to satisfy them without dependence on others. As I discussed in chapter 2, Rousseau's natural goodness is not a moral phenomenon but is instead a physical one. In turn, the Vicar argument for "moral goodness" is quite different. Answering the presumed question of whether we are naturally good or wicked, he turns to the youth: "Let us return to ourselves, my young friend. Let us examine, all personal interest aside, where our inclinations lead us." He then presents several tests cases: whether we are gratified more by the spectacle of others' suffering or happiness, whether we prefer to see a beneficent or a wicked act, whether we find friendship sweet, admire heroic actions, and so on. "Take this love of the beautiful from our hearts, and you take all the charm from life" (287). While it may be possible to reconcile the Vicar's appeal to the love of the beautiful or a kind of moral aesthetics with Rousseau's argument for the natural goodness of man, they are not the same argument.[31]

The Vicar turns from an appeal to the inward testimony of our aestheticized love of virtue to external evidence and ends by asserting that the principle of conscience is the explanation for these alleged moral facts. There is almost nobody whose love for virtue is extinguished despite the crimes they commit when led astray by self-interest. Where our own interest is not at stake we are indignant at wickedness—for example, in reading of the crimes of Catiline—and we also cheer virtuous acts. The cry of remorse is the voice of nature, which testifies to our hatred of the vicious actions we commit. We long for the serenity experienced by the just man, the reward for virtue. Finally: "Cast your eyes on all the nations of the world, go through all the histories. Among so many inhuman and bizarre cults, among the prodigious diversity of morals [*moeurs*] and characters, you will find everywhere the same ideas of justice and decency, everywhere the same notions of good and bad." All of this points to the naturalness of the conscience, he claims. "There is in the depths of souls, then, an innate principle of justice and virtue, according to which, in spite of our own maxims, we judge our actions and those of others as good or bad, and it is to this principle that I give the name *conscience*" (287–89).

One might expect that after this lengthy windup that the Vicar would expand on his understanding of the conscience, but instead he once again combats those who would doubt it, as though he needs to reassure himself.[32] The "allegedly wise" reject the innate principle of conscience because they argue that everything in the human mind is introduced by sense experience. Of course, Rousseau himself follows Lockean epistemology in rejecting innate ideas and in arguing that all knowledge originates from the senses. As we have seen, his own understanding of the conscience derives from the ordered development of our natural sentiments working with reason, not as an "innate principle." The Vicar also argues that the philosophers reject the "evident and universal accord of all nations" concerning good and evil, citing in particular Montaigne's eagerness to find examples of bizarre customs of peoples to refute the "general induction drawn from the concurrence of all peoples." Further, he argues that the philosophers who reduce everything to self-interest cannot explain why the just man contributes to the public good even against his private interest or why we admire virtue. Finally, he states that he will not enter into "metaphysical discussions" to explain how the "voice of nature" speaks to us even against our self-interest and instead asks the youth to "consult your heart" as testimony. "Were all the philosophers to prove that I am wrong, if you sense that I am right, I do not wish for more" (288–89). The proof lies with our interior assent to something we cannot help but believe.

The Vicar's language about the limits of philosophy and the appeal to the heart echoes the very beginning of his inquiry, where he states that he will appeal to the "inner light." He asks the youth to distinguish between the ideas we acquire from the senses and our "natural sentiments" based on which our will judges what is good or bad for us. This distinction roughly parallels his earlier distinction between our "passive" and "active" principles, or the incipient dualism he posits. "The acts of the conscience are not judgments but sentiments," he argues—that is, sentiments that "evaluate" what we ought or ought not to do. "To exist, for us, is to sense; our sensibility is incontestably anterior to our intelligence, and we had sentiments before ideas." The sentiments concerned with our preservation are innate. "These sentiments, as far as the individual is concerned, are the love of self, the fear of pain, the horror of death, the desire for well-being," he continues. "But if, as cannot be doubted, man is by his nature sociable, or at least made to become so, he can be so only by means of other innate sentiments relative to his species. . . . It is from the moral system formed by this double relation to oneself and to one's fellows that the impulse of conscience is born." Let us resist the temptation to interrupt the Vicar and instead allow him to complete his thought. "Thus, I do not believe, my friend, that it is impossible to explain, by the consequences of our nature, the immediate principle of the conscience independently of reason itself," he states in still another direct address to the youth. "Yet even if others deny this principle," we can still continue to believe based on our "inner witness and the voice of conscience" (289–90). The reasoning here is of course circular: the proof that the conscience exists is that we believe it exists. Then the famous peroration:

> Conscience, conscience! Divine instinct, immortal and celestial voice, certain guide of a being that is ignorant and limited but intelligent and free; infallible judge of good and bad which makes man like unto God; it is you who make the excellence of his nature and the morality of his actions. Without you I sense nothing in me that raises me above the beasts. (290)[33]

Recall that the Vicar earlier congratulated his species, in a moment of pride signaled there by the mention of *amour-propre*, on the power and intelligence that raised them above the beasts (see 277). Now it is the supposedly "certain guide" and "infallible judge" of the conscience that renders us godlike. Perhaps the emphatic character of the Vicar's hymn to conscience wards off the doubts that his repeated addresses to the youth and forestalled interruption of him in this context may signal.

Now let us conclude by comparing the Vicar's claims about human nature and the conscience to Rousseau's stated views on these matters. As for human nature, the priest's key claim is the following: "But if, as cannot be doubted, man is by his nature sociable, or at least made to become so, he can be so only by means of other innate sentiments relative to his species. " To put the point bluntly: Rousseau not only doubts that man is by nature sociable; he denies it. What about the Vicar's concession: "or at least made to become so"? Here the comparison is more complicated, depending on the meaning of "sociable" as well as "made to become so." While it is true that Rousseau argues that humans develop the capacities that enable them to interact with their fellow human beings in "sociable" ways, capacities such as language and love, the core question is whether we become "sociable" in a strong sense or whether we remain fundamentally asocial. Interpreters have pointed to the Vicar's statement about our natural sociability as either (1) evidence that Rousseau himself holds humans are naturally social, or at least made to become so, or (2) an indication that the Savoyard Vicar does not speak for Rousseau on this core matter of human nature.[34] As I am sure is clear by now, my own view is that Rousseau holds human beings to be fundamentally asocial, hence the conflicts we feel in ourselves living in society, and therefore that I take this passage to be proof of the distance between Rousseau and the Vicar on the issue.

As for the divergence between the Vicar's understanding of conscience and what Rousseau says about it in his own name, especially in the main text of *Emile*, I discussed Rousseau's view in chapter 5 and so I limit myself here to recalling the main point. The most important passage concerning the conscience comes earlier in book IV, before the "Profession," where Rousseau writes: "Finally we enter the moral world. . . . If this were the place for it, I would try to show how the first voices of conscience arise out of the first movements of the heart. . . . I would show that *justice* and *goodness* are not merely abstract words—pure moral beings formed by the understanding—but are true affections of the soul enlightened by reason, are hence only an ordered development of our primitive affections" (235). In short, the conscience as Rousseau presents it is a development of self-love and pity guided by reason and not, as the Vicar would have it, an innate principle opposed to the passions and in tension with reason. In this light, the Vicar's claim that "it is from the moral system formed by this double relation to oneself and to one's fellows that the impulse of conscience is born" could be recast in explicitly Rousseauian terms of self-love and pity without recourse to an innate principle of conscience.[35]

In sum, the Vicar's fundamental assumption in his understanding that "man is by his nature sociable, or at least made to become so," is inconsistent with Rousseau's conception of human nature and his system of the natural goodness of man in general. Likewise, his doctrine of the conscience as an innate "principle" and the metaphysical dualism undergirding it are inconsistent with what little Rousseau himself writes on the subject. Moreover, Rousseau's argument concerning the natural goodness of man and his corruption in society, including the transformation of *amour de soi* into *amour-propre*, explains the very dividedness of soul that is experienced by the Vicar and that leads him to the doctrine of conscience. Let me now return to the "Profession" and complete the analysis of the first part of the writing, which concludes with the Vicar's return to the inner conflict he experiences.

RETURN TO HIMSELF: THE VICAR'S CONCLUDING THOUGHTS

After his moving hymn to the moral guide he has discovered, the Vicar moves toward the conclusion of his first speech. He admits that the conscience is difficult to discover and that nature's voice is "timid," is easily "stifled" by prejudices, and is counterfeited by fanaticism. These admissions might make us question his earlier and repeated assertions about the supposedly evident universality of conscience despite the variety of customs across human societies. The Vicar nonetheless reassures himself that he has found the voice of the conscience after losing it for so long, thus returning to the very beginning of his speech and his experience of inner turmoil. "Constantly caught up in the combat between my natural sentiments, which spoke for the common interest, and my reason, which related everything to me, I would have floated [*floté*] all my life in this continual alternation—doing the bad, loving the good, always in contradiction with myself—if new lights had not illuminated my heart, and if the truth, which settled my opinions, had not also made my conduct certain and put me in agreement with myself" (291). The Vicar's self-description is remarkably similar to Rousseau's portrait of the bourgeois at the outset of *Emile*: "always in contradiction with himself, always floating [*flotant*] between his inclinations and his duties" (40).

"O my child!" the Vicar addresses the youth, celebrating the rediscovery of a moral guide that leads to happiness. Yet his inner conflict endures. He cannot understand why his soul is chained to the body, producing disorder. If there were no such disorder man would be happy, or we might say "good" to employ Rousseau's terms, but he would also not have the opportunity to be virtuous by exercising his freedom and combating the voice of the body. The Vicar acknowledges that he is not entirely virtuous, alluding to the faults that resulted in the moral doubt that occasioned the meditations he is relating to the youth. He is unable to overcome the senses, and his solution is striking: "I aspire to the moment when, after being delivered from the shackles of the body, I shall be *me* [*moi*] without contradiction or division, and need only myself [*que de moi*] in order to be happy." With this aspiration avowed, the Vicar concludes his first speech by stating that even if the conclusions—he says "opinions"—he has reached in his search for the truth are false, they are his opinions, and he has sought them in good faith (294).[36]

Conclusion: The Purpose of the "Profession"

What is Rousseau's purpose in including the theological teaching of the first part of the "Profession," both in terms of the textual elements such as its separateness from the main text, dramatis personae, and so on, and in terms of the substance of the Vicar's teaching in the first part of the speech? We can gain some further purchase on these questions with a brief examination of two parts of the text: first, the dramatic interlude between the two parts of the "Profession" and, second, the conclusion of the entire speech. In the next chapter I analyze the second part of the "Profession" and its specific aims.

After the Vicar concludes his theological teaching there is a dramatic interlude in which the supposed author of the essay, writing thirty years after the event, reflects on the speech and reports what he said to the priest. As for the reflection:

> The good priest had spoken with vehemence. He was moved [*ému*], and so was I. I believed I was hearing the divine Orpheus sing the first hymns and teaching men the worship of the gods. Nevertheless, I saw a multitude of objections to make to him. I did not make any of them, because they were less solid than disconcerting, and persuasiveness was on his side. To the extent that he spoke to me according to his conscience, mine seemed to confirm what he had told me. (294)

Several aspects of this reflection deserve note. First, the figure of Orpheus singing to men (and animals) is the subject of the frontispiece related to book IV, which Rousseau placed at the beginning of the third printed volume of *Emile*, which opened with the "Profession": "'Thirty years ago....'" I have analyzed this frontispiece and its relationship to the text elsewhere,[37] so I restrict myself here to pointing out that the Vicar is analogized to Orpheus in trying to persuade his audience. Second, the Vicar is said to have "persuasiveness" on his side, but the youth does not remain fully convinced: "I saw a multitude of objections to make to him." To use the language of the *Social Contract* with regard to the great lawgiver, the Vicar is attempting "to persuade without convincing." Third, the Vicar has given his profession according to his own lights and without appealing to any other authority than his own judgment, and he has asked the youth to judge for himself.

With this retrospective reflection stated, the author of the essay reports what he said to the Vicar, here in indirect discourse. "The sentiments you have just expounded to me, I said to him, appear more novel in what you admit you do not know than in what you say you believe. I see in them pretty nearly the theism or the natural religion that the Christians claim to confound with atheism or irreligiousness, which is the directly contrary doctrine. But in the present condition of my faith I have to ascend rather than descend in order to adopt your opinions" (263). The youth, whom we are told in the dramatic introduction was headed toward "the morals of a tramp and the morality of an atheist" (263), recognizes the "present condition" of his faith and his need for a religious teaching of the sort the Vicar has provided. In other words, the Vicar's speech is tailored to the needs of its audience. Whatever the nature of the "multitudes of objections" he elects not to pose, the youth says he agrees with him that he "ought to be guided by the inner sentiment" and that he will continue to reflect on the speech and determine what parts of it he finds convincing. In other words, the youth will do precisely what the Vicar asks him to do: judge for himself.

Let me now turn to the end of the "Profession," where we again see the emphasis on the intended persuasive and emotional effects of the speech for its intended audience as well as the stress on using one's own judgment rather than depending on the authority of others. As we have seen, the Vicar reveals his sentiments regarding theology and religion to the young proselyte because he believes they will be useful to the youth given the present condition of his soul. If the Vicar offers his profession to the youth alone, Rousseau offers the "Profession" to any reader. We now get a sense of Rousseau's intention in doing so from what Vicar says next.

> So long as there remains some sound belief among men, one must not disturb peaceful souls or alarm the faith of simple people with

> difficulties which they cannot resolve and which upset them without enlightening them. But once everything is shaken, one ought to preserve the trunk at the expense of the branches. Consciences which are agitated, uncertain, almost extinguished, and in the condition in which I have seen yours, need to be reinforced and awakened; and in order to put them back on the foundations of eternal truths, it is necessary to complete the job of ripping out the shaky pillars to which they think they are still attached. (310)

On this occasion I almost dare affirm that the Vicar is ventriloquizing Rousseau. Rousseau offers the "Profession" to his readers because their consciences are "agitated, uncertain, almost extinguished," like the youth's. Put differently, because they are no longer naturally good but instead are corrupted by society, their souls are divided and require a teaching that accounts for that dividedness and endeavors to palliate it in such a way that offers consolation and hope.

One of the forces that unsettles the consciences and disturbs the beliefs of Rousseau's contemporaries is the proud disputes of the philosophers, and especially the materialists. Recall that in the *Letter to Beaumont* Rousseau explains that an aim of the first part of the "Profession" is to combat modern materialism (*Beaumont*, 75). The Vicar concludes his speech by warning the youth—and Rousseau thereby warns his readers—to avoid their disputes. "Flee those who sow dispiriting doctrines in men's hearts under the pretext of explaining nature. Their apparent skepticism is a hundred times more assertive and more dogmatic than the decided tone of their adversaries." So to speak, echoing Rousseau's argument in the *Discourse on the Sciences and the Arts*, the Vicar says that, in addition to their "haughty" view that they alone are enlightened, these philosophers subvert the opinions, including religious opinions, on which popular morality is founded. "Moreover, by overturning, destroying, and trampling on all that men respect, they deprive the afflicted of the last consolation of their misery and the powerful and the rich of the only brake on their passions. . . . They say that the truth is never harmful to men. I believe it as much as they do, and in my opinion this is a great proof that what they teach is not the truth" (312). We know, however, that Rousseau himself does not believe that the truth is never harmful to men. As Jeffrey Macy states, "The Vicar's belief in truth and its relationship to happiness and the good is too naïve and unreliable a doctrine for Rousseau to endorse or to follow in his own theological-political teaching."[38] Whatever the truth of the Vicar's speech, its utility is manifest: to console the afflicted and check the wicked.

We have seen Rousseau uses the notes he adds as editor as a running skirmish with modern materialism, but this note is by far the lengthiest in the "Profession," and also the most revealing about his polemics. He begins by characterizing the polemics between the "two parties" as tendentious. The "philosophic party" wants to compare a "people of true philosophers with a people of bad Christians," but the true question is what effect philosophy as it is practiced has on peoples, a subject he first took up in the *Discourse on the Sciences and the Arts*. "But I do know that as soon as it is a question of peoples it is necessary to suppose one which will abuse philosophy without religion, just as our peoples abuse religion without philosophy." Despite Bayle's proof that fanaticism is more pernicious than atheism, a proof that he says he finds incontestable, Rousseau quite remarkably states that "fanaticism, although sanguinary and cruel, is nevertheless a grand and strong passion which elevates the heart of man." In turn, "irreligion—and the reasoning and philosophic spirit in general"—has enervating effects and "concentrates all the passions in the baseness of private interest, in the abjectness of the human I, and thus quietly saps the true foundations of every society" (312–14n). The *true* foundations of *every* society. As he states in defense of *Emile*, "Religion is useful and even necessary for peoples" (*Mountain*, 140). The "secret egoism" of the philosophers and their "indifference" to common virtues are corrosive of popular virtues, including their foundation in religion. Fanaticism is much less dangerous than the "philosophic spirit" in its consequences. "From the point of view of principles," he concludes, "there is nothing that philosophy can do well that religion does not do still better, and religion does many things that philosophy could not do" (312–14n).

If religion is superior to philosophy from the perspective of "principles," what about practice? "Practice is something else," says Rousseau. Even if no individual entirely follows the tenets of his or her religion, nonetheless "it is indubitable that religious motives often prevent them from doing harm and produce virtues and laudable actions which would not have occurred without these motives." In other words, whatever the truth of religious doctrines, they are useful because they provide a check on the wicked and an incentive to virtue. This statement echoes the Vicar's argument that philosophic doctrines "deprive the afflicted of the last consolation of their misery and the powerful and the rich the only brake on their passions" (312–14n). Similarly, in the *Dialogues* Rousseau says of atheism: "This convenient philosophy of the happy and the rich, who make their paradise in this world, cannot long serve as that of the multitude who are the victim of their passions, who—for lack of happiness in this life—need to find in it at least the hope and consolations of which that barbarous doctrine deprives them" (*CW*, 1:241).

The consolation afforded to the afflicted and the punishments meted out to the wicked are what the doctrines of the afterlife found in many religions provide, including the Vicar's. Rousseau offers some remarks on such doctrines in two religions. Christianity provides modern governments with "more solid authority and less frequent revolutions and made these governments less sanguinary," he claims, especially when compared to ancient governments. We will have to await his discussion in the chapter "On Civil Religion" in the *Social Contract* of the political utility of pagan religions in comparison to Christianity to determine whether what he says here about Christianity is meant as a compliment. The positive example he offers here is from Islam. He does so with a lengthy quotation from Chardin concerning a bridge over which everyone must pass after the universal resurrection, a bridge called Poul-Serrho, on which the final judgment of the good and wicked will occur. Rousseau comments: "Should I believe that the idea [*idée*] of this bridge, which corrects so many iniquities, never prevents any? If one took away this idea from the Persians by persuading them that there is no Poul-Serrho or any place like it where the oppressed wreak vengeance on their tyrants after death, is it not clear that this would put the latter very much at their ease and would deliver them from the care of placating these unfortunates?" (313–14n). In short, the myth is useful, even though Rousseau surely does not consider it to be true.

Most interestingly, after writing this, Rousseau references the Vicar's claim that a truth cannot be harmful, that utility and truth are not at variance: "It is false, therefore, that this doctrine [*doctrine*] would not be harmful; this doctrine would therefore not be the truth" (314n) This passage is somewhat obscure, but we can unravel it by noting that the "idea" of the myth of the bridge of judgment is not the "doctrine" that is not true because it is false that it is not harmful. The doctrine in question is that of the philosophers who hold that the truth is always useful, especially against superstition, which is how the note began, specifically with reference to Bayle. That this is the doctrine he has in mind is made clearer by how Rousseau continued the passage ending in a draft: "I respond to Bayle with his own principle and even by the same manner of arguing" (*OC*, 4:1600, n (*b*) to 635). Contra Bayle, a society of atheists is not preferable to at least certain superstitions, and combating superstitions in the name of truth can be deleterious. Rousseau concludes the note by addressing his interlocutor(s): "Philosopher, your moral laws are very fine, but I beg you to show me their sanction. Stop beating around the bush for a moment, and tell me plainly what you put in the place of Poul-Serrho" (312–14n). The tension between the truth and the utility of theological doctrines runs throughout this astonishing passage.

Philosophy, the truth, must be supplemented or even replaced by the sanctions provided by religion to be useful.[39]

Returning to the main text of the "Profession" and its concluding paragraph, the Vicar makes his final address to the youth and warns him against philosophy. "Good young man, be sincere and without pride. Know how to be ignorant.... Proud philosophy leads to freethinking as blind devoutness leads to fanaticism. Avoid these extremes.... Dare to acknowledge God among the philosophers, dare to preach humanity to the intolerant." And he concludes: "What does matter for man is to fulfill his duties on earth, and it is in forgetting oneself that one works for oneself. My child, private interest deceives us. It is only the hope of the just which never deceives" (313). In short, the Vicar's emphasis is on religion as a support for virtue and a provider of hope, less its truth than its utility.

CHAPTER 7

The Critique— and Revival—of Religion in the "Profession of Faith"

Although the theological teaching of the first part of the "Profession of Faith" has most occupied scholars, it was the critique of religion in the second part that drew the attention of the religious and political authorities who condemned *Emile* and prosecuted its author. As Rousseau explained in defense of his work, the second part "raises doubts and difficulties about revelation in general," while acknowledging the "purity and sanctity" of the moral doctrine of the Gospel, if not its divine authority, with the object of making readers "more circumspect from within his own religion about accusing others of bad faith within theirs" (*Beaumont*, 75). Neither Throne nor Altar heeded the lesson concerning the dangers of religious zeal or the admonition to toleration.

What astonished Rousseau's contemporaries was less the contents of the second part of the "Profession," for the critique of religion sketched there is largely a pastiche of arguments familiar to readers of Hobbes, Spinoza, Locke, Bayle, and others, than the fact that he had the audacity to publish them under his own name. For whatever the status of the Savoyard Vicar and the "Profession," they were contained in a book that announced his authorship on the title page. Rousseau refused to play the game of anonymity almost universally practiced by his predecessors and contemporaries, aided and often abetted by censors and officials.[1] Perhaps the most adept player of the game was Voltaire, whose voluminous writings almost all appeared either anonymously or under a veritable Hugoesque cast of pseudonymous characters. Indeed, the master paid Rousseau the unusual compliment of reproducing the second part of the "Profession" in his 1765 *Necessary Collection; With the Gospel of Reason* (*Recueil nécessaire, Avec l'évangile de la raison*), which collected a number of pieces written and previously published by Voltaire himself with two writings by other authors, including Rousseau's, a work needless to say published anonymously. Voltaire was not impressed with *Emile* as a whole or with the first part of the "Profession," as snide comments in the margins of his copy attest, but he admired at least the audacity of the second part. His summary judgment: "a hodgepodge by a silly wet nurse in four volumes, with some forty pages against Christianity, the boldest which have ever been written."[2]

Largely because the second part of the "Profession" is less systematic and less original than the first part, by Rousseau's own admission, it has received only cursory attention from scholars.[3] In addition, since Rousseau largely embraces most of the arguments put forward by the Vicar in the second part of the "Profession," scholars tend to take the Vicar's position on these matters as speaking for Rousseau. Thus, in this chapter I will have little quarrel with other interpretations. While I sketch the main points of the Vicar's argument and relate them to what Rousseau writes elsewhere, my main interest is in the avowed aims of the inquiry, as stated by both the Vicar and Rousseau himself. To frame my argument in terms of the criteria of truth and utility: in the second part of the "Profession" the emphasis is on the limitations of what we can know as the truth in matters of revelation, miracles, Scripture, and related subjects, with the declared aim of the utility of the inquiry in making readers less pridefully presumptuous and more tolerant in religion. In addition, and in keeping with how both Rousseau and the Vicar characterize the "Profession" as a whole, a related aim of the second part is to vest the auditor or readers with the authority to judge for themselves. Perhaps it is this investiture of authority in individuals which most threatened the religious and political authorities who so quickly and vigorously combated the writing.

Yet the critique of religion offered by the Vicar, and seconded by Rousseau, is joined with the Vicar's promotion of a religion of the morality of the Gospel, also seconded by Rousseau. The Vicar and Rousseau therefore set the stage for a religious revival through promoting a true and salutary form of what they term the religion of the Gospel, a religion limited to what reason can affirm and directed at morality. My argument builds on Arthur Melzer's excellent article, in which he writes: "Rousseau's religious writings are the veritable Rosetta Stone because they are the only texts that somehow embrace both sides of the ideological divide. On the one hand, they contain, indeed initiate, the post-Enlightenment renewal of Christianity; on the other, they restate, indeed bring to fullest expression, the scathing Enlightenment critique of it."[4]

The Impetus of the Inquiry

The Vicar's turn to address questions concerning matters that go beyond the natural religion expounded in the first part of the "Profession" is spurred by the youth's desire to hear more, as expressed at the end of the dramatic interlude: "Speak to me of revelation, of the scriptures, of those obscure dogmas through which I have been wandering since childhood, without being able either to conceive or to believe them and without knowing how I could either accept or reject them." In reply, the Vicar embraces the youth and explains that "the desire of which you give witness to me was necessary to authorize my having no reserve with you" (*Emile*, 294–95).[5]

What is the youth's "desire" and why does expressing it "authorize" the Vicar to broach these subjects, about which presumably he would have otherwise remained silent? Are the youth's motives to hear about these subjects limited to curiosity? As we shall see shortly, the Vicar himself recounts that his own inquiries into these subjects was spurred by *amour-propre*, his prideful desire to have particular knowledge of the divinity. We know from the narrative framing story that the youth is also infected by *amour-propre*, so perhaps he too is actuated by pride. If so, the Vicar may be "authorized" to take up these subjects because it is in the service of his project of effecting a cure for the youth's corruption. Such an intention is suggested when the Vicar explains his hesitation in addressing such obscure and doubtful subjects: "If your sentiments were more stable, I would hesitate to expound mine to you. But in your present condition you will profit from thinking as I do." As we saw in the previous chapter, Rousseau adds a note to this passage, which reads: "This is, I believe, what the good vicar could say to the public at present" (295 and n).[6] Once again, then, we have some indication of the audience and aim of the discussion. Finally, we also know from the narrative framing story that the youth observes that the Vicar privately expresses views on religious subjects at variance with his public words and deeds in his role as a priest, so perhaps the youth is still curious about how the Vicar can square the apparent contradiction between his private and public selves. In sum, the second part of the "Profession" raises the same questions of character, rhetoric, audience, and so on, that we have seen from the outset of interpreting the writing.

The Vicar's broad aims in speaking of these subjects are evident when he begins his lesson by stating that such a lesson shouldn't even be necessary. "You see in my exposition only natural religion," he says to the youth, referring to the first part of his speech. "It is very strange that any other is needed." Natural religion as the religion universally available to every individual through witnessing the spectacle of nature and hearing the divine voice within should alone suffice. But it does not, because of human pride. "What more will men tell us? Their revelations have only the effect of degrading God by giving Him human passions. I see that particular dogmas, far from clarifying the notions of the great Being . . . make man proud, intolerant, and cruel." The effects of such particular dogmas and revelations are at the same time their cause. Each people makes God "speak in its own way, and made Him say what it wanted." The Vicar develops the sociopsychological roots of religion, or a natural history of religion, in an autobiographical register. "I did not begin with all these reflections. I was carried along by the prejudices of education and by that dangerous *amour-propre* which always wants to carry man above his sphere." In addition to the sort of *amour-propre* he has associated with philosophical speculation and disputes, his own prideful motives concern him as an individual. "I wanted more immediate communications, more particular instructions; not content with making God like man, I wanted supernatural understanding in order that I myself would be privileged among my fellows, I wanted an exclusive form of worship; I wanted God to have said to me what He had not said to others" (295–96).[7] In short, the causes and effects of particular religions involve human pride, both for the Vicar in particular and for men in general.

Religious Authority

The Vicar recounts his inquiry by beginning with his observation that while the truth is one and universal, religions are many. Religions are a matter of custom. "Their choice is the effect of chance; to blame them for it is iniquitous. It is to reward or punish them for being born in this or that country" (297). Rousseau says the same thing himself just before the "Profession." "The faith of children and many men is a question of geography," he explains, but he then makes a concession to the accidents of place and time: "A child has to be raised in his father's religion" (258, 260). As we shall see, the Vicar will also recommend to the young proselyte that he return to the religion of his fathers, worshipping the divinity in his heart and practicing the rituals of the religion so long as they do not contradict the true worship of natural religion. Returning to the beginning of the Vicar's inquiry, he explains: "Are we, then, sincerely seeking the truth? Let us grant nothing to the right of birth and to the authority of fathers and pastors." He will not submit his reason to authority. "They may well cry out, 'Subject your reason.' He who deceives me can say as much. I need reasons for subjecting my reason." Since the subjects he is about to explore exceed the reach of human reason, they must be based on the authority of men. The word of God? Miracles? Scripture? In the end, all rely on human testimony. "So many men between God and me!" (297). The Vicar rejects this authority, and this rejection will be a cornerstone of his inquiry.

Much of the Vicar's inquiry is occupied with his remarks on the very difficulties it faces. The first obstacle he takes up at some length is verifying the miracles that allegedly testify to the truth of prophecies, revelations, and Scriptures. Aside from requiring knowledge of the laws of nature to judge these alleged miracles are truly such, the fact that they are said to occur in only one corner of the universe and before a small set of witnesses raises questions about the justice of a divinity who would offer such proofs for belief and especially punishment for disbelief. Similarly, if a religious doctrine is to be proved by miracles, and only miracles that conform to doctrine are judged as veritable miracles, for Scripture states that the Pharaoh's priests also performed miracles in the presence of Moses, then we have a vicious circle. "Doctrine coming from God ought to bear the sacred character of the divinity. Not only should it clarify for us the confused ideas which reasoning draws in our mind, but it should also propound a form of worship, a morality, and maxims that are suitable to the attributes with which we conceive his essence on our own." The Vicar illustrates the conflict between the authority of reason and the authority of men through an imagined dialogue between THE INSPIRED MAN and THE REASONER. Of course, THE REASONER gets the last word, insisting that he must use his reason to judge the authority of alleged prophecies. The Vicar comments: "See, then, what your supposed supernatural proofs, your miracles and prophecies come down to. To believe all this on the faith of others, and to subject the authority of God, speaking to my reason, to the authority of men" (299–301). In other words, only doctrines that conform to the natural religion we discover through reason, such as propounded in the first part of the "Profession," are to be embraced as true.

Rousseau affirms and extends the Vicar's argument concerning miracles in the *Letters Written from the Mountain* when defending his publication of the "Profession." As in the *Letter to Beaumont*, Rousseau generally insists on distinguishing between what he writes in his own name from what the Vicar says (e.g., *Mountain*, 159–61 and n, 168 note *, 183–84), but in the case of miracles he speaks for himself. His argument has two main prongs. The first prong is his argument that the authenticity of miracles that testify to revelation, including in Scripture, derives from the truth of the doctrine. However, his conception of the proper "doctrine" by which to judge a potential miracle avoids the vicious circle identified by the Vicar. For by "doctrine" Rousseau explains: "that is from its utility, its beauty, its sanctity, its truth, its depth" (166). This doctrine is not what is authorized by a church or any other authority, but the moral doctrine accessible to reason alone—that is, natural religion. Insofar as the moral teaching of the Gospel accords with the moral doctrine discovered by reason it can be considered true. The second prong concerns the question of whether Scripture holds that miracles are necessary to confirm the truth of Christianity—that is, the truth of the Gospel. Rousseau denies it. Jesus "did not proclaim himself at first by miracles, but by preaching" (168). Based on passages he quotes from Scripture he concludes: "The proof is in the word, then, and not in the miracles" (171). "You see, Sir, that it is attested by Scripture itself that, in the mission of Jesus Christ, miracles are not a sign so necessary to faith that we cannot have it without accepting them." Although he admits that the Gospel speaks of miracles, all the doubts concerning the meaning of the text, testimonies, and so on take him back to the authority of reason: "And so I chose, making use of my right, the one of these meanings that appeared to me the most reasonable and the clearest." Each individual is his own authority in interpreting Scripture (172–73).

Returning to the "Profession," the Vicar finds similar difficulties in assessing religious texts. He speaks of the need to learn ancient languages, many of them lost, to evaluate manuscripts, to engage in hermeneutics, and other endeavors to assess not only the Bible, but the scriptural texts of all religions. Most important, however, is the question of the justice of confining the truth to a book not accessible to everyone. "I shall never be able to conceive that what every man is obliged to know is contained in books, and that someone who does not have access to these books, or to those who understand them, is punished for an ignorance which is involuntary. Always books! What a mania. Because Europe is full of books, Europeans regard them as indispensable, without thinking that in three-quarters of the earth they have never been seen? Were not all books written by men?" (303). (The Vicar echoes Rousseau's remarks on books with regard to Emile: "I hate books. They only teach one to talk about what one does not know" [184].) Taking up the three principal monotheistic religions of Europe, the Vicar begins with Catholicism and its appeal to the authority of the Church in matters of Scripture and doctrine. The archbishop of Paris quite correctly saw the Vicar's rejection of any authority beyond his reason as a frontal assault on the Church. As for the Jews, he says we will never truly know what they have to say until they are free to speak. The situation is reversed among the Turks, where they speak openly about their religion, but Christians dare not speak freely about theirs. Yet three-quarters of mankind do not adhere to any of these three religions. To condemn them for not even hearing the Gospel preached, much less for believing it, would be iniquitous. "If there were only a single man in the whole universe who had never been preached to about Jesus Christ, the objection would be as strong for that single man as for a quarter of mankind." Indeed, even the Jews who heard Jesus himself preach did not believe him. All religions are subject to the same objections. "Do you want to modify this method and give the least hold to authority of men? At that moment you surrender everything to it," says the Vicar (303–6). Note that the Vicar does not speak here about Protestantism, for as he—and Rousseau—characterize the Reformed religions, chiefly Calvinism, they join him in rejecting intermediaries in religion and authorizing individuals to judge for themselves. I will return to Rousseau's characterization of Protestantism. As Alberg notes, Rousseau manages to join in the Vicar an Enlightenment distrust of authority with a Calvinist distrust of human mediation.[8]

At this point in his speech, the Vicar pauses to address the youth and summarizes where his inquiries into revelation, Scripture, and other subjects have led him so far. Recall that it was his "dangerous *amour-propre*" that led him to want immediate communications and particular instructions from the divinity. Also recall that I suggested in the previous chapter that these direct addresses to the youth appear to function as signals to the reader to be alert to the speaker's motives and to consider alternatives to his arguments. In this case what is emphasized is the Vicar's *amour-propre*, even if he himself is aware of it in this instance. "You see, my son, to what absurdity pride and intolerance lead, when each man is so sure of his position and believes he is right to the exclusion of the rest of mankind? All my researches have been sincere—I take as my witness that God of peace whom I adore and whom I proclaim to you. But when I saw that these researches were and always would be unsuccessful, and that I was being swallowed up in an ocean without shores, I retraced my steps and restricted my faith to my primary notions." Rather than keep swimming, the Vicar returns to the shores of the natural religion he propounded in the first part of his speech. "I therefore closed all the books. There is one open to all eyes: it is the book of nature. It is from this great and sublime book that I learn to serve and worship its divine Author. No one can be excused for not reading it, because it speaks to all men a language that is intelligible to all minds." We have seen that Rousseau does not entirely agree with the Vicar concerning the legibility of the book of nature for all men, but he does agree with him in rejecting the authority of men and asserting the authority of each individual's reason. As for revelation, the Vicar states: "I neither accept it nor reject it. I reject only the obligation to acknowledge it" as being incompatible with God's justice. "With this exception, I remain in respectful doubt about this point" (305–7). In defense of the work, Rousseau affirms the Vicar's conclusion (*Mountain*, 184).

The Majesty of the Scriptures and the Morality of the Gospels

At the same time that he states that he remains in "respectful doubt" concerning revelation, the Vicar admits that "the majesty of the Scriptures amazes me, and that the holiness of the Gospel speaks to my heart" (307). Indeed, so moving is his praise that Beaumont declares: "*It would be difficult, My Very Dear Brethren, to pay a more beautiful language to the authenticity of the Gospel*" (*Beaumont*, 73, quoting the "Pastoral Letter"). "What gentleness, what purity in his morals!" gushes the Vicar. "What touching grace in his teachings! What elevation in his maxims! What profound wisdom in his speeches! What presence of mind, what finesse, and what exactness in his responses! What dominion over his passions!" (307).

The Vicar illustrates the majesty of the Gospels through an interesting comparison of Jesus and Socrates. He introduces the comparison by remarking on the similarity of Jesus to the "imaginary just man" depicted by Plato, "covered with all the opprobrium of crime and worthy of all the rewards of virtue," a similarity also noted by the Church Fathers. (The Vicar curiously omits the fact that Plato's just man is crucified.[9]) Turning to the comparison, the Vicar admits its audacity: "What prejudices, what blindness one must have to dare to compare the son of Sophroniscus to the son of Mary? What a distance from one to the other!" Yet such prejudices and blindness would cease to be such if both Socrates and Jesus were treated as mere mortals, which is in fact how the Vicar proceeds. The comparison favors Jesus. "Socrates, dying without pain and without ignominy, easily sticks to his character to the end." If Socrates investigated morality, others practiced it. "But where did Jesus find among his own people that elevated and pure morality of which he alone gave the lessons and the example?" Their deaths testify to their characters. "The death of Socrates, philosophizing tranquilly with his friends, is the sweetest one could desire; that of Jesus, expiring in torment, insulted, jeered at, cursed by a whole people, is the most horrible one could fear.... Yes, if the life and death of Socrates are those of a wise man, the life and death of Jesus are those of a god" (308). That said, the Vicar does not admit the divinity of Christ as evidence in the trial; if Jesus's life and death are godly, he remains a man.[10]

What testifies to the "divinity" of the Gospels and its subject is its moral teaching: "so great, so striking, so perfecting inimitable." Yet, "the same Gospel is full of unbelievable things, of things repugnant to reason and impossible for any sensible man to conceive or to accept" (308). Rousseau affirms the same: "As for myself, I see facts attested in the holy Scriptures.... But because they are in the Scriptures I do not reject them at all. I do not accept them either, because my reason refuses to do so and because my decision on this matter does not concern my salvation. No judicious Christian can believe everything in the Bible is inspired.... What we ought to believe inspired is everything that relates to our duties" (*Mountain*, 184). As for the Vicar, despite the majesty of the Scriptures and its "hero," he remains in an "involuntary skepticism" concerning these matters, a skepticism that he claims is "in no way painful for me, because it does not extend to the points essential to practice and because I am quite decided on the principles of my duties" (308). The Vicar thus circles back to the very beginning of his account of his inquiries and the unbearable skepticism from which he sought release (267). The moral guidance he sought through his reason now serves as the touchstone for assessing the "divinity" of the moral teachings found in the Gospel. One is tempted to say of the Gospel in the hands of the Vicar what Rousseau says of the one book he allows Emile to read, *Robinson Crusoe*: that it must be stripped of its "rigmarole" (*fratras*) to be useful (185).

Once again, in his own name Rousseau concurs with the Vicar concerning the majesty of the Scriptures and the morality of the Gospel. As we saw in chapter 1 when analyzing Rousseau's claims about his religious beliefs, again while distinguishing them from what the Vicar says, he writes to Beaumont: "Your Grace, I am Christian, and sincerely Christian, according to the doctrine of the Gospel," with that "doctrine" being limited to moral duties and good works while putting aside all doctrinal "subtleties." Furthermore, he professes to be a Protestant: "I take Scripture and reason for the unique rules of my belief," nonetheless taking Scripture as a rule only insofar as it accords with reason, neither affirming nor denying what reason cannot confirm (*Beaumont*, 47–48). Similarly, in the *Letters Written from the Mountain* he writes of the imagined adherents of the "Profession of Faith" in some small corner of the world: "Our proselytes will have two rules of faith that make up only one, reason and the Gospel. The latter will be all the more immutable because it will base itself only on the former." When asked if they accept the entirety of the Gospel, Rousseau has them reply: "We accept all the teachings given by Jesus Christ. The utility, the necessity of most of these teachings strikes us, and we try to conform to them.... Many things in the Gospel go beyond our reason and even shock it. Yet we do not reject them. Convinced of the weakness of our understanding, we know how to respect what we cannot conceive" (*Mountain*, 142–43). His profession that he remains a Protestant has a similar thrust: "Each remains the sole judge of [doctrines] for himself, and does not acknowledge any authority in them other than his own" (154–55).

Returning to Oneself: The Conclusion of the Vicar's Speech

With his account of his inquiry into particular revelations and religious doctrines complete, the Vicar applies the lessons of the "involuntary skepticism" in which he remains and the moral guidance he has discovered through reason by returning to himself. His explanation of what he has learned through his inquiry involves a distinction between what is private or interior and what is public or exterior. "I serve God in the simplicity of my heart. I seek to know only what is important for my conduct," says the Vicar. Or a few sentences later: "The essential worship is that of the heart." By contrast, the Vicar explains, as for dogmas that do not pertain to morality, he does not trouble himself about them. "I regard all the particular religions as so many salutary institutions which prescribe in each country a uniform matter of honoring God by public worship" (308). Recall in this light the observations of the youth conveyed in the narrative framing story concerning the difference between what the Vicar does and says publicly in his role as a priest and what he says—and does—privately in the youth's presence.

Yet the Vicar's *métier* is that of a priest, a priest who is expected to follow "the form of worship which I profess," and so he follows those forms punctiliously. "My conscience would reproach me for voluntarily failing to do so on any point." Perhaps we are meant to reflect on the potentially casuistic character of the Vicar's conscience when it comes to justifying his proclivity for sleeping with unmarried women. In fact, the Vicar alludes to this matter, for he speaks of having been permitted to return to his sacerdotal duties after a long interdict following his punishment for his failing. Formerly, that is, prior to the theological and religious inquiry he has just recounted, the Vicar relates that he performed his priestly duty with a nonchalant "lightness." "But since adopting my new principles, I celebrate it with more veneration. . . . Bearing in mind that I bring to Him the prayers of the people in a prescribed form, I carefully follow all the rites, I recite attentively, I take care never to omit either the least word or the least ceremony." In other words, he does and says these things without actually believing them. To be sure, he emphasizes the core moral teaching. "I shall always preach virtue to men; I shall always exhort them to do good; and insofar as I am able, I shall set them a good example." Similarly, he states that when instructing his flock "I would be less attached to the spirit of the Church than to the spirit of the Gospel, in which the dogma is simple and the morality sublime, and in which one sees few religious practice and many works of charity." Still, he conceals his private beliefs from his flock when performing his public. Indeed, he tells the youth that he is the sole person to have ever heard his profession of faith (309–10). Others hear and see what he is prescribed to say and do.

Is the Vicar a liar? In my previous treatment of the issue, I began with a contemporary critic of *Emile*, a bishop who posed the problem bluntly: "Here we have, not a Protestant, but a deist dressed up as a Catholic priest who performs all of his functions and who . . . does not omit a single action, a single syllable of a liturgy of which he does not believe a single word. . . . How is it not obvious that he discredits his entire doctrine by making its apostle a libertine priest, one who combines deism with the mass, and the most remarkable of hypocrites [*fourbes*]?"[11] For my own part, I suggested that insofar as the Vicar leads his flock to presume that he believes the doctrines he expounds and the ceremonies he performs, he is at minimum guilty of a lie of omission. Given that he states that he performs these rites with all the devotion he can muster despite his doubts and that he does so in good conscience, or so he claims, then it would also seem the Vicar is not a hypocrite, at least not in the strict sense of the term. In short, I concluded that the Vicar might be characterized as a sort of sincere liar.[12]

Let me build on these thoughts by addressing the question from a somewhat different angle here given the emphasis on truth and utility throughout my investigation of Rousseau's theological and religious thought. As for truth, the Vicar's explanation for his not entirely sincere performance of his priestly duties is, first, that he emphasizes the moral doctrines found in the Gospels insofar as he has found them to be true through his reason; second, that the other particular doctrines he professes despite not holding them to be true are indifferent matters of salutary conventions that prescribe a uniform manner of worship; third, that he will not preach any doctrines contrary to the moral doctrine—for example, "the cruel dogma of intolerance." Indeed, Rousseau adds a note to the Vicar's remark about intolerance: "The duty to follow and love the religion of one's country does not extend to dogmas contrary to good morals, such as that of intolerance" (309 and n). Overall, the Vicar's explanation is very similar to Rousseau's own claims in the *Reveries* concerning when we are obliged to tell the truth and when we are permitted to depart from it. Namely, he adheres strictly to the truth when it is useful, here with regard to the moral doctrines he preaches to his flock, and he permits himself a kind of "moral fable" by preaching the particular dogmas he does not believe because doing so is also useful, in this case socially useful in establishing uniform religious practices.

As for utility, in addition to the utility of preaching morally and socially useful doctrines, whether they are true or not, the Vicar's actions are meant to be useful for his audience. Here we can distinguish between two audiences: the young proselyte and his flock. As for the youth, the Vicar justifies opening his heart to him, and him alone, because doing so is useful to him given the condition of his heart and mind. We already saw the Vicar begin the second part of his speech by saying: "But in your present condition you will profit from thinking as I do" (295). Now at the end of his speech he explains: "Consciences which are agitated, uncertain, almost extinguished, and in the condition in which I have seen yours, need to be reinforced and awakened; and in order to put them back on the foundation of eternal truths, it is necessary to complete the job of ripping out the shaky pillars to which they think they are still attached." The corollary of this principle applies to the Vicar's other audience, his flock: "So long as there remains some sound belief among men, one must not disturb peaceful souls or alarm the faith of simple people with difficulties which they cannot resolve and which upset them without enlightening them" (310). Propounding his profession of faith to his flock would not be useful for them, and in fact would be injurious.

Conclusion

In the previous chapter I concluded my discussion of the first part of the "Profession" by examining the conclusion of the "Profession" as a whole to assess Rousseau's intentions in publishing the writing, and so here I restrict myself to a few remarks about his aims with regard to the critique of religion in the second part of the "Profession." First, we can extend the above analysis of the Vicar's intentions with respect to the two audiences he addresses, the youth and his flock, to Rousseau's decision to publish the "Profession" as a whole and the second part in particular. Namely, when justifying his speech to the youth, after stating that peaceful souls should not be disturbed, the Vicar states: "But once everything is shaken, one ought to preserve the trunk at the expense of the branches," and continues with the passage quoted above (and mixing his metaphor) about needing in such cases to rip out the shaky pillars (310). Like the youth who listens to the Vicar's speech, the readers of *Emile* need a theological and religious inquiry such as is found in the "Profession." As Rousseau explains in the *Letter to Beaumont*, "A great good is accomplished for peoples in this delirium by teaching them to reason about religion, for it is bringing them closer to the duties of man, removing the dagger from intolerance, giving back to humanity all its right" (*Beaumont*, 55). Second, and related, in conclusion the Vicar both encourages the youth to judge for himself what he has professed to him and urges him to return to the religion of his fathers, that is, Calvinism, which the priest characterizes as a religion which has "the purest morality and which is the most satisfactory to religion" (311). Given that Rousseau characterizes the "spirit of Christianity" in general and especially the "spirit of Protestantism" as consisting in the morality of the Gospel as authorized by the reason of every individual, the Vicar's counsel amounts to adhering to a natural religion such as he sketched in the first part of his profession while following the particular practices of his religion insofar as they do not contradict the moral doctrines discovered by reason. Such is Rousseau's counsel to his readers as well.

CHAPTER 8

On Civil Religion

The chapter "On Civil Religion" (IV.8) of the *Social Contract* attracted considerable attention in Rousseau's day and continues to do so in our own, most of it decidedly negative. The critique of Christianity from the perspective of politics stoked the ire of Rousseau's contemporaries and was one of the principal reasons cited by the authorities of his native Geneva for condemning the treatise (although the application of its political principles to the oligarchic usurpation of sovereign authority in the city did not escape their notice). In turn, readers of the *Social Contract* over the past century have often found the work objectionable for entirely different reasons. They have grappled with understanding how the champion of democratic sovereignty, liberty, and equality could conclude his treatise with such a seemingly illiberal insistence on the citizens being required to profess the dogmas of a civil religion, even at the pain of death. Some have argued that this civil religion and related elements of Rousseau's political theory, such as the figure of the great lawgiver, reveal the illiberal and even totalitarian thrust of his thought.[1] In contrast, others have argued that the minimal positive content of the dogmas of civil religion and especially the dogma prohibiting intolerance reveal a more pluralist and even liberal aspect of Rousseau's political theory.[2]

My aim in this chapter is to analyze Rousseau's argument in the chapter "On Civil Religion" and his intentions in including it in the *Social Contract*, both in relation to his theological and religious thought and within the context of his political theory. Thus, I will neither condemn Rousseau nor try to exculpate him from the charges brought against him on this account. In the first section I contextualize the treatment of civil religion within his theological and religious thought, returning to some of the issues that have arisen in this study. In the second section I contextualize it within his political theory, especially in the *Social Con-*

tract. I turn to his discussion of civil religion in the third section. After a discussion of how the placement of the chapter "On Civil Religion" within his political treatise suggests its intended aim, I turn to an analysis of the chapter itself. I frame my analysis as addressing the reasons why Rousseau prefaces his brief discussion of the topic of the chapter— namely, the dogmas required by civil religion—with a lengthy sketch of the history of religions and an analysis of the available alternatives (the religion of the citizen, the religion of man, and the religion of the priest) from the perspective of politics. I suggest that this historical sketch and schematic analysis reveal the ultimately irresolvable situation in which we find ourselves with regard to the relationship of politics and religion, and that Rousseau's civil religion is advanced by him as the best available means to address the motivational problem of politics while promoting religious toleration.

Civil Religion within Rousseau's Theological and Religious Thought

A few observations concerning Rousseau's theological and religious thought I have already discussed will help contextualize the substance and aims of the "purely civic profession of faith" he proposes. Rousseau's interest in the subject predates the *Social Contract*. As we saw in chapter 3, at the end of the *Letter to Voltaire* he proposes that the sworn enemy of *l'infâme* should lend his pen to writing a "Catechism of the Citizen." "There is, I admit, a sort of profession of faith that the laws can impose," he writes, "but beyond the principles of morality and natural right, it ought to be purely negative, because there can exist religions which attack the foundation of society, and because it is necessary to begin by exterminating those religions in order to assure the peace of the state." Such are religions that are intolerant and produce fanaticism, and Rousseau includes among them "intolerant unbelievers." "I would therefore wish that in each state one might have a moral code or a sort of civil profession of faith, which contained positively the social maxims that everyone would be bound to admit, and negatively the fanatical maxims that one would be bound to reject, not as impious, but as seditious" (*Voltaire*, 119–20). Rousseau does not propound the positive or negative maxims of such a "moral code" or the "civil profession of faith" as true, but as politically useful. As we shall see, the articles of civil religion he sketches in the *Social Contract* are similar in substance and, more importantly, are presented as politically salutary.

Rousseau speaks to the relationship between religion and politics in the *Letter to Beaumont*, although not with direct reference to the *Social*

Contract. His concern with the utility of religion in relation to politics is signaled by the fact that his remarks on the subject come immediately after he outlines the two criteria for assessing religions, truth and utility, a subject I discussed in chapter 1. "Why does one man have the right of inspection over another man's belief, and why does the state have it over the belief of the citizens?" he asks. "It is because it is assumed that what men believe determines their morality, and that their conduct in this life is dependent on their idea about the life to come.... In society everyone has the right to find out whether another person believes himself obligated to be just, and the sovereign has the right to examine the reasons on which each person bases this obligation." However, this inspection is limited to reasons or beliefs related to morality. Opinions not related to morality are left to each individual's own judgment (*Beaumont*, 56–57).

Rousseau speaks directly about the chapter "On Civil Religion" when defending the treatise against its condemnation by Geneva. As with the *Letter to Beaumont*, in the *Letters Written from the Mountain* his remarks follow immediately after the argument that religions should be assessed by the criteria of both their truth and their utility. "Religion is useful and even necessary for peoples," he writes, and he then goes on to clarify his argument in his political treatise that Christianity is not useful from the perspective of politics. As for truth, he explains that the religion of "reason and the Gospel" is true—again, as he interprets it. However, this universalistic religion cannot as such "contribute to good specific institutions"—that is, to political associations, which are, by their nature, particularistic. "Yet it is important for the state not to be without religion, and it is important for serious reasons, upon which I have strongly insisted throughout" (*Mountain*, 140–48). He will face this intractable dilemma concerning truth and utility in the chapter "On Civil Religion."

"What ought a wise lawgiver to do with these alternatives?" asks Rousseau. "One of two things. The first is to establish a purely civil religion, which includes the fundamental dogmas of every good religion, all dogmas truly useful to either a universal or a particular society." All other doctrines not essential to morality should be omitted, and he singles out the doctrine of original sin for exclusion. "Although true Christianity is an institution of peace," he explains, "who does not see that dogmatic or theological Christianity ... is a permanent battlefield between men?" This first alternative is more or less what he proposes in the *Social Contract*. As for the second alternative: "The other expedient is to leave Christianity as it is in its genuine spirit, disengaged from all bonds of flesh, with no other obligation than that of conscience, no other constraint in its dogmas than morals and laws. The Christian religion, through the purity of its morality, is always good and healthy in the state, provided that it is not made part of its constitution." Such a solution would inspire humanity, but not patriotism (148–49). This religion would be politically salutary if it were tolerant by principle, such as Rousseau argues is the case for true Christianity. Of course, such a proposal would require adopting Rousseau's version of the religion of the Gospel as ascertained by reason.

Finally, when explaining his aims in the chapter "On Civil Religion" Rousseau reveals that he is fighting on two fronts: against both intolerant religions and philosophical atheism. In this regard, then, the discussion of civil religion shares the aim of the "Profession of Faith," but within a political framework absent from the Vicar's speech. Rousseau claims to be sanguine about his project, although it is unclear which of the two alternatives he laid out earlier in the *Letters Written from the Mountain* he has in mind, perhaps both. "The enterprise was bold, but it was not rash, and without circumstances that it was hard to foresee, it ought naturally to succeed." Enlightened individuals and illustrious magistrates have thought as he did, he claims, without identifying any of his supposed fellow travelers. "Consider the religious condition of Europe at the moment I published my book, and you will see that it was more than probable that it would be welcomed everywhere. Religion, discredited everywhere by philosophy, had lost its ascendancy even over the people. The clergy, obstinate about propping it up on its weak side, had let all the rest be undermined, and, being out of plumb, the entire edifice was ready to collapse." Enter Jean-Jacques Rousseau. "What more fortunate moment for establishing universal peace solidly than the one in which the suspended animosity of the parties left everyone in a condition to listen to reason?" Perhaps a rhetorical question? Alas. "How many evils on the point of being reborn would not have been prevented if they had listened to me!" (227–28). Whether or not he seriously believed anyone would listen aside, the thrust of his proposal is clear: if religions are "useful and even necessary for peoples," then a civil religion that is tolerant by principle must be established. If the "great problem of politics"—"*To find a form of government that places the law above man*" can be compared to squaring the circle in geometry, as Rousseau wrote five years after the publication of the *Social Contract*, then a similar challenge of quadrature is posed by the relationship between religion and politics.[3]

Civil Religion within Rousseau's Political Theory

As a number of interpreters have noted, Rousseau's political theory has two main elements: the principles of political right and the science of the legislator or lawgiver.[4] The principles of political right are the theoretical foundation of a legitimate state, and include concepts such as the social contract, sovereignty, general will, law, and government. The science of the lawgiver includes the "maxims of politics" relating to founding and maintaining the state, and especially those formal and informal institutions necessary for forming a people capable of self-legislation and motivating citizens to obey the laws, including civil religion. Interpreters sometimes focus on the principles of political right alone, putting aside the science of the lawgiver as unnecessary, outdated, or just plain dangerous.[5] However that may be, Rousseau himself considered extralegal institutions such as the lawgiver and the formation of proper morals, customs, and opinions through civic education and civil religion as essential to the formation and maintenance of a legitimate political association. They are essential because of the inevitable tension between the particular will the individual has as a "man" and the general will he has as a "citizen." If the conformity of the particular will and the general will is the definition of political virtue ("Discourse on Political Economy," *CW*, 3:149), then these extralegal institutions are necessary precisely because they promote such virtue by working against the grain of nature. If we were to cast these two main elements of Rousseau's political theory in the now-familiar terms of truth and utility, we might say that the principles of political right are true and the extralegal institutions of the lawgiver are useful, politically useful. Let me now turn to a sketch of the two elements of Rousseau's political theory as a preparation for investigating the substance and aims of his discussion of civil religion.

THE PRINCIPLES OF POLITICAL RIGHT

The subtitle of Rousseau's political treatise announces its subject: "Principles of Political Right." After some ground clearing of incorrect notions about the origin of political authority, he begins the exposition of the proper principles in the aptly titled chapter "On the Social Compact" (I.6). He famously argues that the form of association must leave the members as free as they were before, and that paradoxically this is achieved through the total alienation of each associate with all his rights to the whole community. "*Each of us puts his person and all his power in common under the supreme direction of the general will; and as a body we receive each member as an indivisible part of the whole.*" The effect of this act is miraculous: "Instantly, in place of the particular person of each contracting party, this act of association produces a moral and collective body made up of as many members as there are voices in the assembly, which receives from this same act its unity, its common *self*, its life and its will" (I.6). In the following chapter, "On the Sovereign," he explains that the sovereign people cannot alienate any part of itself or subject itself to another power owing to the nature of sovereignty and to "the sanctity of the contract" (I.7). In what way the social contract is "sanctified" is not clear, but at the very beginning of his treatise Rousseau states that "the social order is a sacred right that serves as the basis for all the others. Yet this right does not come from nature; it is therefore based on conventions" (I.1). The conventional act of association itself is somehow "sacred" or "sanctified," and does not receive that character from nature, much less from the divinity.

The point to be emphasized, as Bruno Bernardi forcefully argues, is that religion does not play any role in the *foundation* of the state, which consists in the principles of political right, even if it does in its *formation* through the act of the great lawgiver, as we shall see.[6] A revealing exception of religious language employed when articulating the principles of political right that proves the rule occurs in the chapter "On the Law" (II.6). The social compact gives existence and life to the body politic, but now it is a question of giving it movement and will through legislation. "What is good and in accordance with order is so by the nature of things and independently of human conventions," Rousseau writes. "All justice comes from God; he alone is its source. But if we knew how to receive it from on high, we would need neither government nor laws. Without doubt, there is a universal justice emanating from reason alone. But in order to be acknowledged among us, this justice must be reciprocal. Considering things from a human standpoint, the laws of justice are ineffectual among men for want of a natural sanction" (II.6). What he means by all justice coming from God is enigmatic, but his remark that "there is a universal justice emanating from reason alone" suggests that he has in mind something like the moral law found by reason and coincident with the religion of the Gospel.[7] Justice and morality are "divine" in this sense, and it seems in this sense alone. In any case, human beings are left to their own devices both epistemologically and legally; the sovereign people must legislate for itself as best it can in identifying justice and codifying it as law. This is the work of the general will.[8]

THE MOTIVATIONAL PROBLEM

How to motivate the citizens to make the particular wills conform to the general will? The principles of political right are in themselves insufficient to motivate the citizens, according to Rousseau. To illustrate the motivational problem two passages from the *Social Contract*, both notorious, will suffice. First, having laid out the solution to the problem of finding an association through a social contract that places the citizens under the general will enacted in their capacity as sovereign, Rousseau admits a problem. "Indeed, each individual can, as a man, have a particular will contrary to or differing from the general will he has as a citizen. His particular interest can speak to him entirely differently than the common interest." What to do? "Therefore, in order for the social compact not to be an empty formality, it tacitly encompasses the following commitment, which alone can give force to the rest: that whoever does refuse to obey the general will be constrained to do so by the whole body, which means nothing else but that he be forced to be free" (I.7). Second, after explaining that the only legitimate source of law is the general will of the citizens acting as sovereign, Rousseau acknowledges a related difficulty: "How will a blind multitude, which often does not know what it wants because it rarely knows what is good for it, carry out by itself an undertaking as vast, as difficult as a system of legislation?" The solution? "From this arises the need for a lawgiver" (II.6).

The project of making a people capable of self-legislation and of ensuring that they are motivated to obey the general will is all the more difficult because human beings are not, in fact, by nature citizens. The task of the lawgiver is to make the individual "man" who by nature follows his particular will into a "citizen" who heeds the general will he has qua citizen. "He who dares to undertake to establish a people's institutions must feel that he is capable of changing, so to speak, human nature; of transforming each individual, who by himself is a complete and solitary whole, into a part of a greater whole from which this individual receives as it were his life and his being." (II.7). As Rousseau explains in *Emile*, "Good social institutions are those that best know how to denature man, to take his absolute existence from him in order to give him a relative one and transport the *I* into the common unity, with the result that each individual believes himself no longer one but a part of the unity and no longer feels except within the whole" (40). The lawgiver must remake the identity of the individual into that of a citizen by redirecting natural self-love into love of the whole of which the citizen identifies as a part. Rousseau does not rely upon the self-interest of the associates of the social contract, or their long-term "self-interest rightly understood." Indeed, this was more or less what he attempted to do in the original draft of his political treatise through his confrontation with the "violent reasoner" who refuses to submit to the social contract for want of assured reciprocity from others ("Geneva Manuscript," *CW*, 4:79–81). The attempt ends with a kind of impasse, and Rousseau excised the discussion from the final version. In the *Social Contract*, then, he instead calls for transforming the "self" to instill love of the fatherland and love of one's duty as a citizen.

CHAPTER EIGHT

THE LAWGIVER

The extraordinary mission of the lawgiver is complicated by the fact that he cannot draft the laws, for legislation is by right limited to the sovereign people. Nor can he use force, for to do so would be to violate their liberty. Finally, and most importantly for the present purposes, he cannot use reason because the "general views" and "remote objectives" he has in mind exceed the narrow self-interest and myopic vision of the citizens before they are fully formed. "Hence, therefore, since the lawgiver can use neither force nor reasoning, he must of necessity have recourse to an authority of a different order which ought to be able to motivate without violence and to persuade without convincing" (II.7). We have seen the language of "persuasion" and "conviction" in Rousseau's writings on theology and religion. For example, in the *Letter to Voltaire*, when weighing this materialist explanation of the order of nature against the alternative of order by design of the divinity, he writes: "While both the one and the other seem equally convincing to me, the last alone persuades me" (117–18). Similarly, in the dramatic interlude in the "Profession of Faith," the youth recalls that he saw a "multitude of objections" to make to the Vicar—that is, he was not convinced: "I did not make any of them, because they were less solid than disconcerting, and persuasiveness was on his side" (*Emile*, 294). Finally, in the *Reveries* when recounting his dealings with his former friends the materialist philosophers, he says: "They had not persuaded me, but they had troubled me. Their arguments had shaken me without having ever convinced me" (21). In each of these cases we have seen how the scale tips to the side of persuasion.

There might be several ways available to the lawgiver to persuade the people, but Rousseau emphasizes religion. "This is what has at all times forced the fathers of nations to resort to the intervention of heaven and to honor the gods with their own wisdom, so that peoples—subject to the laws of state as to those of nature, and recognizing the same power in the formation of man as in that of the city—obey with freedom and bear the yoke of public felicity with docility." The lawgiver puts his proposals "into the mouth of the immortals" to "motivate by divine authority those who could not be swayed by human prudence" (II.7). How the people can "obey with freedom" given the apparently heteronomous nature of the lawgiver's appeal to heaven is unclear, but what is clear is that it is the lawgiver's "own wisdom" concerning the laws and institutions that he persuades them to accept as their own, and that the resort to heaven's intervention is meant to supply a motivation to do so.

To the statement about motivating citizens by an appeal to divine authority, Rousseau adds a note in which he quotes Machiavelli: "And truly ... there was never an orderer of extraordinary laws for a people who did not have recourse to God, because otherwise they would not have been accepted. For a prudent individual knows many goods that do not have in themselves evident reasons with which one can persuade others" (II.7 n, quoting Machiavelli, *Discourses on Livy*, I.11). In this context, Machiavelli is discoursing on the religious orders introduced by Numa, but he attributes the same actions to Lycurgus and Solon. Rousseau, too, refers to Numa and Lycurgus, but also Moses and Mohammed.[9] If anything, then, Rousseau is more forthright than his predecessor about the political uses of religion beyond ancient paganism. The successful lawgiver cannot be a charlatan, but rather acts foremost through the "great soul," which proclaims his mission of founding "enduring establishments." Finally, he concludes the chapter by clarifying the relationship between politics and religion. Arguing against Warburton, who claimed that politics and religion have a common goal, he states that "at the origin of nations the one serves as the instrument of the other" (II.7). In the "Geneva Manuscript," in a continuation of the passage cut from the final version, he explains: "As for the contribution of religion to the civil establishment, one also sees that it is no less useful to be able to give the moral tie an internal force which reaches into the soul" (*CW*, 4:104). Religion is a useful instrument for politics—at least at the *formation* of the state. Once again, these appeals to religion are absent from the *foundation* of the state in the principles of political right.

Rousseau returns to the lawgiver's task in a discussion closely related to the use of religion for the aims of politics. After a few chapters devoted to various considerations about the character of the people to be founded, climate, terrain, and other factors that should be considered by the "wise founder," he turns to a discussion of different kinds of laws—political, civil, and criminal. To these he says a fourth sort may be added, "the most important of all," even if not, precisely speaking, a law at all:

> One which is not engraved on marble or bronze, but in the hearts of the citizens; which is the genuine constitution of the state; which daily acquires more force; which, when the other laws grow old or die out, revives them or replaces them, preserves the people in the spirit of its institution and imperceptibly substitutes the force of habit for that of authority. I speak of morals [*moeurs*], customs, and especially opinions—a part of the laws unknown to our politicians, but upon which the success of the others depends, a part to which the great lawgiver attends in secret while he appears to restrict himself to particular regulations which are merely the sides of the arch of which morals—slower to arise—ultimately form the unshakeable keystone. (II.12)

Once again, the fact that the lawgiver builds this edifice "in secret" and forms the people's morals, customs, and opinions without their knowledge or consent raises the question of how such heteronomous elements can be reconciled with the autonomous self-legislation of the citizens.

The lawgiver's appeal to heaven to motivate the people to accept his legislation and his formation of their morals, customs, and opinions are, whatever concerns we may have about them, clearly meant to form the people so that they are capable of self-legislation in their role as citizens and to motivate them to obey the laws. Civil religion clearly has a similar aim. But does the lawgiver establish the "purely civil profession of faith"? It is certainly tempting to suppose as much.[10] The fact that the original draft of the chapter was hastily scribbled on the verso of the manuscript of the chapter "On the Lawgiver" further encourages the assumption, and numerous scholars have duly pointed to this circumstantial evidence.[11] On the other hand, we know that the chapter on civil religion was a late addition to the work, sent to the publisher after the author had submitted the rest of the manuscript.[12] We do not know anything about his original intentions, but if Rousseau did not initially envision including it in his treatise, then there would appear to be something of a gap between the chapters on the lawgiver and on civil religion. This gap is widened when we consider the physical distance between the two chapters in the final version, and also when we note that there are no internal references in either chapter to the other. Finally, some scholars have suggested a substantive caesura, for the grandiose action of the lawgiver calling the gods down to earth finds a very feeble echo in the comparatively tepid dogmas of the civil religion Rousseau proposes, and these very limited dogmas do not seem up to the Mosaic mission confronting the lawgiver.[13] The relationship between the lawgiver and civil religion, both as elements of the text and in terms of substance, is something of a mystery. I will try to shed some light on this mystery, if not solve it, in the next section by distinguishing between forming the state and maintaining it, with the first being the task of the lawgiver and the second being the role of civil religion.

"On Civil Religion"

Let us now turn to the chapter "On Civil Religion" in the *Social Contract*. We can restrict our focus of Rousseau's treatment of civil religion to his treatise for a simple reason: there is no sustained discussion of civil religion outside of the *Social Contract*.[14] There are two exceptions to this assertion that do not disprove the rule: first, he does discuss civil religion in the draft version of the chapter in the "Geneva Manuscript";

second, he makes some brief remarks in the *Letters Written from the Mountain* when defending the treatment of the subject in his political treatise, remarks I have already discussed. What he does address beyond the *Social Contract* are the other elements of the lawgiver's art—namely, the formation of citizens through morals, customs, and opinions. I begin with some remarks on how the placement of the chapter "On Civil Religion" within his treatise sheds light on its aims, then turn to address the question of what precisely "civil religion" refers to, and then analyze the substance and aims of his discussion of the relationship between politics and religion and the "purely civil profession of faith" he proposes.

THE CHAPTER "ON CIVIL RELIGION" WITHIN THE SOCIAL CONTRACT

The chapter "On Civil Religion" (IV.8) is the longest chapter in the *Social Contract* and, with the exception of a brief concluding chapter, the last. The chapter comes as a bit of a surprise, and its location has prompted some head-scratching. Indeed, book IV as whole is often viewed as ancillary, and many interpreters simply skip the lengthy discussion of Roman institutions to get straight to the discussion of civil religion.[15]

Yet let us begin with book IV. The contents of the four books of the *Social Contract* are summarized by Rousseau in the table of contents, an element he insisted on including but one almost always omitted from editions of the work.[16] The contents of book IV follow from those of book III. Book III is characterized by the author as "discussing political laws, that is, the form of the government" (158). A major theme of the book is how the government (that is, the executive power) tends to usurp sovereignty (that is, the legislative power) and how to forestall that tendency. One reason for this tendency is the gradual divergence of the particular will from the general will among the citizens, and so Rousseau's discussion in book III is concerned with the motivational problem that makes formal and informal institutions, including civil religion, necessary. Book IV is summarized as follows: "While continuing the discussion of political laws, the means for strengthening the constitution of the state are explained" (159). In keeping with the theme of the decay and eventual death of the state begun in book III, the overall trend of book IV is one of decline, beginning with the image of a primitive political society so simple and unified that the general will almost doesn't need to be enunciated and concluding with a state "close to its ruin," which "continues to subsist in an illusory and empty form, when the social bond is broken in all hearts" (IV.1). Rousseau then illustrates how to adapt political laws, notably systems of voting, to the "current state of morals and the health of the body politic"—namely, as it declines over time (IV.2). He does so through an extensive discussion of Roman institutions (IV.2–7). The last chapter in this sequence is "On the Censorship" (IV.7), and what Rousseau emphasizes about this Roman institution is its role in maintaining salutary opinions. "Public opinion is a type of law of which the censor is the minister and which he does no more than apply to particular cases," he explains. "The opinions of a people arise from its constitution. Although law does not regulate morals, it is legislation which causes them to arise. When legislation grows weak, morals degenerate, but by then the censor's judgment will not be able to do what the force of the laws has not done." The censor can therefore work to preserve morals, but not to restore them. The "artfulness" with which the censor does so is "entirely forgotten among the moderns" (IV.7). Perhaps these opinions include the ones introduced by the lawgiver. At any rate, it is at this point that he turns to civil religion.

The placement of the chapter "On Civil Religion" in this context is significant for understanding Rousseau's aims. Here I build on Bruno Bernardi's excellent discussion of this issue.[17] First, one might surmise from both the contents of the chapter and the fact that the original draft was written on the verso of the manuscript of what became the chapter "On the Lawgiver" (II.7) that the chapter devoted to civil religion would logically follow from the discussion of the lawgiver, especially given Rousseau's remarks on how the lawgiver must appeal to the authority of the gods when *forming* a people. Whatever Rousseau's original intention, he instead chose to position the discussion of civil religion within a broad treatment of *maintaining* the political community by instilling opinions or beliefs in the citizens that motivate them to do their duty. The fact that the chapter "On Civil Religion" follows the chapter "On the Censorship" is telling in this regard, and Bernardi therefore suggests that we read that chapter as a continuation of the prior chapter.[18] To this I would add that the principal problem concerning the relationship of politics and religion that Rousseau identifies in the chapter "On Civil Religion" is post-Roman, owing to the advent of Christianity within the Roman context, and that the chapter therefore logically follows his discussion of Roman institutions and the inability of such institutions to address the political problematic consequences of the Christian religion. Let me now turn to the chapter itself.

WHAT IS "CIVIL RELIGION"?

First a word about the title. Even if the question of the relationship between religion and political or civil society has a long history, the term "civil religion" (*religion civile*) is Rousseau's own coinage.[19] To anticipate, he thinks a new concept is necessary to address a new situation regarding the relationship between politics and religion.

Does the term refer to the contents of the entirety of the chapter—that is, the entire discussion of religion as it is related to politics? Or does it refer to a part—namely, the concluding discussion of the "purely civil profession of faith"? The only time he uses the phrase in the chapter (and the entire treatise) is when discussing the dogmas of the "purely civil profession of faith" authorized by the right the sovereign possesses to inquire into those opinions of the citizens that matter to the community: "The dogmas of the civil religion should be simple, few in number," and so on (IV.8). In the original draft of the chapter there is one more instance, when he writes concerning the supposed excellence of Christian troops as witnessed by the Crusades: "They were citizens of the Church fighting for their spiritual country. Properly understood, this amounts to paganism; since the Gospel is not a *civil religion*, any war of religion is impossible among Christians" ("Geneva Manuscript," CW, 4:120; emphasis added). His terminology in the draft is ambiguous, as "civil religion" is not distinct from "paganism." He corrected this in the final draft: "Strictly speaking, this should be included under paganism. Since the Gospel does not establish a *national religion*, a holy war is impossible among Christians" (IV.8; emphasis added). In short, he confines "civil religion" to the "purely civil profession of faith" to which he turns at the end of the chapter. The part becomes the title for the whole through an act of synecdoche.

As for the chapter, it is divided into three parts. The first part consists of a history of the relationship between religion and politics, beginning with the first societies, progressing through paganism, and concluding with the advent of Christianity and the challenges it poses for that relationship. The first part comprises nearly the first half of the chapter (fourteen paragraphs out of thirty-five total). The second part undertakes an investigation of "religion considered in relation to society," and focuses on three available alternatives: (1) the religion of the citizen, or ancient pagan religions; (2) the religion of man, or the religion of the Gospel as Rousseau interprets it; (3) the religion of the priest, principally Roman Catholicism. The second part comprises nearly the remaining half of the chapter (sixteen paragraphs). The third part consists of the remaining five paragraphs and is devoted to sketching "a purely civil profession of faith," which the sovereign can demand from the citizens.

A HISTORY OF RELIGIONS

Why does Rousseau choose to devote the first half of the chapter to a historical sketch of the relationship between politics and religion, beginning with ancient pagan religions and ending with the advent of Christianity? This question is apt because the first draft of the chapter does not include any equivalent discussion, even though the remainder of the draft and the final version are fairly close.

The first draft of the chapter begins with a paragraph on the motivational problem in politics as it is addressed by religion, and then the draft turns straightaway to an analysis of the types of religion "considered in relation to society," or what in the final version becomes the second main part of the chapter. Let me begin by quoting the first paragraph in the original version.

> As soon as men live in society, they must have a religion that keeps them there. A people has never subsisted nor ever will subsist without religion, and if it were not given one, it would make one itself or would soon be destroyed. In every state that can require its members to sacrifice their lives, anyone who does not believe in the afterlife is necessarily a coward or a madman. But we know only too well the esteem to which the hope of an afterlife can bring a fanatic to scorn this life. Take away this fanatic's visions and give him the same faith as the reward for virtue, and you will turn him into a true citizen. ("Geneva Manuscript," *CW*, 4:117)

In the final version of the chapter only an echo of one phrase of this paragraph survives. There are several claims here. First: "A people has never subsisted nor ever will subsist without religion."[20] This claim, at once historical and predictive, appears to be directed against Bayle's infamous proposition regarding the possibility of a state composed of virtuous atheists. Rousseau in fact refers briefly to Bayle and his proposition at the very end of the historical sketch found in the final version, and this is the surviving echo to which I just referred: "One would prove to [Bayle] that no state has ever been founded except with religion as its base" (IV.8). Second: a state cannot survive without religion because it requires that the citizens sacrifice their lives when needed, and that sacrifice would be impossible or insane without the hope of an afterlife as reward for doing so. This claim resembles the moral (and not specifically political) argument Rousseau makes in the long final note to the "Profession of Faith," also directed in part against Bayle, in which he asks the philosophers what equivalent they have to the myth of Poul-Serrho to prevent or correct the iniquities of this life (*Emile*, 312–14n). At any rate, this claim goes to the heart of the motivational problem faced by politics. Third: there is an unstated claim that there is a natural religiosity in humans that can be directed toward fanaticism or civic virtue.

This assumption also echoes the note to the "Profession of Faith" and Rousseau's favorable estimation of the possibilities provided by the fiery passions of fanaticism in comparison to the tepidness of atheism (312–14n). This claim would be the psychological basis for solving the motivational problem faced by politics through religion, as well as the basis for the problem of the fanaticism or intolerance that threatens the state. In short, the claims in this paragraph neatly set up the need for a "purely civil profession of faith" and the positive and negative dogmas Rousseau recommends. Yet this paragraph is absent in the final version.

What, then, is the purpose of the conjectural history of religion in the final version? The first paragraph may offer a clue. "Men at first had no other kings than the gods, nor any other governments than a theocratic one. They reasoned like Caligula, and in this case they reasoned correctly. A lengthy degeneration of sentiments and ideas is needed before they could bring themselves to accept their fellow human as a master, and to flatter themselves that this would be a good thing" (IV.8). Two things are noteworthy about this passage for our purposes. First, he establishes the separation between theocratic or religious authority and political authority, and the potential tension between them. As such, he foreshadows the problem of the contestation of religious and secular authority that characterizes the Christian world, the main problem he will address. Second, he introduces the issue of inequality and subjection, the central problem of the *Social Contract* itself. Perhaps the thought is that religion has been used as a justification for inequality and subjection, and the puzzle is how religious authority can be introduced into the state without violating the equality and freedom of the citizens. Overall, then, when compared to the introductory paragraph of the original draft, the emphasis shifts from the potentiality of religion as a solution to the motivational problems of politics to the problematic relationship between politics and religion. The ensuing conceptual history of religions therefore serves to outline the development of this increasingly problematic relationship over time and thereby to prepare his discussion of civil religion and especially the dogma against intolerance.[21]

First up is paganism. "By the sole fact that god was placed at the head of each political society," he begins, "it followed that there were as many gods as peoples. . . . Thus from national divisions resulted polytheism, and from it theological and civil intolerance, which are naturally the same thing, as will be stated below." Indeed, he will again reject the supposed distinction between these two forms of intolerance when he proscribes intolerance from the "purely civil profession of faith" at the end of the chapter. The corollary to the lack of such a distinction is that the notion that there were no wars of religion under paganism is false because there was no distinction between political and theological war. The pagans warred alongside their gods, and conquest meant submission of men and gods alike to the victorious. Among the Romans, as more gods came under Jupiter's command through their conquests, "the peoples of that vast empire imperceptibly found themselves with multitudes of gods and forms of worship, more or less everywhere the same. And this is how paganism eventually became one and the same religion throughout the known world" (IV.8).

The most interesting aspect of Rousseau's treatment of paganism is how he handles the apparently exceptional case of the Jews. His first sally is to include them among the pagan religions, and he cites a speech by Jephthah to the Ammonites recognizing what belongs to Chamos "your god" (Judges 11:24). Indeed, this is the only citation from Scripture in the entire chapter, and he even goes to the trouble of adding a note criticizing the French translation by Carrières for softening the passage (IV.8 and n). The thrust of his argument is clear: if all governments were originally theocratic, then the Jews are no exception. Rousseau thereby closes off the theologico-political route taken by Spinoza of appearing first to cede the special status of the Jews as having a theocratic state ruled directly by God, only then to deny its application to any other state. The situation becomes more complicated in Rousseau's second sally. Unlike other peoples, when vanquished the Jews refused to submit to the gods of their conquerors, initially under the Babylonians and then under the Romans. This refusal was regarded as an act of rebellion—a political offense—and this brought down upon them persecutions not seen again until Christianity (IV.8). Yet Rousseau's point here is not that the Jews were the monotheistic ancestors of the Christians, but that the persecutions they both experienced were political. Rather, as we shall see, he treats the Christians as a fundamentally different case than the Jews in terms of his conceptual analysis of the relationship between politics and religion. Doing so cuts the legs out from under someone like Warburton, whom he cited in the chapter "On the Lawgiver" and whom he will cite again shortly, who views the "divine legation of Moses" (to cite the title of his major work) as a divine dispensation that extends to Christianity.

The empire of the Romans and the ubiquity of polytheism set the stage for the turning point in Rousseau's history. "It was under these circumstances that Jesus came to establish a spiritual kingdom on earth, which, by separating the theological system from the political system, made it so that the state ceased to be a unity, and caused the intestine quarrels which have never ceased to convulse Christian peoples." Like the Jews before them, the Christians seemed to be veritable rebels in the eyes of the pagans, rebels who cloaked their ambition "beneath a hypocritical submission" while they awaited the opportunity to make themselves masters. Such was the cause of persecutions. Whatever the intentions of the early Christians, once they got the upper hand they changed their tune and brought their otherworldly kingdom down to earth in the form of the Church. The dual power of Throne and Altar "has resulted in a perpetual conflict over jurisdiction which has made any good polity impossible in Christian states." Attempts to maintain or restore the previous system have all failed, for "the spirit of Christianity has won out over everything." By the "spirit of Christianity" Rousseau appears to mean its essentially "spiritual" character, and in particular its lack of any essential tie to any political system, for he explains: "The sacred cult has always remained or become independent of the sovereign and without any necessary tie to the body of the state" (IV.8).

Rousseau cites Islam as an interesting study in contrast that then becomes one of convergence. Mohammed successfully tied the political system together well, and this system endured as long as his successors the caliphs ruled, under which "this government was strictly unified, and good for that reason" (IV.8). His positive treatment of Islam is notable in his contemporary context, and it fits with his earlier discussion of Mohammed in the chapter on the lawgiver, where he states, in a swipe directed at Voltaire and his play *Fanaticism, or Mohammed*, that "whereas proud philosophy or the blind spirit of partisanship sees in [Moses and Mohammed] merely lucky imposters, the true politician admires in their institutions that great and powerful genius that presides over enduring institutions" (II.7). But once the conquering Arabs were conquered in turn, a division between the temporal and spiritual powers began anew, and sectarian divisions arose such as are found among the Christians. Rousseau's treatment of Islam's similar fate seems to be premised on it being a monotheistic religion that has no essential relation to the body politic, thus always encouraging the rise of a separate spiritual authority that is opposed to political authority. The English and the czars failed for the same reasons. "Wherever the clergy constitutes a body," he explains, "it is the master and the lawgiver in its dominion. There are therefore two powers, two sovereigns, in England and in Russia, just as everywhere else" (IV.8).

Another who underestimated the "spirit of Christianity" was Hobbes, "the only one who clearly saw the disease and the remedy, who dared to propose reuniting the two heads of the eagle and the complete return of political unity, without which neither state nor government will ever be well constituted." Rousseau refers to Hobbes's proposal to unify both secular and spiritual power under a single sovereign, as exemplified in the frontispiece of *Leviathan* with its awesome sovereign wielding both sword and crozier. "But he should have seen that the domineering spirit of Christianity was incompatible with his system and that the interest of the priest would always be stronger than that of the state." Part of Rousseau's criticism of his predecessor here would seem to be that by seeking to establish a national church, or to put the Anglican Church on a different theoretical footing, Hobbes left the priests in their pulpits. In this way, then, the "domineering spirit of Christianity"—the combination of a religion without necessary ties to the state and the inevitable rise of those ambitious to exercise authority over men apart from or in opposition to the state—would ultimately prevail.[22] This line of criticism suggests two challenges for Rousseau's civil religion. First, how to encourage a religion without priests, or what would be the very radical Protestantism feared by Hobbes because of the authority it grants to every individual to judge. Second, how to forge a tie between the state and an otherwise otherworldly religion. Rousseau concludes his discussion of Hobbes: "It is not so much what is horrible and false in his politics as what is correct and true that has made it so odious" (IV.8). On this a book could be written.

Finally, Rousseau ends his review with a concluding paragraph that provides a bridge to the second part of the chapter. "I believe that by elaborating on the historical facts from this point of view," namely, the conjectural historical perspective he has adopted, "it would be easy to refute the opposing sentiments of Bayle and Warburton, the first of whom claims that no religion is useful to the body politic, and the latter of whom maintains on the contrary that Christianity is its firmest support." As to Bayle, we have already seen his answer: "No state has ever been founded except with religion as its base." As for Warburton, he responds: "The Christian law is at bottom more harmful than useful to the strong constitution of the state." With this said, he turns to an assessment of the available politico-religious alternatives, including foremost Christianity, thereby giving "a little more precision to the overly vague ideas about religion relative to my subject" (IV.8). In other words, the first part of the chapter, which he added, provides the historical setting for the conceptual analysis of the available alternatives that follows.

ASSAYING THE AVAILABLE ALTERNATIVES

"Religion considered in relation to society, which is either general or particular, can also be divided into two types: namely, the religion of man and that of the citizen" (IV.8). Rousseau begins his analysis by announcing its subject: "religion considered in relation to society." This is a broader inquiry than religion considered in relation to politics or the state. The "religion of man" relates to "general" society, and the "religion of the citizen" to "particular" society.

I linger over this point because Rousseau did as well in defense of his treatise, and specifically in defense of his treatment of Christianity as a religion unfit for political societies. "Might there be some new ambiguity here, by means of which I was portrayed as more guilty or crazier than I am? This word *Society* offers a slightly vague meaning," he explains in his defense. In fact, the terms "society," "social," and so on were relatively new to French when Rousseau was writing, to the point that he included instructions to his printers not to change the word for more familiar ones. (Recall that in chapter 2 I remarked that the term "moral," as in "moral inequality" or "moral love," means something more like what we would call "social," and one reason Rousseau may not have used "social" is that it was not entirely current.) At any rate, he goes on to argue that what is good for one type of society may be injurious for another. In the case of Christianity, because it is "in its principle a universal religion" it cannot be made into a "national religion" without harming both the religion and the state. In turn, "perfect Christianity is the universal social institution." By making men just, moderate, and friends of peace, Christianity "is very favorable to the general society. But it weakens the force of the political spring, it complicates the movements of the machine, it breaks the unity of the moral body, and since it is not sufficiently united to it, it must either degenerate or remain a foreign and cumbersome component" (*Mountain*, 146–48).[23] Having anticipated the argument of the *Social Contract*, let me return to the work.

Rousseau elaborates on the "religion of man" and the "religion of the citizen." As for the first: "Without temples, without altars, without rites, limited to the purely internal form of worship of the supreme God and to the eternal duties of morality—[it] is the pure religion of the Gospel, true theism, and what might be called divine natural right." In other words, this is the natural religion ascertained by reason and found in the Gospel as interpreted by Rousseau. The second, by contrast, is "inscribed in a single country, gives it its gods, its own tutelary patrons. It has its dogmas, its rites, its exterior form of worship prescribed by the laws. Outside the single nation that follows it, everything for it is infidel, alien, barbarous. It does not extend the duties and the rights of man any farther than its altars. Such were all the religions of the earliest peoples, to which the name of civil or positive divine right may be given" (IV.8).

To these two categories of religion Rousseau adds a third, as though an afterthought. "There is a third, more bizarre sort of religion, which, by giving men two bodies of legislation, two leaders, two fatherlands, subjects them to contradictory duties and prevents them from being able to be simultaneously devout men and citizens" (IV.8). Although Roman Catholicism is his main example, he mentions the religion of the lamas and the Japanese as well. It is tempting to suggest that the category includes a far larger number of members, even perhaps almost all existing Christian sects. If so, the apparent afterthought is in actuality foremost in Rousseau's mind.[24] "This sort can be called the religion of the priest. It results in a sort of mixed and unsociable right which has no name" (IV.8).

With these three categories of religion in place, Rousseau narrows his inquiry: "Considering these three sorts of religion in terms of politics, they all have their defects." Before turning to his assessment, we should recall his argument concerning the criteria by which religions should be evaluating, as discussed in chapter 1: truth and utility. The key point here is Rousseau's argument that these criteria do not necessarily coincide. In fact, as we shall see with his assessment of the three available alternatives the point is precisely that the criteria of truth and utility are in conflict.

Rousseau disposes of the third sort of religion, that of the priest, right away as "so manifestly bad that it is a waste of time to amuse oneself with demonstrating it. Everything that destroys social unity is worthless. All institutions that put man in contradiction with himself are worthless" (IV.8). This summary dispatch nonetheless reveals two aims of a proper religion in relation to politics: it should promote social unity and the psychic unity of the individual. In terms of the evaluative criteria, then, the religion of the priest is both untrue and useless or, worse, harmful.

The religion of the citizen, in turn, is useful but untrue. It "is good in that it combines divine worship and the love of the laws" and "it makes the fatherland the object of the citizens' worship." Further, the religion solves the motivational problem facing the polity: "To die for one's country is to be martyred, to violate the laws is to be impious." However, "it is bad in that, being founded on error and falsehood, it deceives men, makes them credulous, superstitious, and drowns the true worship of the divinity in empty ceremony." Such a religion is false because it is particular, like the state in which it is inscribed, whereas the true religion is universal. It is also potentially harmful. "It is also bad when, becoming exclusive and tyrannical, it makes a people bloodthirsty and intolerant." Further, it puts a people into a natural state of war with other peoples, which undermines its own security (IV.8). Interestingly, Rousseau seems to forget the success of Rome in conquering the world, as discussed in the first part of the chapter. The danger the empire faced came from within: "When the cross had driven out the eagle, all Roman valor disappeared" (IV.8), he writes later in the chapter, taking a page from Machiavelli.

Before turning to the religion of man, I note that in the original version Rousseau included a paragraph at this point offering a summary judgment of the religion of the citizen. "Now if pagan superstition, despite this mutual tolerance and in the midst of culture and a thousand virtues, engendered so many cruelties, I do not see how it is possible to separate those very cruelties from that very zeal, and to reconcile the rights of a national religion with those of humanity. It is better, then, to bind the citizens to the state by weaker and gentler ties, and to have neither heroes nor fanatics" ("Geneva Manuscript," *CW*, 4:119). The last sentence here seems to foreshadow the dogma of the civil religion concerning the sanctity of the social contract and the laws, which is a much "weaker and gentler" tie of the citizens to the state than found in pagan religions. It also evinces a more optimistic tone concerning the problematic relationship between politics and religion than the final version.

Finally, returning to the *Social* Contract, as for the religion of man, it is true but not useful from the perspective of politics. Rousseau's discussion of "religion of man or Christianity" is lengthy, but the main lines of the argument are clear. First, he begins by distinguishing his version of the religion of the Gospel from Christianity as it is actually practiced as "altogether different." His judgment appears to include all Christian sects, not just the "religion of the priest" exhibited in Roman Catholicism. The religion of the Gospel is a "genuine religion" in which all men "recognize one another as brothers and the society that unites them does not dissolve even at death." However, its very universality and otherworldliness renders it politically not useful. "But this religion, since it has no particular relation to the body politic, leaves the laws with only the force they derive from themselves without adding any other force to them, and, due to this, one of the great bonds of any particular society remains ineffectual. What is more, far from attaching the citizens' hearts to the state, it detaches them from it as it does from all earthly things. I know of nothing more contrary to the social spirit" (IV.8).

With his overall assessment of the truth and utility of the religion of man stated, he addresses a number of arguments claiming that Christianity is in fact a suitable religion for politics. Recall in this light that when he concludes his historical sketch and turns to the analysis of "religion considered in relation to society" he mentions Warburton in particular as someone who made such a claim for Christianity. "We are told that a people of true Christians would form the most perfect society that could be imagined," he begins. He replies that such a society "would no longer be a society of men," or, in other words, a people of true Christians has never been seen and never will be seen because it exceeds the capacity of human beings. Moreover, its perfection would render it fragile in various ways. "By dint of being perfect, it would lack cohesion: its fatal vice would lie in its very perfection." To be sure, the citizens of this society would fulfill their duty and obey the laws. However, their hearts would not be fully engaged. "Christianity is a wholly spiritual religion, exclusively concerned with the things of Heaven: the Christian's fatherland is not of this world." Further, Rousseau claims that this imagined society would be vulnerable to "a single ambitious person, a single hypocrite," for "Christian charity does not easily allow one to think ill of one's neighbor." As for war, Christian soldiers would do their duty, but without passion and with an indifference to the outcome, since all things are in the hands of providence. A Christian republic would be no match for a Sparta or Rome. "But I am mistaken in speaking of a Christian republic: each of these two words excludes the other. Christianity preaches nothing but servitude and dependence. . . . True Christians are made to be slaves. They know it and are scarcely moved by it; this brief life has too little value in their eyes." We are told that Christian soldiers are excellent, he relates, but replies that he does not know of any such Christian troops. As mentioned above, the example of the Crusades he denies because these troops were not fighting as Christians, but as citizens of the Church, a veritable instance of paganism (IV.8).

Rousseau's argument that the religion of man or true Christianity is useless and even harmful when viewed from the perspective of politics is less a historical claim than the entertainment of a hypothesis, for the simple reason that there is no such society. And there perhaps aren't any "true Christians" either. "If it were permitted to draw from the actions of men the proof of their sentiments, it would be necessary to say that there is not a single Christian on earth," he writes in the "Preface" to *Narcissus* (*CW*, 2:188). As for Christianity as it is actually practiced in its various forms, he criticizes it for different reasons, principally for dividing men's loyalties by giving them two fatherlands and for the intolerance it engenders. Perhaps insofar as actual Christians resemble the true Christians of his imagination, the same defects he finds in the religion of man would also apply. In any case, his critique of Christianity is even more relentless than that found in one of the thinkers who clearly inspired him: Machiavelli. "Thinking then whence it can arise that in those ancient times peoples were more lovers of freedom than these, I believe it arises from the same cause that makes men less strong now, which I believe is the difference between our education and the ancient, founded on the difference between our religion and the ancient," writes Machiavelli in the *Discourses on Livy*. "For our religion, having shown the truth and the true way, makes us esteem less the honor of the world, whereas the Gentiles, esteeming it very much and having placed the highest good in it, were more ferocious in their actions."[25]

In sum, the analysis of religions in relation to society and especially in terms of politics, ends with an aporia.[26] Of the three available alternatives, the "religion of the citizen" is untrue but useful, the "religion of man" is true but not useful, and the "religion of the priest" is both untrue and not useful. Does Rousseau's turn to a "purely civil profession of faith" constitute a solution?

THE PURELY CIVIL PROFESSION OF FAITH

"But leaving aside political considerations, let us return to right and determine what principles obtain concerning this important point" (IV.8). In this way Rousseau commences his concluding discussion of civil religion. I take the "important point" to be the consideration with which he ended the historical sketch and transitioned to his analysis of the available alternatives of religion from the perspective of politics: that no state has ever been founded without religion as a base, contra Bayle, and that Christianity is more harmful than useful for the constitution of a state, contra Warburton. In other words, Rousseau's state needs religion, given the motivational problem facing any polity. Yet, that religion cannot be any form of Christianity, despite its truth in the pure form. And a return to the religion of the citizen seen among the ancients would appear to be impossible in the present circumstances in Rousseau's estimation, and in any case undesirable.

The way in which he commences his discussion of civil religion indicates that the first question to be answered is what "principles" obtain concerning religion according to "right"—that is, according to the principles of political right as defined in his political treatise. "The right the social compact gives to the sovereign over the subjects does not, as I have said, exceed the bounds of public utility. The subjects therefore do not owe the sovereign an account of their opinions except insofar as those opinions matter to the community." Such is the limit. "Now, it is certainly important to the state that each citizen have a religion which makes him love his duties, but the dogmas of that religion are of no interest either to the state or its members except insofar as those dogmas relate to morality and to the duties which anyone who professes it is bound to fulfill toward others" (IV.8). The unstated premise here is stated in the *Letter to Beaumont*: "It is because it is assumed that what men believe determines their morality, and that their conduct in this life is dependent on their idea about the life to come" (56). Beyond opinions relating to morality, the state has no need or right to know, provided the subjects are "good citizens" in this life (IV.8). The "purely civil profession of faith" Rousseau is about to articulate must be confined within the bounds determined by right.

"There is, therefore, a purely civil profession of faith whose articles it belongs to the sovereign to determine, not precisely as dogmas of religion but as sentiments of sociability, without which it is impossible to be a good citizen or a loyal subject." Several things should be noted about this sentence. First, it is the sovereign—the people itself—which determines the articles of this profession of faith. Whatever the role of the lawgiver, of whom there is no mention here, civil religion is a matter of self-legislation of the citizens binding themselves as subjects. Second, these dogmas are less dogmas than "sentiments of sociability," which seems to be a gloss of what he wrote in the previous paragraph: "Those dogmas relate to morality and to the duties which anyone who professes it is bound to fulfill toward others." If our actions are determined by our opinions or "sentiments," then the dogmas must reach to the heart. Third, such sentiments are necessary to be a "good citizen" and a "loyal subject." These relate to the two main motivational challenges facing politics: how to make a people capable of self-legislation ("good citizens") and inclined to obey the laws they make ("loyal subjects"). As Bernardi remarks, "This restatement of dogmas of civil religion as sentiments of sociability implies that they are settled on not as a function of their truth but of their utility."[27]

No one can "obligate" the citizens to believe these dogmas, Rousseau explains. This for two reasons. First, belief or opinion is not something that can be obligated by its very nature. Second, obligation in the political context can come only from law. All the law can do is obligate the subject to profess these dogmas and, more importantly, to act in accordance with them. The state can banish anyone who does not believe them, or more precisely he who refuses to profess them. "It may banish him, not as impious but as unsociable, as incapable of sincerely loving the laws, justice, and if need be of sacrificing his life to his duty." Here we are back to the motivational problem, which was how Rousseau began the original draft of the chapter: the state may require the citizens to sacrifice their lives. Finally, if anyone publicly acknowledges these dogmas and then behaves as though he does not believe them, "let him be punished with death. He has committed the greatest of crimes: he has lied before the laws" (IV.8). The dogmas are promulgated as a law made by the sovereign, and laws have sanctions. Like all other laws, the cognizance of the state is restricted to actions—in this case, public profession and actions—and does not extend to private beliefs. That said, the threats of banishment and death for not professing these dogmas are what especially has led to charges against Rousseau that the requirements of a "purely civil profession of faith," as minimalist as it might be, introduce a heteronomous element into his theory at odds with the freedom and autonomy upon which he insists or that this required profession reveals the illiberal or even totalitarian thrust of his thought.

What are the dogmas that must be professed? "The dogmas of the civil religion should be simple, few in number, stated with precision, without explanation or commentaries." This is the sole use of the term "civil religion" in the chapter "On Civil Religion." And Rousseau is good to his word concerning the lack of explanation or commentary on the dogmas, the "positive" ones at least. There are four "positive dogmas" (by my enumeration) and one "negative" one:

1. The existence of a powerful, intelligent, beneficent, foresighted, and provident divinity;
2. The life to come;
3. The happiness of the just, the punishment of the wicked;
4. The sanctity of the social contract and the laws;
5. The prohibition of intolerance.

Rousseau simply lists the first four dogmas in a single sentence, with commas rather than the semicolons I have just employed. Most scholars would probably agree with David Williams that these dogmas are "logically linked."[28] However, as Charles Griswold notes, "Rousseau says nothing explicitly about how these dogmas are related, and it is unclear whether the order in which he lists them is ordinal (though the first would indeed seem naturally placed before the second and third)." Further, among other things, Griswold notes that Rousseau's laconic phrasing renders the third article ambiguous: Are the just happy and the wicked punished in this life, as a consequence of their very justice or wickedness, or will they be so in the life to come, as a reward or compensation for what happens in this life?[29] We saw a similar ambiguity in the "Profession of Faith" concerning the life to come.

Let us begin with the obvious. As Griswold emphasizes, "It is important to note that Rousseau says not a word to show that the first three of these dogmas are *true*; indeed, he does not even assert here that the positive dogmas are true."[30] In fact, when defending the chapter, Rousseau goes as far as to say that "what is at issue here is not at all to consider religions as true or false, nor even as good or bad in themselves, but to consider them uniquely in relation to political bodies and as parts of legislation" (*Mountain*, 147). Whatever their truth, the dogmas of civil religion are promulgated as useful.

That the first three positive dogmas are strikingly similar to the articles of faith found in the "Profession of Faith" has not escaped notice, and I will return to the question of the relationship between the "Profession" and the chapter "On Civil Religion." What has also not escaped notice is that there is no equivalent in the Vicar's speech to the fourth dogma: the sanctity of the social contract and the laws.[31] What does Rousseau mean by the "sanctity" of the social contract and the laws? Earlier I discussed an instance of him speaking of the "sanctity of the contract," when discussing the reason the sovereign cannot alienate any part of itself or subject itself to another power (I.7), and also mentioned a passage where he states that "the social order is a sacred right that serves as the basis for all the others. Yet this right does not come from nature; it is therefore based on conventions" (I.1). I concluded that the social contract itself is somehow "sacred" or "sanctified," and, more importantly, that it does not receive that character from nature, much less the divinity. What, then, about the dogma of civil religion concerning the "sanctity" of the social contract and the laws? Although it is listed after the first three dogmas concerning the existence of the divinity, the life to come, and the happiness of the just and punishment of the wicked, this fourth dogma does not seem to follow logically from them. To begin, the first three dogmas are universalistic theological dogmas consistent with natural religion, whereas the fourth dogma is particularistic, the sanctity of the social contract and laws of a particular political association. The fourth dogma is political, not theological. If so, then the social contract and laws do not get their "sanctified" status from the divinity, but, as with the other instances discussed above, from the social compact itself. As Guénard explains, "It is before the laws, not before God, that they engage themselves."[32]

The fifth dogma prohibiting intolerance does receive commentary by Rousseau. First, he states that intolerance "belongs with the forms of worship we have excluded." He does not specify which forms of worship have been excluded, but he characterized both the religion of the citizen and the religion of the priest as intolerant. In turn, the religion of man, or true Christianity, is tolerant by principle, but Rousseau rejects it as the basis of the state for different reasons. Second, at the beginning of the chapter, when speaking of polytheism, he argued that civil intolerance and theological intolerance should not be distinguished, and promised to return to the point, which he now does. Whom he has in mind who does argue that they should be distinguished he does not say.[33] "These two intolerances are inseparable. It is impossible to live in peace with people one believes are damned; to love them would be to hate God who punishes them; they absolutely must be brought into the fold or tormented. Wherever theological intolerance is allowed, it is impossible for it not to have some civil effect." Third, his exclusion of intolerance is entailed by the historical sketch of the relationship between politics and religion of the first part of the chapter. "Now that there are no longer and can no longer be an exclusive national religion, all those which tolerate all the others should be tolerated insofar as their dogmas contain nothing contrary to the duties of the citizen" (IV.8). Christianity, in both its actual and "true" forms, has made exclusive national religions impossible, but Rousseau borrows from the genuine religion of the Gospel the principled tolerance for the civil religion he propounds.

What are we to make of Rousseau's civil religion, including in terms of truth and utility? A number of interpreters suggest that his civil religion is an attempt to combine the positive features of the religion of the citizen and the religion of man, and therefore to combine truth with utility. For example, Céline Spector emphasizes that religion for Rousseau is ultimately a matter of utility, moral utility in the case of the "Profession" and political utility in the case of civil religion. As for civil religion, she explains: "Once again, Rousseau acts as a modern critic of modernity: he intends to delineate a new civil religion for the Moderns."[34] Such an interpretation has a strong but ultimately questionable advocate in Rousseau himself. In the original version of the chapter on civil religion, Rousseau includes a paragraph in the concluding discussion of intolerance missing from the final version, which reads in part: "Thus the advantages of the religion of man and the religion of the citizen will be combined. The state will have its cult and will not be the enemy of anyone else's. With divine and human laws being always united on the same object, the most pious theists will also be the most zealous citizens, and the defense of the holy laws will be the glory of the God of men" ("Geneva Manuscript," *CW*, 4:122).[35] Yet this passage is missing from the definitive version. So, too, is the optimistic tone.

A related interpretive question concerns the relationship between the chapter "On Civil Religion" and the "Profession of Faith," an issue I promised I would address. As I noted, the first three "positive dogmas" of the civil profession of faith are very similar to the articles of faith advanced by the Vicar. Some interpreters have therefore seen the civil religion of the *Social Contract* and the natural religion of the "Profession" as largely congruent and argue that Rousseau's aim is to combine the universalism of natural religion with the particularism of national religions, with the question being how successfully.[36] Others have pointed in particular to the fourth positive dogma, the one concerning the sanctity of the social contract and the laws, as an indication that the chapter "On Civil Religion" and the "Profession" are incompatible. Under this interpretation these two different religions serve the very different aims of forming "citizens" in the case of the *Social Contract* and forming "men" in the case of *Emile* and the "Profession."[37] One important difference between the two treatments of religion is nonetheless clear: the articles of faith propounded by the Vicar are left to the judgment of his audience, whether the young proselyte or the reader of *Emile*, as matters of belief, whereas, by contrast, the dogmas of the "purely civil profession of faith" are imposed as legally binding and subject to punishment for noncompliance.[38] Perhaps ironically, then, Rousseau's seeming softening of the articles of the civil profession of faith by characterizing them as "sentiments of sociability" actually hardens them, for it authorizes the sword of justice.

Conclusion

Rousseau's civil religion faces at least two challenges, without even talking about the potential dangers it may pose theoretically (heteronomy) and practically (illiberality). First, can the universalism of the first three dogmas, which are effectively those of natural religion, be combined with the particularism of the fourth dogma, a particularism Rousseau argues is necessary for any civil association? Will the universalism ultimately undermine the particularism, or vice versa? Of course, this tension runs through Rousseau's entire political theory in the form of the inevitable tension between the particular will we have as natural individuals and the general will we have as citizens. The motivational problem of politics that civil religion and other extralegal institutions are meant to address remains just that: a problem.

Second, how can his theory avoid the fate he assigned to Hobbes's attempt to reunify the two heads of the eagle due to the "domineering spirit of Christianity"? More broadly, the historical sketch of the relationship between politics and religion that Rousseau provides before addressing the available alternatives we face and before offering his civil religion as what is possible within the scope of the principles of political right and the historical context reveals the limits of finding a solution. If Christianity is here to stay for the foreseeable future, then it poses a constant challenge to the creation and maintenance of a legitimate state in both its "true" but impossible form and its "false" but actual forms. In conclusion, then, I am inclined to agree with Blaise Bachofen when he says of Rousseau's civil religion that rather than solving the theologico-political problem it should be considered as revealing it as an "impossible problem."[39]

Conclusion

In this study I have explored the relationship between Rousseau's philosophy of the natural goodness of man and his corruption in society, on the one hand, and his theological and religious thought, on the other. I have argued that there is not a straightforward relationship between these two subjects, with, for example, his justification of nature and nature's god through his doctrine of the natural goodness of man somehow leading logically to the theological and religious views he propounds, largely in the mouth of the Savoyard Vicar and not in his own name. In fact, I have stressed the tensions between these two subjects and have sought to explain the source of these tensions. My exploration has revolved around two oppositions. The first opposition involves the differing needs and attributes of *natural man* and *social or moral man*, and I have argued that Rousseau's solution to the problem of evil, and therewith his justification of nature, extends only to natural man, and that this justification does not suffice for perfected and therefore corrupted human beings, except under the most exceptional of cases. The second opposition follows from the first opposition. Namely, Rousseau states that theological and religious doctrines and practices must be judged according to two criteria, criteria that may not be in accord: *truth* and *utility*. I have argued that the theological and religious views he expresses throughout his writings, whether in his own name or in the voice of the Savoyard Vicar or others, are offered by him as less *true* than *useful*. They are propounded as *useful* in various ways depending on the context: psychologically, morally, or politically. The consistent intention of offering useful teachings in his writings on theology and religion explains the tension between these writings and the core philosophical principle of the natural goodness of man.

Let me conclude this book by returning to the extraordinary final note Rousseau adds to the "Profession of Faith" in his role as editor, a note I discussed in chapter 6, but do so here to illustrate the broad concerns of his philosophy and his mission as a writer. The note is added to a passage at the very end of the Vicar's speech in which he counsels the young proselyte to flee the "dispiriting doctrines" of the modern philosophers, who, "overturning, destroying, and trampling on all that men respect . . . , deprive the afflicted of the last consolation of their misery and the powerful and rich of the only brake on their passions." Their doctrines cannot be true, claims the Vicar, because the truth is never harmful to men (*Emile*, 312). This passage captures the crux of my entire argument in this book. On the one hand, Rousseau and the Vicar both battle the philosophers because of the effects of what they both characterize as their materialism and atheism. Their doctrines are "dispiriting," undermine "all that men respect"—that is, popular opinions and beliefs—and banish salutary or useful beliefs that console the oppressed and check the wicked. Rousseau may agree that these doctrines may not be true, but his emphasis is on utility. On the other hand, whereas the Vicar claims these inimical effects prove these doctrines cannot be true, Rousseau is not so sanguine.

The issue of truth and utility is central to the note he adds to the Vicar's claim about salutary effects of the truth in which Rousseau launches his own assault on the philosophers. The "philosophic party" attacks religious fanaticism, as does Rousseau, although for fairness' sake he puts in a good word for it: "Fanaticism, although sanguinary and cruel, is nevertheless a grand and strong passion which elevates the heart of man." The philosophic spirit is one of "secret egoism" and "indifference," a spirit that saps our concern for virtue, in part by undermining the popular opinions and beliefs that ground the virtues of man and citizen. "From the point of view of principles," he states, "there is nothing that philosophy can do well that religion does not do better, and religion does many things that philosophy could not do" (*Emile*, 312n). The "principles" he has in mind are not clear, but I suggest that he has both the cause and the effect in mind: "principles" understood as the motive causes of our action, such as the self-love and pity of the *Discourse on Inequality*, and "principles" understood as our judgment of the effects or results of the opinions and beliefs we hold as seen from the perspective of morality and politics. The judgment he renders of philosophy and religion, even of fanaticism, is pragmatic: what is useful.

The note concludes with a Persian story, the story of Poul-Serrho, on which the final judgment of the good and wicked will occur. "Should I believe that the idea of this bridge, which corrects so many iniquities, never prevents any? If one took away this idea from the Persians by persuading them that there is no Poul-Serrho or any place like it where the oppressed wreak vengeance on their tyrants after death?" The "idea"—the myth—of the bridge is useful, even if surely it is not true. Having said this, Rousseau echoes the Vicar's statement about doctrines that must be false because they are harmful only to invert it: "It is false, therefore, that this doctrine would not be harmful; it would therefore not be the truth." Put differently, contrary to the doctrine that we should always promulgate the truth against superstition because doing so cannot be harmful, dispelling the salutary myth would be harmful, so the doctrine concerning telling the truth is itself not true. "Philosopher, your moral laws are very fine, but I beg you to show me their sanction," he concludes. "Stop beating around the bush for a moment, and tell me plainly what you put in the place of Poul-Serrho" (*Emile*, 313–14n). Ultimately, then, Rousseau counsels leaving the myth despite it not being true, for philosophy offers nothing to put in its place. Thus spoke the author who adopted the motto *Vitam impendere vero*.

ACKNOWLEDGMENTS

My interest in the subject of this book began almost forty years ago when I was an undergraduate. Roger Masters first introduced me to Rousseau and encouraged me to do my honors thesis on religion in Rousseau's thought, persuaded that my announced antipathy for the thinker and the subject would propel me through the project. If only he knew how far. Joseph Cropsey and Nathan Tarcov further fostered my interest in political philosophy in graduate school. Scholars whom I greatly admire have lent more than a helping hand along the way, among them Allan Bloom, Christopher Kelly, and Ourida Mostefai. John Warner and Emma Planinc have read drafts of portions of this book and made helpful suggestions. Jonathan Dahlsten did a marvelous job of creating the index. Chuck Myers's masterful midwifing was essential to bringing my work to see the light, a process brought to completion by Sara Doskow. Throughout this entire journey has been my wife, Adrienne, whose support and love made this and everything else possible, and I gratefully dedicate this book to her.

Two chapters of this book are much-revised versions of previously published works. Chapter 2 is based on "The Theodicy of the *Second Discourse*: The 'Pure State of Nature' and Rousseau's Political Thought," *American Political Science Review* 86 (1992): 686–711. Chapter 3 is based on "Pride and Providence: Religion in Rousseau's *Letter to Voltaire*," in *Rousseau and l'Infâme: Religion, Toleration, and Fanaticism in the Age of Enlightenment*, ed. Ourida Mostefai and John T. Scott (Amsterdam: Rodopi, 2009), 115–36.

NOTES

Introduction

1. Rousseau to the Marquise de Créqui, June 7, 1762, CC, 11:38–39. See Zaretsky and Scott, *Philosophers' Quarrel*, 29–30.
2. For the best work on the natural goodness of man in Rousseau, see Melzer, *Natural Goodness of Man*.
3. See, e.g., Warner, *Rousseau and the Problem of Human Relations*.
4. Cassirer, *Philosophy of the Enlightenment*, 137–53. See Neiman, *Evil in Modern Thought*.
5. See Cassirer, *Question of Jean-Jacques Rousseau*.
6. Cassirer, *Philosophy of the Enlightenment*, 154–55.
7. Augustine, *Confessions*, VIII.7–8, 12.
8. Another parallel to Augustine's reading of the Gospels occurs at the end of book VIII, where Rousseau relates that he resolved to withdraw from Paris and the corrupting effects of his friends, the *philosophes*, who had shaken his beliefs. In this context, he states that his reading of the Gospels had led him to see in them the true moral doctrines, or what we will see in chapter 1 he describes as equivalent to the natural religion accessible by reason alone, and to reject the rest (*Confessions*, CW, 5:329). In this case he joins Augustine in appreciating the Gospels but takes this appreciation in the entirely opposite direction.
9. Pascal, *Pensées*, no. 164 [42].
10. On the general will, see Bertram, "Rousseau's Legacy in Two Conceptions of the General Will."
11. E.g., Dent, *Rousseau*.
12. Brooke, *Philosophic Pride*.
13. Israel, *Radical Enlightenment*, 269. See 717–20.
14. Israel, 720.
15. Starobinski, *Transparency and Obstruction*, 6, 12–13, 182, 198.
16. Kavanagh, *Writing the Truth*, 55, 154–55.
17. Taylor, *Ethics of Authenticity*, chap. 3, and *Sources of the Self*, 362–63; Berman, *Politics of Authenticity*; Neidleman, *Rousseau's Ethics of Truth*, esp. chap. 3.
18. Grimsley, *Rousseau and the Religious Quest*, 52.
19. Burgelin, Introduction to *Emile*, OC, 4:cxxiv.
20. E.g., metaphysical dualism: Douglass, "Free Will and the Problem of Evil"; O'Hagan. "Taking Rousseau Seriously," 83. Freedom: Cassirer, *Question of Jean-Jacques Rousseau*, esp.

118; Douglass, "Free Will and the Problem of Evil"; MacLean, *Free Animal*. Sociability: Burgelin, *Philosophie de l'existence de J.-J. Rousseau*, 239; Derathé, *Rationalisme de J.-J. Rousseau*, 14, 81. Conscience: Cooper, *Rousseau, Nature, and the Problem of the Good Life*, 4–11; Dent, *Rousseau*, 229; Williams, *Rousseau's Platonic Enlightenment*, 73–76.

21. Masters, *Political Philosophy of Rousseau*, 56ff.

22. E.g., De Man, *Allegories of Reading*, 226; Emberley, "Rousseau versus the Savoyard Vicar"; Meier, *On the Happiness of the Philosophic Life*, esp. 224.

23. E.g., Cooper, *Rousseau, Nature, and the Problem of the Good Life*, 84–89; Masson, *Religion de J.-J. Rousseau*, 167; Masters, *Political Philosophy of Rousseau*, 54–55; Williams, *Rousseau's Platonic Enlightenment*, 63.

24. For Habermas, see *Structural Transformation of the Public Sphere*.

25. Brant, *Eighteenth-Century Letters and British Culture*, 5.

26. King, *Writing to the World*, 4.

27. See Spacks, *Privacy*.

28. King, *Writing to the World*, 7–8. I wish to thank Caroline Winterer for her guidance.

29. See Smith, "Naming the Un-'Familiar.'"

30. Notably Masters, *Political Philosophy of Rousseau*, chap. 5; Meier, *On the Happiness of the Philosophic Life*; Melzer, *Philosophy between the Lines*, 141, 274–75; Strauss, "On the Intention of Rousseau." See Kelly's discussion of the issue in *Rousseau as Author*, 142–54.

31. Rousseau's importance and influence in theology are signaled by Karl Barth, perhaps the most influential Protestant theologian of the twentieth century, in the title of his book: *Protestant Thought from Rousseau to Ritschl*.

Chapter 1

1. For a summary of the scholarly debate, see Scott, *Rousseau's Reader*, 27 and n1.

2. See Strauss, *Natural Right and History* (255–63) for a similar interpretation. I appear to have unconsciously absorbed his use of the term "disproportion" in this regard (261).

3. Henceforth in this section all references in the text are to the *Discourse on the Sciences and the Arts* (*Sciences*) unless otherwise noted.

4. For examinations of the complex argument of the *Discourse on the Sciences and the Arts*, see esp. Campbell and Scott, "Politic Argument"; Scott, *Rousseau's Reader*, chap. 1.

5. See *Reply [by the King of Poland]*, in *CW*, 2:29; *Refutation of the Observations* [Lecat], in *CW*, 2:56–57; *Refutation by an Academician* [Lecat], in *CW*, 2:134, 171–72.

6. In an early essay predating the *Discourse*, "Idée de la méthode dans la composition d'un livre," Rousseau states that one should begin one's argument by appearing to agree with accepted opinion (*OC*, 2:1242–44). See Goldschmidt (*Anthropologie et politique*, 21ff.) for a reading of the *Discourse* that takes this early essay for its guide. See also Yamashita, *Rousseau face au publique*, 39–40.

7. For a fuller analysis of how Rousseau proceeds in the *Discourse*, see Scott, *Rousseau's Reader*, chap. 1.

8. See Masters, *Political Philosophy of Rousseau*, chap. 5.

9. For a sustained analysis of the *Observations* as a whole, see Tully and Scott, "Rousseau's *Observations*," on which the following discussion draws in part.

10. For the same distinction between the few truly learned and the people, see also *Letter to Grimm* (*CW*, 1:85), *Final Reply* (*CW*, 1:111), and "Preface" to *Narcissus* (*CW*, 1:191, 194–95).

11. Both Kelly (*Rousseau as Author*, 142–54) and Melzer (*Philosophy between the Lines*, 112–13, 141, 274–75) point to this passage among others as evidence that Rousseau himself

also wrote esoterically. In turn, Williams takes it to be a criticism of esotericism (*Rousseau's Platonic Enlightenment*, 64).

12. A probable source for what Rousseau claims about the "interior doctrine," including the argument that the Chinese also practiced it, is Pierre Bayle's article "Spinoza" (Remark B) for the *Historical Critical Dictionary*.

13. Juvenal, *Satires* 4.91. Rousseau first uses this motto, and so translates it, in his *Letter to d'Alembert* (*CW*, 10:348n).

14. Henceforth in this section all references in the text are to the *Reveries of the Solitary Walker* (*Reveries*) unless otherwise noted.

15. See Plutarch, *Life of Solon*, sect. 2, 31.

16. See Butterworth, "Interpretative Essay" (esp. 181–89) for this observation and a useful analysis of these two "Walks." See also Gourevitch, "Rousseau on Lying"; Meier, *On the Happiness of the Philosophic Life*, 59–62. Williams (*Rousseau's Platonic Enlightenment*, 64) disputes this reading of the two walks, suggesting that they are separate and should not be read together, and also argues that Rousseau is opposed to esoteric readings.

17. Butterworth, "Interpretative Essay," 173.

18. See Black, *Rousseau's Critique of Science*, 146–50; Kavanagh, *Writing the Truth*, 125–29; Masters, *Political Philosophy of Rousseau*, 225–26. For my own discussion of the frontispiece to the *Discourse on the Sciences and the Arts*, see Scott, *Rousseau's Reader*, 36–42.

19. Rousseau's discussion of injurious lies and noninjurious or even salutary lies can be usefully compared to Socrates's treatment of lying in Plato's *Republic*. Saying to Adeimantus that all gods and humans "hate the true lie [*alēthōs pseudos*], if that expression can be used," Socrates explains to his confused interlocutor that a "true lie" is a falsehood that is injurious to the soul, and that this "would most correctly be called truly a lie—the ignorance in the soul of the man who has been lied to" (2.382a-b). Of course, Socrates will later say that the city will require a "noble lie" (*pseudos gennaios*), which is justified because it unifies the city and makes it just (3.414b-15d).

20. Interestingly, the "magnanimous lie" in Tasso's *Jerusalem Delivered* (2.22) is on a religious theme: the Christ-like sacrifice of the maiden Sophronia, who falsely takes responsibility for a desecration to save her fellow Christians, for which she is condemned by the Muslim prince of Jerusalem to be burned at the stake.

21. Henceforth in this section all references in the text are to the *Letter to Beaumont* (*Beaumont*) unless otherwise noted.

22. Rousseau employed the same strategy a few years earlier in his *Letter to d'Alembert*, identifying himself as the simple "Citizen of Geneva" as against d'Alembert and all his memberships in illustrious academies.

23. For a useful summary of the context of the *Letter to Beaumont* and insightful analysis of Rousseau's polemical stance, see Mostefai, *Jean-Jacques Rousseau, écrivain polémique*, chap. 4.

24. O'Hagan does not notice the distinction Rousseau maintains here between himself and the Vicar, and instead takes him to be equating them: "Although Rousseau puts the 'Profession of Faith' in the mouth of a fictional character, he makes it clear in the *Letter to Beaumont* that it represents his own views," citing this passage as evidence (*Rousseau*, 238).

25. Hobbes, *On the Citizen* (*De Cive*), 1.2 and addendum.

26. Rousseau to Sidoine-Charles-François Séguier, marquis de Saint-Brisson, July 22, 1764, *CC*, 20:315.

27. Rousseau to Ferdinand-Olivier Petitpierre, July 1763, *CC*, 20:279–80.

28. Waterlot remarks: "In one sense, the pure Evangel has at its disposal an advantage over natural religion because it is a concrete illustration of it and because Jesus, a divine and

sublime man, can constitute a model, a perceptible figure to which one directs one's conduct" ("Discours des prosélytes du vicaire," 56).

29. Bernardi emphasizes the centrality of exercising one's own reason without any other authority to Rousseau's "spirit of the Reformation" as well as his conscious departure from the historical facts ("Christianisme de Jean-Jacques Rousseau," 68–73).

30. See Waterlot, "Discours des prosélytes du vicaire," 53–58.

Chapter 2

1. Henceforth in this chapter all references in the text are to the *Discourse on Inequality* (*Inequality*) unless otherwise noted.

2. See esp. Velkley, *Freedom and the End of Reason*.

3. Kant, "Remarks," 96.

4. Kant, "Remarks," 104–5.

5. Kant, "Conjectural Beginning of Human History," 169; emphasis original.

6. Cassirer, *Question of Jean-Jacques Rousseau*, 75–76, 104–6, 96. Cassirer's argument is based mainly on his interpretation of *Emile* and the *Social Contract*, for he claims (56–57) that Rousseau abandoned the naturalistic account of the *Discourse on Inequality* and its thesis that historical progress was a decline, and instead "decided unconditionally for 'spirit' and against nature," making the "ethical will" primary. See also Cassirer, *Philosophy of the Enlightenment*, 153–58.

7. Neuhouser, *Rousseau's Theodicy of Self-Love*. See especially his clear sketch of the argument in the introduction. Cladis (*Public Vision, Private Lives*, 81, 111–13) offers an analogous argument, suggesting that Rousseau's depiction in the *Discourse on Inequality* of the state of nature amounts to a "scientific theodicy," but that in later works, for example, the *Letter to Voltaire*, he seeks the source of evil in free will. Cladis sees Rousseau as uneasily combining "Enlightenment optimism" (the "scientific theodicy") and "Augustinian pessimism" (the source of evil in free will) (*Public Vision, Private Lives*, esp. chap. 6).

8. E.g., Colletti, *From Rousseau to Lenin*; Horowitz, *Rousseau, Nature, and History*; Rapaczynski, *Nature and Politics*.

9. E.g., Masters, *Political Philosophy of Rousseau*, 113–15. See Plato, *Republic* 10.611b–d.

10. See Descartes, *Discourse on the Method*, Part 5, beginning; *The World*, chaps. 6–7 (in *Philosophical Writings*, 1:90–98). See Goldschmidt, *Anthropologie et politique*, 132–33.

11. See Cooper, *Rousseau, Nature, and the Problem of the Good Life*, 39; Masters, *Political Philosophy of Rousseau*, 106–18; Goldschmidt, *Anthropologie et politique*; Plattner, *Rousseau's State of Nature*, 17–25, 31–34; Strauss, *Natural Right and History*, 267n32.

12. E.g., O'Hagan characterizes the pure state of nature as "an ideal type" or "thought experiment," and as a "hypothetical world" (*Rousseau*, 37, 40). See also, among others, Charvet, *Social Problem in Rousseau*, 15; Gourevitch, "Rousseau's Pure State of Nature," 32–33.

13. Neuhouser, *Rousseau's Theodicy of Self-Love*, 36, 38.

14. Neuhouser largely follows Dent, especially in his argument about *amour-propre*. Dent himself focuses more on *Emile* than the *Discourse on Inequality*, since he argues it supersedes the account in the earlier work and also because he finds it richer and more compelling, and so he has little to say about the status and function of the pure state of nature (*Rousseau*, esp. 52ff., 79–81).

15. Spector, *Rousseau*, 16–17.

16. Cooper argues that there are core attributes of human nature that still exist in the "present nature of man," but he is less interested in our physical being than those attributes that

enable humans to develop and flourish (*Rousseau, Nature, and the Problem of the Good Life*, esp. 41–47).

17. See Goldschmidt, *Anthropologie et politique*, 125–28; Masters, *Political Philosophy of Rousseau*, 118; O'Hagan, *Rousseau*, 38; Spector, *Rousseau*, 16–17.

18. Strauss explains: "Rousseau's reflection on the state of nature, in contradistinction to Hobbes's reflection, takes on the character of a 'physical' investigation" (*Natural Right and History*, 268).

19. For background on the "state of nature" and the "pure state of nature" in the natural law tradition, see Gierke, *Natural Law*, 96–105 and notes; Gourevitch, "Rousseau's Pure State of Nature," 25–33; Strauss, *Natural Right and History*, 184–85. For the original formulations, see Aquinas, *Summa theologica*, I–II, qu. 109.8, and 102.3–12, 109.2–4; Suarez, *De legibus ac Deo legislatore*, 1.3.11–12, 2.8.8–9; Hooker, *Of the Laws of Ecclesiastical Polity*, 1.10.1; Grotius, *De jure belli ac pacis*, 2.5.15, 3.7.1; Pufendorf, *De officio hominis et civis*, 2.1.1–7, and *De jure naturae et gentium*, 2.2.1–4.

20. Pufendorf, *On the Duty of Man and Citizen*, 2.1 (ed. Tully, 115).

21. Pufendorf, 2.1 (115–16).

22. See Pufendorf, *Of the Law of Nature and Nations*, 1.1.7 [ed. Kennett, 7] and 2.2 [ibid., 149–69].

23. See Goldschmidt, *Anthropologie et politique*, 177–79. See also Douglass, *Rousseau and Hobbes*, 37–46.

24. The only other scholar to discuss Castel's work and the allegedly commonplace distinction between the "physical" and the "moral" is Wokler, "Rousseau's Two Concepts of Liberty," 90–92.

25. Castel, *L'homme moral opposé à l'homme physique*, 129, 182.

26. Castel, 144–45, 263–65.

27. Castel, 136, 159–89, 316–24.

28. Castel, 167.

29. Aristotle, *Metaphysics* 12.1072a–b; *Nicomachean Ethics* 10.1176b–79a. See Goldschmidt, *Anthropologie et politique*, 243–44.

30. Hobbes, *Leviathan*, chap. 11 [57–58].

31. Locke, *Two Treatises*, 2, chap. 5.

32. See Pangle, *Spirit of Modern Republicanism*, chap. 14.

33. Pufendorf, *On the Duty of Man and Citizen*, 2.2.8; *On the Right of Nature and of Men*, 2.5.2.

34. See Derathé, *Rationalisme de J.-J. Rousseau*, 10; Rosenblatt, *Rousseau and Geneva*, 173–77.

35. Diderot, "Droit naturel," in *Oeuvres complètes*, 7:25. Diderot may be drawing on Shaftesbury for his conception of "animal goodness," as he terms it in his translation of Shaftesbury's *Inquiry Concerning Virtue and Merit* as *Principes de la philosophie morale, ou Essai de M. S*** sur le mérite et la vertu, Avec réflexions* (1745), an inscribed copy of which he gave to Rousseau. See Scott, "En vertu de la bonté."

36. Hobbes, *Leviathan*, chap. 13 [77].

37. Hobbes, *On the Citizen*, Preface to the Readers [11]. In this same context in the work Hobbes denies that he is arguing man is naturally evil.

38. See Melzer, *Natural Goodness of Man*.

39. See Dent, *Rousseau*, 109–12.

40. See Charvet, *Social Problem in the Philosophy of Rousseau*, 18–19; Masters, *Political Philosophy of Rousseau*, 156–57.

41. See Schwarze and Scott, "Mutual Sympathy and the Moral Economy."

42. Rousseau follows Buffon in distinguishing between "physical" and "moral" aspects of the sexual passion, but he develops this distinction and makes it central to his own analysis of human nature as a whole. See Goldschmidt, *Anthropologie et politique*, 268–69, 362–69.

43. See Locke, *Two Treatises*, 2.79–80. Rousseau is quoting a French translation originally published in 1691 under the title *Du gouvernement civil*, which is how Rousseau refers to the work here. The translation is generally quite accurate.

44. See esp. Dent, *Rousseau*, chaps. 2–3.

45. The most extensive study of Rousseau's abandoned work is Menin, *Morale sensitive de Rousseau*.

46. See Scott, "Rousseau and the Melodious Language of Freedom" and "'Morale sensitive' dans l'*Essai*."

Chapter 3

1. Neiman makes the Lisbon earthquake the central episode in *Evil in Modern Thought*. For Voltaire's reaction, see Besterman, "Voltaire et le désastre de Lisbonne." For a history of the Lisbon earthquake, including its reverberations in the intellectual world, see Molesky, *This Gulf of Fire*, esp. chap. 10.

2. For a detailed account of the history of Rousseau's letter, see Havens, "Voltaire, Rousseau, and the 'Lettre sur la providence,'" and Leigh, "Rousseau's Letter to Voltaire on Optimism."

3. Gourevitch, "Rousseau on Providence," 566.

4. Masson, *Religion de J.-J. Rousseau*, 2:47, 49. Masson comes to the same conclusion regarding the "Moral Letters" and *Julie* (2:54–59, 65–74).

5. E.g., Gouhier, *Méditations métaphysiques de Jean-Jacques Rousseau*, 86; Grimsley, *Rousseau and the Religious Quest*, 17–18; Hendel, *Moralist*, 1:231–32; 2:129–30.

6. Gourevitch, "Rousseau on Providence," 566. In a discussion of the spectrum of Rousseau's letters from strictly private letters on the one end to open letters such as the *Letter to d'Alembert* on the other, Leigh concludes that the *Letter to Voltaire* occupies a position near the middle, although he also states that "it is clear that, right from the start, Rousseau wanted to publish it" ("Rousseau's Letter to Voltaire on Optimism," 250).

7. Gourevitch, "Rousseau on Providence."

8. Voltaire, "Poëme sur le désastre de Lisbonne," in *Oeuvres complètes*, vol. 45A:323.

9. Voltaire, "Poëme sur le désastre de Lisbonne," 335.

10. Pope, *Essay on Man*, 1.1–2.

11. Gourevitch, "Rousseau on Providence," 578.

12. Henceforth in this chapter all references in the text are to the *Letter to Voltaire*, unless otherwise noted.

13. Voltaire, "Poëme sur le désastre de Lisbonne," 344.

14. Voltaire, "Poëme sur la loi naturelle," in *Oeuvres complètes*, vol. 32B:85.

15. Pope, *Essay on Man*, 1.16 [289–94].

16. Voltaire, "Poëme sur le désastre de Lisbonne," 341.

17. Voltaire, "Poëme sur le désastre de Lisbonne," 348.

18. Gourevitch summarizes: "The *Poem*'s clearly intended effect is, therefore, the very opposite of its ostensible aim, and Voltaire's protestations to the contrary . . . only reinforces the reader's impression that this is a poem *against* Providence" ("Rousseau on Providence," 577). Gourevitch provides a clear summary of the philosophical and theological contents of Voltaire's poem (566–79).

19. See Gourevitch, "Rousseau on Providence," 571.

20. Aristotle, *Politics* 3.6, 1278b25–30.

21. Cicero, *De senectute* 23.84. Rousseau probably quotes Cicero via Erasmus, to whom he refers in the paragraph in which this citation is found. See Erasmus, "Godly Feast," in *Ten Colloquies*, 155–58.
22. Pope, *Essay on Man*, 1.1–18.
23. Voltaire, "Poëme sur le désastre de Lisbonne," 339.
24. Voltaire, "Poëme sur le désastre de Lisbonne," 353.
25. Rousseau to François de Conzié, January 17, 1742, *CC*, 1:132–39.
26. See Gourevitch, "Rousseau on Providence," 580–82.
27. Voltaire, "Poëme sur le désastre de Lisbonne," 346. The image of weighing reasons in a scale is drawn from Bayle's article "Buridan" in the *Historical Critical Dictionary*.
28. Voltaire, *Éléments de la philosophie de Newton*, pt. 3, chap. 6. Both Voltaire and Rousseau may also have been familiar with d'Alembert's recent contribution to the theory of celestial mechanics in the *Traité de dynamique* (1753) as a dynamic rather than a static system of forces, including advancing what is now known as "D'Alembert's Principle."
29. Voltaire, "Poëme sur le désastre de Lisbonne," 325.
30. Voltaire, "Poëme sur le désastre de Lisbonne," 337.
31. Voltaire, "Poëme sur le désastre de Lisbonne," 341.
32. Cicero, *De senectute*, 23.84–85.
33. See the similar separation in Locke, *Reasonableness of Christianity*, §228; and Leibniz, *Theodicy*, 2nd Part, §217.
34. Shklar, *Men and Citizens*, xiii.
35. As we shall see, Rousseau will analogize the order of the universe due to change to the composition of Voltaire's *Henriade* to chance. In the *Pensées philosophiques* Diderot uses the *Iliad* as his example. The argument and analogy go back to at least Cicero in his *De natura deorum*.
36. For the "Profession of Faith," see below chapter 5. In the letter to Franquières he uses the *Aeneid* as the example, and while he acknowledges that the outcome of the order of the universe coming about by chance is "not impossible," he says that the "internal sentiment" cannot believe it (January 15/March 25, 1769, *CW*, 8:264).
37. Gourevitch notes that Bayle argues: "Proofs of sentiment settle nothing. . . . Every people is imbued with proofs of sentiment for its religion; they are therefore more often false than truth" ("Rousseau on Providence," 599n68, quoting Bayle's *Continuation des pensées diverses sur le comète*).
38. Gourevitch, "Rousseau on Providence," 596.

Chapter 4

1. Henceforth in this section all references in the text are to the *Discourse on Inequality* (*Inequality*) unless otherwise noted.
2. Quoted in Goldschmidt, *Anthropologie et politique*, 267n50.
3. Quoted in Goldschmidt, 267n51.
4. See Douglass, "Free Will and the Problem of Evil," and *Rousseau and Hobbes*, 76–82; MacLean, *Free Animal*, esp. chap. 1; O'Hagan, "Taking Rousseau Seriously." Kantian interpretations also place emphasis on freedom, but without any metaphysical claims (e.g., Cassirer, *Question of Jean-Jacques Rousseau*). For scholars who argue Rousseau abandons freedom for a metaphysically neutral claim about perfectibility, see Masters, *Political Philosophy of Rousseau*, 69–71; Plattner, *Rousseau's State of Nature*, 43–46; Strauss, *Natural Right and History*, 265–66.
5. E.g., O'Hagan, *Rousseau*, esp. chap. 1.
6. Goldschmidt, *Anthropologie et politique*, 281–83, 350–56. Shklar characterizes Rous-

seau's conception of free will as a "logical" rather than "metaphysical" question, meaning by "logical" something like what I have termed "phenomenological" (*Men and Citizens*, 70–71). Similarly, Horowitz writes: "If Rousseau does assert that what separates human life from other animal life is 'free agency,' this distinction is not elevated to the status of an ontological dualism" (*Rousseau, Nature, and History*, 64).

7. That *perfectibilité* is Rousseau's neologism is supported by the Littré *Dictionnaire de la langue française*, and is generally accepted by scholars.

8. See Goldschmidt, *Anthropologie et politique*, 292.

9. See Pufendorf, *The Whole Duty of Man According to the Law of Man*, 1.3.7–8, and *De jure naturae et gentium*, 2.3.15.

10. Spector, *Rousseau*, 22.

11. See Goldschmidt, *Anthropologie et politique*, 296–97.

12. Hobbes, *Leviathan*, chap. 8 [41].

13. Hume, *Treatise of Human Nature*, 3.3.3.

14. Charvet makes the connection between the "consciousness" of freedom and self-consciousness, but suggests that natural man must therefore have some form of self-consciousness (*Social Problem in the Philosophy of Rousseau*, 10–11).

15. Henceforth in this section all references in the text are to *Emile* unless otherwise noted.

16. Rousseau to Philibert Cramer, October 13, 1764, *CC*, 21:248.

17. There is a lively debate over whether Emile is educated to be a "man" alone or to be a "citizen" as well, whether a citizen of a legitimate polity such as is described in the *Social Contract* or in a more attenuated sense. This debate is beyond my present purpose.

18. Numerous interpreters have emphasized that unity of soul or wholeness is Rousseau's objective, in *Emile* and throughout his writings. E.g., see Melzer, *Natural Goodness of Man*; Scott, "Theodicy of the *Second Discourse*."

19. A view shared by Burgelin, *Philosophie de l'existence*, 361. He also points to *Julie* as the practical application of the theory.

20. Hanley, "Rousseau's Virtue Epistemology."

21. O'Hagan, "Morale sensitive de Jean-Jacques Rousseau," 344–45. O'Hagan argues that, as a psychologist, Rousseau "adheres to a psychological modern closer to monism than dualism," but that "as a moralist, by contrast, Rousseau tends to accept a dualist metaphysics of substances," drawing most of his evidence from the "Profession of Faith."

22. On natural man in the pure state of nature as a formal model of psychic unity, see Scott, "Theodicy of the *Second Discourse*." On the development of "civilized naturalness" and the argument that there are two criteria for assessing developed humans, psychic unity and expansiveness, see Cooper, *Rousseau, Nature, and the Problem of the Good Life*.

23. In the *Dialogues* he distinguishes between two types of "sensitivity" or "sensibility" (*sensibilité*): first, "a purely passive physical and organic sensitivity which seems to have as its end only the preservation of our bodies and of our species through the direction of pleasure and pain," and, second, "another sensitivity that I call active and moral which is nothing other than the faculty of attaching our affections to beings who are foreign to us," which can take both positive and negative forms, especially in the case of *amour-propre* (*CW*, 1:112–13).

24. A point also noted by Lenne-Cornuez, *Etre à sa place*, 386.

25. Cooper treats Rousseau's conception of the conscience as a form of sublimation of the primitive principles of *amour de soi* and pity (*Rousseau, Nature, and the Problem of the Good Life*, 4–11, 80–105). Shklar also discusses it in terms of an expansion of self-love through an erotic force (*Men and Citizens*, 61).

26. E.g., Douglass, "Free Will and the Problem of Evil," 655.

27. Horowitz devotes an interesting chapter to the subject titled "*Julie* and the Pathology of Conscience" (*Rousseau, Nature, and History*, chap. 6).

28. As Lenne-Cornuez argues (*Etre à sa place*, 383–84).

29. E.g., Cooper, *Rousseau, Nature, and the Problem of the Good Life*, 86–89; Hendel, *Moralist*, vol. 1, chap. 12; Masson, *Religion de Jean-Jacques Rousseau*, 54–59; Williams, *Rousseau's Platonic Enlightenment*, 74–76. Shklar goes so far as to claim it contains "the clearest and most reliable account of Rousseau's real beliefs" (*Men and Citizens*, 229–30), although she also remarks on the distance between the "Moral Letters" and the "Profession" (xiv).

30. Hence Philonenko states: "These letters are, at bottom, destined for Jean-Jacques Rousseau himself, much more so than for the 'generous Sophie'" (*Jean-Jacques Rousseau et la pensée du malheur*, 2:250).

31. As Shklar suggests (*Men and Citizens*, 120).

32. A similar passage is found in the Favre version of *Emile* within the Vicar's own speech (*OC*, 4:220).

33. As also noted by Gouhier, *Méditations métaphysiques de Jean-Jacques Rousseau*, 172.

Chapter 5

1. For the assumption about different dates of composition, see esp. Jimack, *La Genèse et la rédaction de l'Emile*. For more recent studies of the composition of the work, see Bernardi, Gittler, and Swenson, editors' introduction to Rousseau, *Emile, Premières versions (manuscrits Favre)*.

2. See Masson, *Religion de J.-J. Rousseau*, 65–75. For Julie's profession, see *Julie*, 6.11, *CW*, 6:586–88.

3. Gouhier, *Méditations métaphysiques de Jean-Jacques Rousseau*, 85, 89. Grimsley calls the "Profession" "a true synthesis of his belief" (*Rousseau and the Religious Quest*, 24). Williams argues that the Vicar's views are congruent with what Rousseau writes in his own voice and rejects those who suggest otherwise (*Rousseau's Platonic Enlightenment*, 62–64). See also Dickstein, "Faith of a Vicar"; Hendel, *Moralist*, 2:139–62; O'Hagan, *Rousseau*, chaps. 11–12; Viroli, *Jean-Jacques Rousseau and the Well-Ordered Society*, esp. 17–29.

4. E.g., in his editor's introduction to the Pléiade edition of *Emile*, Burgelin comments: "He sought to attenuate his responsibility" by presenting himself as the "editor" of the "Profession" (*OC*, 4:cxxxiv).

5. E.g.: Dent states: "Although Rousseau puts the 'Profession of Faith' in the mouth of a fictional character, he makes it clear in the *Letter to Beaumont* that it represents his own views" (*Rousseau*, 238). Douglass claims: "Although this is done through the mouthpiece of the Savoyard Vicar, Rousseau's autobiographical writings clarify that the 'Profession of Faith' represented his own views" ("Free Will and the Problem of Evil," 646n). Gouhier asserts "this priest is the spokesperson for Rousseau" (*Méditations métaphysiques de Jean-Jacques Rousseau*, 35); Grimsley the Vicar is Rousseau's "mouth-piece" (*Rousseau and the Religious Quest*, 1, 37); O'Hagan, Rousseau conceals his views "behind a *persona ficta*" (*Rousseau*, 250). See also Masson, *Religion de J.-J. Rousseau*, esp. 119, 161.

6. E.g., Cooper, *Rousseau, Nature, and the Problem of the Good Life*, esp. 84; Menin, *Morale sensitive*, chap. 3.

7. Masters, *Political Philosophy of Rousseau*, 56ff.

8. Brooke, *Philosophic Pride*, chap. 8. O'Hagan advances a similar developmental argument (*Rousseau*, esp. chaps. 1 and 12). Vargas voices surprise at the apparent contradictions and concludes that the divergences center on the Vicar's argument that man was made to be sociable

and Rousseau's attempt to account for the divisions we feel in society (*Introduction à l'"Emile,"* chap. 6). Charvet is similarly perplexed and concludes that Rousseau became aware that he could not reconcile the contradictions (*Social Problem in the Philosophy of Rousseau*, 106–11).

9. E.g., De Man, *Allegories of Reading*, 226; Emberley, "Rousseau versus the Savoyard Vicar"; Meier, *On the Happiness of the Philosophic Life*, esp. 224.

10. Other scholars who emphasize Rousseau's invitation to his readers to judge include Melzer, "Origin of the Counter-Enlightenment"; and Schaeffer, *Rousseau on Education, Freedom, and Judgment*, chap. 5.

11. Juvenal, *Satires* 4.91. The context of the line in Juvenal may be revealing. The dictate to dedicate life to telling the truth is ironically said of Quintus Crispus, a bottle companion of the emperors who is said by Juvenal to have been capable of giving good advice but instead remained quiet out of caution.

12. See Scott, *Rousseau's Reader*, 197–200.

13. See Scott, *Rousseau's Reader*, 197–200, 214–16. Schaeffer also emphasizes judgment in assessing the "Profession" on the reader's part (*Rousseau on Education, Judgment, and Freedom*, esp. 129).

14. E.g., Burgelin, "Second Education of Emile"; Gilden, Rousseau's "Social Contract," 189; Lenne-Cornuez, *Etre à sa place*, 148, 347–49.

15. E.g., Burgelin, in Rousseau, *OC*, 4:cxxxiv.

16. Ellenburg, *Rousseau's Political Philosophy*, 298–99.

17. Spector, *Rousseau*, 120–23.

18. Meier, *On the Happiness of the Philosophic Life*, 229.

19. See Cooper, *Rousseau, Nature, and the Problem of the Good Life*, 127; Shklar, *Men and Citizens*, xiv.

20. See Mall, *Emile, ou les figures de la fiction*, chap. 9.

21. Meier, *On the Happiness of the Philosophic Life*, 233–35.

22. E.g., Cooper, "Nearer My True Self to Thee," 470–71; Dent, *Rousseau*, 235; Ellrich, *Rousseau and His Reader*, 58–60; Nichols, "Rousseau's Novel Education in *Emile*," 545; Strong, *Jean-Jacques Rousseau*, who states: "The narrator of the story drops the third person and tells the reader that the young man is actually the same *I* as the *I* of the tutor" (125). Schaeffer also makes this assumption, although she does note the "narrative slippage" (*Rousseau on Education, Judgment, and Freedom*, 108).

23. See Masson, *"Profession de foi du vicaire savoyard,"* 39–46.

24. Rousseau's views on sex and marriage are admittedly more complex than this simple appeal to his argument concerning physical love allows, but at issue here is the Vicar's appeal to the naturalness of marriage. For a full discussion of Rousseau's understanding of sexuality, marriage, and related topics, see Schwartz, *Sexual Politics of Jean-Jacques Rousseau*.

25. Meier states that the Vicar's argument about the naturalness of marriage is the first case in the "Profession" of a blatant contradiction of what Rousseau writes in his own name, here in the *Discourse on Inequality* (*On the Happiness of the Philosophic Life*, 239).

26. Emberley makes a similar argument about the dividedness of the Vicar's soul ("Rousseau versus the Savoyard Vicar," esp. 309). Meier notes the issue but does not pursue it (*On the Happiness of the Philosophic Life*, 234–35). Shklar characterizes the Vicar as "self-divided" and even "neurotic," apparently due to his *amour-propre* (*Men and Citizens*, 182).

27. Lenne-Cornuez, *Etre à sa place*, 349–52, 359–60.

28. Lenne-Cornuez, *Etre à sa place*, 364.

29. Schaeffer also compares these other sunrise stories to the setting of the "Profession" in terms of the erotic longing associated with our notions of the divinity (*Rousseau on Education, Judgment, and Freedom*, 110–11).

30. Rousseau to the maréchal de Luxembourg, February 20, 1763, *CC*, 15:48.

31. Alberg argues that the audience of Vicar's speech is unclear, and may or may not be the young Jean-Jacques, is certainly not Emile, but is most importantly for the reader of *Emile* (*Reinterpretation of Rousseau*, 58).

Chapter 6

1. Henceforth in this chapter all references in the text are to *Emile* unless otherwise noted.

2. An interesting exception is Alberg, who argues that the scandalous effective denial of Christ's intercession for our sins in the second part of the "Profession" is the decisively important point of the work (*Reinterpretation of Rousseau*, esp. 62–64). It might be said that Alberg's interpretation faithfully follows Beaumont's lead.

3. Scott, *Rousseau's Reader*, chap. 5.

4. Gouhier, *Méditations métaphysiques de Jean-Jacques Rousseau*, chap. 2; Philonenko, *Jean-Jacques Rousseau et la pensée du malheur*, vol. 3, chap. 10. Vargas remarks on the difference between Descartes and the Vicar concerning doubt (*Introduction à l'"Emile,"* 260–61).

5. Descartes, *Discourse on the Method*, Part 1, beginning.

6. Descartes, *Discourse on the Method*, Part 6, beginning.

7. Descartes, *Discourse on the Method*, Part 3, beginning.

8. Descartes, *Discourse on the Method*, Part 3, toward end.

9. Descartes, *Discourse on the Method*, Part 1.

10. Derathé, *Rationalisme de J.-J. Rousseau*, 62.

11. Melzer, "Origin of the Counter-Enlightenment," 354.

12. Rousseau echoes this passage in his 1769 letter to Franquières, bringing forward Plato along with Clarke, and pronounces their teachings "a doctrine so beautiful, so sublime, so mild, and so consoling for every just man would have really stirred all men to virtue" and humanity (January 15/March 25, 1769, *CW*, 8:261–62).

13. Grimsley, *Rousseau and the Religious Quest*, 46. See also Masson, *Religion de J.-J. Rousseau*, 105, 113.

14. See Clarke, *Demonstration*, 38, 80–83, 85–86. See also the editor's introduction, xxx. On the difference in method compared to Rousseau, see Masters, "Rousseau and the 'Illustrious Clarke,'" 41–42.

15. Meier makes a similar argument about the attraction of Clarke's teaching being a matter of its consoling effect (*On the Happiness of the Philosophic Life*, 242–43).

16. Descartes, *Discourse on Method*, Part 4, beginning; *Meditations on First Philosophy*, Part 1, end.

17. Melzer, "Origin of the Counter-Enlightenment," 354.

18. Meier terms the Vicar's distinction between "active" and "passive" principles his "first dualism" (*On the Happiness of the Philosophic Life*, 244).

19. The article "Evidence" appeared in volume 5 of the *Encyclopédie*, and the argument that judgment is reducible to sensation occurs near the beginning. The article was written by the physiocrat Quesnay.

20. Philonenko notes that the Vicar's argument is inconsistent with Newton (*Jean-Jacques Rousseau et la pensée du malheur*, 3:219). Oddly, the editor of the Pléiade edition of *Emile* states that the Vicar's argument "is a way of enunciating the principle of inertia" (*OC*, 4:1525n1).

21. An appeal to Newton would make better sense when the Vicar derives his second article of faith concerning an ordered universe being evidence for an intelligence, given Newton's "General Scholium" to the *Principia* arguing that the lawlike motion of matter must be due to God, an argument Clarke also makes (*Demonstration*, 61–63). Furthermore, such a point

would cohere with the Vicar's agnosticism at that point in his argument regarding whether matter is created ex nihilo by the divinity or exists independently of a divinity who orders it (276–77).

22. Compare Lenne-Cornuez, who notes the Vicar's pride but then exonerates him (*Etre à sa place*, 366).

23. Lenne-Cornuez argues on this point: "The Vicar's dualism is less a substantial dualism than the expression of the sentiment and the proof of an internal contradiction. To name this contradiction 'soul' and 'body' is convenient, but should not lead without prudence to hypostasize them" (*Etre à sa place*, 395–96). For similar reasons, Menin claims that the Vicar's dualism is not an "ontological dualism," but is instead what he terms a "spontaneous dualism" (*Morale sensitive de Rousseau*, 109).

24. Recall that the sole reference to the "Profession" within the main text of *Emile* concerns the necessity of attributing goodness to the divinity, so the reference is to this passage. The context of the reference is Rousseau's programmatic statement concerning the natural goodness of man (see 67). In a letter Rousseau explains that the "love of order" is of itself an insufficient motivation for virtuous action because it is counterbalanced too strongly by self-interest, and therefore a further incentive is necessary (Rousseau to the abbé Alexandre Louis Benoît de Carondelet, March 4, 1764, CC, 19:199–200).

25. In a letter Rousseau explains that the existence of physical order makes us expect moral order as well, and thus an afterlife: "Nature in its entirety guarantees as much to me. It is not in contradiction with itself. I see reigning in it an admirable physical order which never deceives. Moral order ought to correspond to it" (Rousseau to Moultou, February 14, 1769, CC, 37:57).

26. Spector, *Rousseau*, 123.

27. Meier, *On the Happiness of the Philosophic Life*, 264.

28. For an interesting deconstructionist analysis of these binaries, see De Man, *Allegories of Reading*, chap. 10, esp. 230–31.

29. See Scott, *Rousseau's Reader*, 215–16. Gilden also notes the attempted interruption, and comments: "If the young man . . . remembered what had been said earlier, he may well have had a legitimate objection to put to the vicar" ("On Rousseau's Confession of Faith of the Savoyard Vicar," 209–10). Meier does as well and, like me, argues that it is meant as a signal of the precarity of the Vicar's doctrine concerning the conscience (*On the Happiness of the Philosophic Life*, 269)

30. For an examination of a number of notes Rousseau adds to the "Profession" and an argument that they often undercut the Vicar's claims, see Macy, "'God Helps Those Who Help Themselves.'" Macy does not, however, discuss this particular note.

31. Meier makes a similar point (*Happiness of the Philosophic Life*, 269).

32. DeMan notes the Vicar's alternation between assertion and doubt (*Allegories of Reading*, 237).

33. A number of interpreters have seen the emphatic and lyrical language concerning the conscience as evidence that it is also the centerpiece of Rousseau's moral theory. E.g., Hendel, *Moralist*, 2:152–56; Grimsley, *Rousseau and the Religious Quest*, 61.

34. Among those who accept the Vicar's statement about man being sociable by nature as representing Rousseau's view are Burgelin, *Philosophie de l'existence de J.-J. Rousseau*, 239; Derathé, *Rationalisme de J.-J. Rousseau*, 14, 81. Among those who argue that the Vicar's argument is inconsistent with Rousseau's position are Meier, *On the Happiness of the Philosophic Life*, 292; Melzer, "Origin of the Counter-Enlightenment," 355; Vargas, *Introduction à l'"Emile*," 181–21.

35. For similar arguments concerning the distance between Rousseau and the Vicar on

conscience, see De Man, *Allegories of Reading*, 222; Marks, "Divine Instinct?"; Spector, *Rousseau*, 133.

36. De Man comments: "Rousseau never claimed that good faith suffices to give authority of truth to a statement or a knowledge" (*Allegories of Reading*, 228).

37. See Scott, *Rousseau's Reader*, 181–84.

38. Macy, "'God Helps Those Who Help Themselves,'" 626.

39. See Macy, "'God Helps Those Who Help Themselves,'" esp. 623–26.

Chapter 7

1. For Rousseau's reasons for taking responsibility for his books by proclaiming his authorship, see Kelly, *Rousseau as Author*.

2. Voltaire to Etienne-Noel Damilaville, June 14, 1762, quoted by Havens, *Voltaire's Marginalia on the Pages of Rousseau*, 72. For a discussion of Voltaire's *Recueil necessaire* in relation to the "Profession," see Scott, "Between Religious Fanaticism and Philosophical Fanaticism."

3. See Alberg, *Reinterpretation of Rousseau*, 65–71; Grimsley, *Rousseau and the Religious Quest*, 68–76; Hendel, *Moralist*, 2:157–62; Masson, *Religion de Jean-Jacques Rousseau*, 2:103–12; Masters, *Political Philosophy of Rousseau*, 86–8; O'Hagan, *Rousseau*, 238–41, 257–59; Spector, *Rousseau*, 125–27; Vargas, *Introduction à l'"Emile*," 186–93.

4. Melzer, "Origin of the Counter-Enlightenment," 344.

5. Henceforth in this chapter all references in the text are to *Emile* unless otherwise noted.

6. Meier advances a similar reading, first saying of the Vicar that "he considered necessary a circumspect preparation and a particular authorization, namely the discernible need and explicit desire of the addressee," and, second, with regard to both the Vicar in relation to the youth and Rousseau to the public: "They orient their speeches about revelation as well as about Natural Religion toward the concrete state of the individual or to the concrete historical state" (*On the Happiness of the Philosophic Life*, 283–84).

7. For a similar reading, see Meier, *On the Happiness of the Philosophic Life*, 287.

8. Alberg, *A Reinterpretation of Rousseau*, 69.

9. See Plato, *Republic* 361d–62a.

10. Socrates suffers a similar fate when Rousseau compares him to Cato. "Let us dare to compare Socrates himself to Cato. One was more a philosopher, the other more a citizen.... Socrates' virtue is that of the wisest of men. But compared to Caesar and Pompey, Cato seems like a God among mortals" ("Political Economy," *CW*, 3:151).

11. Jean-Georges Lefranc de Pompignan, *Instruction pastorale* (1763), quoted in Trousson, *Jean-Jacques Rousseau jugé par ses contemporains*, 259.

12. Scott, *Rousseau's Reader*, 206–7.

Chapter 8

1. For a thorough and fair-minded argument that the chapter "On Civil Religion" is theoretically inconsistent with Rousseau's political principles, see Griswold, "Liberty and Compulsory Civil Religion." For an extensive overview of the totalitarian reading of Rousseau and a rejoinder, see Ball, "Rousseau's Civil Religion Reconsidered."

2. E.g., Bertram, "Toleration and Pluralism in Rousseau's Civil Religion."

3. Rousseau to Victor Riqueti, marquis de Mirabeau, July 26, 1767, *CC*, 33:239–40. After writing this, I discovered that Guénard makes the same comparison ("'Esprit social' et 'choses du ciel,'" 35).

4. See esp. Masters, *Political Philosophy of Rousseau*.

5. E.g., Cohen, *Free Community of Equals*, 57–58; Stilz, *Liberal Loyalty*, chap. 5.

6. Bernardi, "Sur la genèse du concept de religion civile," esp. 121–24. Compare Guillemin: "Thus Rousseau cultivates a dualism with regard to the sources of right, at once transcendental and human, spiritual and temporal" ("Religion politique de Jean-Jacques Rousseau," 112).

7. Other interpreters have argued that the passage about all justice coming from God indicates that the general will is a transcendent principle. See, e.g., Williams, *Rousseau's "Social Contract."*

8. I note that the concept of the "general will" had its origins in late seventeenth- and early eighteenth-century theological disputes over the relationship of the divinity to the realms of nature and grace, disputes that engaged the attention of Malebranche above all, but also Pascal, Arnaud, Leibniz, and others. In this theological context a distinction was drawn between the "particular will" (*volonté particulière*) and the "general will" (*volonté génerale*). The general will was the will by which God governs the realms of nature and grace through general laws—for example, the general laws of nature—whereas the particular will was the will through which He created the universe and intervenes in it through miracles and particular grace or providence, with much of the dispute being over the extent to which he so intervened. This terminology is found in secularized form in Montesquieu and Diderot. Diderot speculated in his article "Natural Right" (*Droit naturel*) on a general will of all humanity, a moral law discoverable by reason, and Rousseau responded to him in the first draft of the *Social Contract*, in a passage omitted from the final version, in which he argued that there was effectively no such universal general will of all men, but only a general will of particular political societies ("Geneva Manuscript," *CW*, 4:76–79). For the theological background, see Riley, *General Will before Rousseau*. For a critique, see Bernardi, who persuasively argues that even if Rousseau adopts the terminology of the "general will" from these theological debates, it is his engagement with Diderot over a thoroughly secularized concept that is most important for understanding his own conception of the general will (*Fabrique des concepts*, chap. 9). Finally, and following on this, one might argue that the sovereign people imitates the divinity by legislating through the general will, and that the social contract and the laws are "sacred" in this respect, although I would suggest in a thoroughly secularized manner. In fact, I have made this argument elsewhere: Scott, "Politics as the Imitation of the Divine."

9. He also refers in this context to Calvin as someone whose political orders were just as important as his theological writings (II.7 n), but he does not expressly connect the religious and political orders and instead emphasizes that Calvin abdicated any political power in Geneva.

10. E.g., Guillemin, "Religion politique de Jean-Jacques Rousseau," 119ff.; Ward, "Gods Would Be Needed."

11. See Derathé, in *OC*, 3:1498.

12. Rousseau to Marc-Michel Rey, December 23, 1761, *CC*, 9:346.

13. E.g., Beiner, *Civil Religion*, 15–16.

14. A point that Ball takes to mean that "On Civil Religion" should be read as a final test by Rousseau to see whether the reader still needs such a religion ("Rousseau's Civil Religion Reconsidered," 127).

15. E.g., Bertram, *Rousseau and "The Social Contract."*

16. For the table of contents, see Rousseau to Marc-Michel Rey, February 28, 1762, *CC*, 10:122.

17. Bernardi, "Sur la genèse du concept de religion civile."

18. Bernardi, "Sur la genèse du concept de religion civile," 126.

19. See Beiner, *Civil Religion*, 11. There is one potential partial antecedent for Rousseau's "civil religion" in Varro. His *Antiquities of Human and Divine Things* is lost, but the relevant portion of the work is quoted and discussed by Augustine in the *City of God*. Augustine relates that Varro distinguished three types of "theology": mythical or fabulous, physical or natural, and civil. The first is the domain of poets, the second of philosophers, and the third of the people. Augustine argues that mythical and civil theology are not distinct, and of course that they are both false, and suggests that Varro distinguished them for prudential reasons. At any rate, the main point is that civil theology was viewed by the philosophers as untrue but politically useful, and on this matter in addition to Varro Augustine cites Seneca, to which one could add Cicero's *De divinatione*, among others. See Augustine, *City of God*, 6.5–10.

20. See Waterlot, "Rousseau démontre-t-il l'affirmation . . . ?"

21. I am indebted here to Bachofen, "Religion civile selon Rousseau."

22. See Melzer, "Origin of the Counter-Enlightenment," 348–50.

23. Similarly, in a letter Rousseau explains: "The great society, human society in general, is founded on humanity, on universal beneficence; I say and I have always said that Christianity is favorable to this society. But particular societies, political and civil societies, have an entirely different principle. They are purely human establishments from which, consequently, true Christianity detaches us as it does from everything merely terrestrial. It is only men's vices which render these establishments necessary, and it is only human passions which preserve it" (Rousseau to Usteri, July 18, 1763, *CC*, 17:62).

24. See Bachofen, "Religion civile," esp. 42–43, 53.

25. Machiavelli, *Discourses* II.2 (ed. Mansfield and Tarcov, 131).

26. As also characterized by Bernardi, "Sur la genèse du concept de religion civile," 116.

27. Bernardi, "Religion civile," 160.

28. Williams, *Rousseau's "Social Contract,"* 200.

29. Griswold, "Liberty and Compulsory Civil Religion," 274–75.

30. Griswold, "Liberty and Compulsory Civil Religion," 277.

31. E.g., Waterlot, "Discours des prosélytes," 58–59, 62–66.

32. Guénard, "'Esprit social' et 'choses du ciel,'" 34.

33. For a discussion of the possible candidates, see Bernardi, "Religion civile," 161–64. A number of scholars suggest the article "Intolérance" from the *Encyclopédie*, but as Bernardi points out it was not published until 1767.

34. Spector, *Rousseau*, 134–38. For other scholars who see civil religion as a blending of the religions of the citizen and of man, see O'Hagan, *Rousseau*, 227; Sherover, "Rousseau's Civil Religion."

35. See also Rousseau's description of how the imagined proselytes of the religion of the "Profession" would behave: "They will say: accept with us the principles of the duties of the man and the citizen. For the rest, believe whatever you please" (*Mountain*, 145). See Waterlot, "Discours des proselytes."

36. Williams treats both versions as effectively identical and uses the "Profession" to explicate the dogmas of civil religion (*Rousseau's "Social Contract,"* 199–201). O'Hagan sees the same minimal deist theology in both writings, with the version in the *Social Contract* being something like an application of the "Profession" to a political context (*Rousseau*, 227). Guillemin and Waterlot are largely in agreement, but note that there remains a tension between the "universalistic" aspirations of the "Profession" when applied to the "particularistic" needs of politics (Guillemin, "Religion politique de Jean-Jacques Rousseau"; Waterlot, "Discours des prosélytes," 65). In turn, Cladis argues that it is precisely on the plane of religion that Rousseau reconciles the tension, offering a minimal civil religion for public worship and

a sphere of private religion, especially of the sort found in the "Profession" (*Public Vision, Private Lives*, esp. chap. 10).

37. E.g., Bachofen, "Religion civile selon Rousseau," 46–47; Burgelin, *Philosophie de l'existence*, 442; Waksman, "'Difficultés étaient dans la nature de la chose,'" 108.

38. Bachofen, "Religion civile selon Rousseau," 46–47.

39. Bachofen, "Religion civile selon Rousseau," 39. See also Guénard, "'Esprit social' et 'choses du ciel,'" 35.

BIBLIOGRAPHY

Rousseau's Works

Rousseau, Jean-Jacques. *Oeuvres complètes*. 5 vols. Bibliothèque de la Pléiade. Paris: Gallimard, 1959–95.
Rousseau, Jean-Jacques. *Correspondence complète*. Ed. Ralph A. Leigh. 50 vols. Oxford: Voltaire Foundation, 1965–91.
Rousseau, Jean-Jacques. *Emile, or On Education*. Trans. Allan Bloom. New York: Basic Books, 1979.
Rousseau, Jean-Jacques. *The Collected Writings of Rousseau*. Ed. Roger D. Masters and Christopher Kelly. 13 vols. Hanover: University Press of New England, 1990–2010.
Rousseau, Jean-Jacques. *The Major Political Writings of Jean-Jacques Rousseau: The Two Discourses and the Social Contract*. Trans. and ed. John T. Scott. Chicago: University of Chicago Press, 2012.

Secondary Sources

Alberg, Jeremiah. *A Reinterpretation of Rousseau: A Religious System*. New York: Palgrave Macmillan, 2007.
Augustine of Hippo. *The City of God*. Trans. Marcus Dods. New York: Random House, 1950.
Augustine of Hippo. *Confessions*. Trans. R. S. Pine-Coffin. Harmondsworth: Penguin, 1961.
Bachofen, Blaise. "La religion civile de Rousseau: Une théologie politique négative." In *La théologie politique de Rousseau*, ed. Ghislain Waterlot, 37–62. Rennes: Presses universitaires de Rennes, 2010.
Ball, Terence. "Rousseau's Civil Religion Reconsidered." In *Reappraising Political Theory: Revisionist Studies in the History of Political Thought*, 107–30. Oxford: Oxford University Press, 1995.
Beiner, Ronald. *Civil Religion: A Dialogue in the History of Political Philosophy*. Cambridge: Cambridge University Press, 2011.
Berman, Marshall. *The Politics of Authenticity: Radical Individualism and the Emergence of Modern Society*. New York: Atheneum, 1970.
Bernardi, Bruno. "Le Christianisme de Jean-Jacques Rousseau." In *La religion, la liberté, la justice: Un commentaire des "Lettres écrites de la montagne" de Jean-Jacques Rousseau*, ed. Bruno Bernardi, Florent Guénard, and Gabriella Silvestrini, 67–85. Paris: Vrin, 2005.

Bernardi, Bruno. *La fabrique des concepts: Recherches sur l'invention conceptuelle chez Rousseau.* Paris: Honoré Champion, 2006.

Bernardi, Bruno. "Sur la genèse du concept de religion civile et sa place dans le *Contrat social* de Jean-Jacques Rousseau." In *La religion philosophique des Lumières*, ed. Mai Lequan, 107–37. Paris: Classiques Garnier, 2016.

Bernardi, Bruno, Bernard Gittler, and James Swenson. Introduction to Rousseau, *Emile, Premières versions (manuscrits Favre)*. In *Oeuvres complètes*, vol. 11A, 17–61. Paris: Garnier, 2021.

Bertram, Christopher. *Rousseau and "The Social Contract."* London: Routledge, 2004.

Bertram, Christopher. "Toleration and Pluralism in Rousseau's Civil Religion." In *Rousseau and l'Infâme: Religion, Toleration, and Fanaticism in the Age of Enlightenment*, ed. Ourida Mostefai and John T. Scott, 137–52. Amsterdam: Rodopi, 2009.

Bertram, Christopher. "Rousseau's Legacy in Two Conceptions of the General Will: Democratic and Transcendent." *Review of Politics* 74 (2012): 403–19.

Besterman, Theodore. "Voltaire et le désastre de Lisbonne: Ou, la mort de l'optimisme." *SVEC* 2 (1956): 7–24.

Black, Jeffrey J. S. *Rousseau's Critique of Science: A Commentary on the "Discourse on the Sciences and the Arts."* Lanham, MD: Lexington Books, 2009.

Bloom, Allan. Introduction to Jean-Jacques Rousseau, *Emile, or On Education*. Ed. and trans. Allan Bloom. New York: Basic Books, 1979.

Brant, Claire. *Eighteenth-Century Letters and British Culture*. New York: Palgrave Macmillan, 2006.

Brooke, Christopher. *Philosophic Pride: Stoicism and Political Thought from Lipsius to Rousseau*. Princeton: Princeton University Press, 2012.

Burgelin, Pierre. *La philosophie de l'existence de J.-J. Rousseau*. Paris: Presses universitaires de France, 1952.

Burgelin, Pierre. "The Second Education of Emile." *Yale French Studies* 28 (1961–62): 106–11.

Butterworth, Charles E. "Interpretative Essay." In Jean-Jacques Rousseau, *Reveries of the Solitary Walker*, trans. Charles E. Butterworth, 145–240. New York: New York University Press, 1979.

Campbell, Sally H., and John T. Scott. "The Politic Argument of Rousseau's *Discourse on the Sciences and the Arts*." *American Journal of Political Science* 49 (2005): 819–29.

Cassirer, Ernst. *The Philosophy of the Enlightenment*. Trans. Fritz C. A. Koelln and James P. Pettegrove. Princeton: Princeton University Press, 1951 [1932].

Cassirer, Ernst. *The Question of Jean-Jacques Rousseau*. Trans. and ed. Peter Gay. 2nd ed. New Haven: Yale University Press, 1989 [1932].

Castel, Louis-Bertrand. *L'homme moral opposé à l'homme physique de Monsieur R***. Lettres philosophiques, où l'on refute le Déisme du jour*. Toulouse, 1756.

Charvet, John. *The Social Problem in the Philosophy of Rousseau*. Cambridge: Cambridge University Press, 1974.

Cladis, Mark S. *Public Vision, Private Lives: Rousseau, Religion, and 21st-Century Democracy*. Oxford: Oxford University Press, 2003.

Clarke, Samuel. *A Demonstration of the Being and Attributes of God and Other Writings*. Ed. Ezio Vailati. Cambridge: Cambridge University Press, 1998.

Cohen, Joshua. *Rousseau: A Free Community of Equals*. Oxford: Oxford University Press, 2010.

Colletti, Lucio. *From Rousseau to Lenin: Studies in Ideology and Society*. Trans. John Merrington and Judith White. London: New Left Books, 1972.

Cooper, Laurence D. *Rousseau, Nature, and the Problem of the Good Life*. University Park: Pennsylvania State University Press, 1999.

Cooper, Laurence D. "Nearer My True Self to Thee: Rousseau's New Spirituality—and Ours." *Review of Politics* 74 (2012): 465–88.

DeMan, Paul. *Allegories of Reading: Figural Language in Rousseau, Nietzsche, Rilke, and Proust*. New Haven: Yale University Press, 1979.

Dent, N. H. J. *Rousseau: An Introduction to His Psychological, Social, and Political Theory*. London: Basil Blackwell, 1988.

Derathé, Robert. *Le rationalisme de J.-J. Rousseau*. Paris: Presses universitaires de France, 1948.

Descartes, René. *Philosophical Writings*. Trans. John Cottingham. 2 vols. Cambridge: Cambridge University Press, 1985.

Dickstein, Morris. "The Faith of a Vicar: Reason and Morality in Rousseau's Religion." *Yale French Studies* 28 (1961–62): 48–54.

Diderot, Denis. "Droit naturel." In *Oeuvres complètes*, ed. John Lough and Jacques Proust, 7:24–29. Paris: Hermann, 1975.

Douglass, Robin. "Free Will and the Problem of Evil: Reconciling Rousseau's Divided Thought." *History of Political Thought* 31 (2010): 639–55.

Douglass, Robin. *Rousseau and Hobbes: Nature, Free Will, and the Passions*. Oxford: Oxford University Press, 2015.

Ellenburg, Stephen. *Rousseau's Political Philosophy: An Interpretation from Within*. Ithaca: Cornell University Press, 1976.

Ellrich, Richard J. *Rousseau and His Reader: The Rhetorical Situation of the Major Works*. Chapel Hill: University of North Carolina Press, 1969.

Emberley, Peter. "Rousseau versus the Savoyard Vicar: The Profession of Faith Considered." *Interpretation* 14 (1986): 299–330.

Erasmus, Desiderius. *Ten Colloquies*. Trans. Craig R. Thompson. Indianapolis: Bobbs-Merrill, 1957.

Gierke, Otto von. *Natural Law and the Theory of Society, 1500–1800*. Trans. Ernest Barker. Cambridge: Cambridge University Press, 1934.

Gilden, Hilail. *Rousseau's "Social Contract": The Design of the Argument*. Chicago: University of Chicago Press, 1983.

Gilden, Hilail. "On Rousseau's Confession of Faith of the Savoyard Vicar." *Interpretation* 43 (2017): 199–214.

Goldschmidt, Victor. *Anthropologie et politique: Les principes du système de Rousseau*. Paris: Vrin, 1974.

Gouhier, Henri. *Les méditations métaphysiques de Jean-Jacques Rousseau*. Paris: Vrin, 1970.

Gourevitch, Victor. "Rousseau on Lying: A Provisional Reading of the Fourth 'Rêverie.'" *Berkshire Review* 15 (1980): 93–107.

Gourevitch, Victor. "Rousseau's Pure State of Nature." *Interpretation* 26 (1988): 23–60.

Gourevitch, Victor. "Rousseau on Providence." *Review of Metaphysics* 53 (2000): 565–611.

Grimsley, Ronald. *Rousseau and the Religious Quest*. Oxford: Oxford University Press, 1968.

Griswold, Charles L. "Liberty and Compulsory Civil Religion in Rousseau's *Social Contract*." *Journal of the History of Philosophy* 53 (2015): 271–300.

Guénard, Florent. "'Esprit social' et 'choses de ciel': Religion et politique dans la pensée de Rousseau." In *La théologie politique de Rousseau*, ed. Ghislain Waterlot, 15–36. Rennes: Presses universitaires de Rennes, 2010.

Guillemin. Maxence. "La religion politique de Jean-Jacques Rousseau: Résolution d'un conflit entre universalisme et particularisme." *Revue du droit des religions* 4 (2017): 107–28.

Habermas, Jürgen. *The Structural Transformation of the Public Sphere: An Inquiry into a Category of Bourgeois Society*. Trans. Thomas Burger and Thomas Lawrence. Cambridge, MA: MIT Press, 1989.

Hanley, Ryan Patrick. "Rousseau's Virtue Epistemology." *Journal of the History of Philosophy* 50 (2012): 239–63.

Havens, George R. *Voltaire's Marginalia on the Pages of Rousseau: A Comparative Study of Ideas*. Columbus: Ohio State University Press, 1933.

Havens, George R. "Voltaire, Rousseau, and the 'Letter sur la providence.'" *PMLA* 59 (1944): 109–30.

Hendel, Charles. *Jean-Jacques Rousseau: Moralist*. 2nd ed. 2 vols. Indianapolis: Bobbs-Merrill, 1962 [1934].

Hobbes, Thomas. *Leviathan*. Ed. Edwin Curley. Indianapolis: Hackett, 1994.

Hobbes, Thomas. *On the Citizen*. Ed. Richard Tuck and Michael Silverthorne. Cambridge: Cambridge University Press, 1998.

Horowitz, Asher. *Rousseau, Nature, and History*. Toronto: University of Toronto Press, 1987.

Israel, Jonathan I. *Radical Enlightenment: Philosophy and the Making of Modernity, 1650–1750*. Oxford: Oxford University Press, 2002.

Jimack, Peter D. *La Genèse et la rédaction de l'Emile de Jean-Jacques Rousseau*. Geneva: Voltaire Foundation, 1960.

Kant, Immanuel. "Conjectural Beginning of Human History." In *Anthropology, History, and Education*, ed. Günter Zöller and Robert B. Louden, 163–75. Cambridge: Cambridge University Press, 2011.

Kant, Immanuel. "Remarks." *Observations on the Feeling of the Beautiful and Sublime and Other Writings*, ed. Patrick Frierson and Paul Guyer, 63–202. Cambridge: Cambridge University Press, 2011.

Kavanagh, Thomas M. *Writing the Truth: Authority and Desire in Rousseau*. Berkeley: University of California Press, 1987.

Kelly, Christopher. *Rousseau's Exemplary Life: The "Confessions" as Political Philosophy*. Ithaca: Cornell University Press, 1987.

Kelly, Christopher. "'To Persuade without Convincing': The Language of Rousseau's Legislator." *American Journal of Political Science* 31 (1987): 321–35.

Kelly, Christopher. *Rousseau as Author: Consecrating One's Life to the Truth*. Chicago: University of Chicago Press, 2003.

Kelly, Christopher. "Rousseau's 'Peut-Etre': Reflections on the Status of the State of Nature." *Modern Intellectual History* 3 (2006): 75–83.

King, Rachael Scarborough. *Writing to the World: Letters and the Origins of Modern Print Genres*. Baltimore: Johns Hopkins University Press, 2018.

Leigh, R. A. "Rousseau's Letter to Voltaire on Optimism (18 August 1756)." *Studies on Voltaire and the Eighteenth Century* 30 (1964): 247–309.

Lenne-Cornuez, Johanna. *Etre à sa place: La formation du sujet dans la philosophie morale de Rousseau*. Paris: Classiques Garnier, 2021.

Machiavelli, Niccolò. *Discourses on Livy*. Trans. Harvey Mansfield and Nathan Tarcov. Chicago: University of Chicago Press, 1996.

MacLean, Lee. *The Free Animal: Rousseau on Free Will and Human Nature*. Toronto: University of Toronto Press, 2013.

Macy, Jeffrey. "'God Helps Those Who Help Themselves': New Light on the Theological-Political Teaching in Rousseau's *Profession of Faith of the Savoyard Vicar*." *Polity* 24 (1992): 615–32.

Mall, Laurence. *Emile, ou les figures de la fiction*. Oxford: Voltaire Foundation, 2002.
Marks, Jonathan. "The Divine Instinct? Rousseau and Conscience." *Review of Politics* 68 (2006): 564–85.
Masson, Pierre-Maurice. *La "Profession de foi du vicaire savoyard" de Jean-Jacques Rousseau: Edition critique*. Paris: Libraire Hachette, 1914.
Masson, Pierre-Maurice. *La religion de J.-J. Rousseau*. 3 vols. Paris: Hachette, 1916.
Masters, Roger D. *The Political Philosophy of Rousseau*. Princeton: Princeton University Press, 1968.
Masters, Roger D. "Rousseau and the 'Illustrious Clarke.'" In *Jean-Jacques Rousseau et son temps*, ed. Michel Launay, 37–50. Paris: Libraire A.-G. Nizet, 1969.
Meier, Heinrich. *On the Happiness of the Philosophic Life: Reflections on Rousseau's "Rêveries" in Two Books*. Trans. Robert Berman. Chicago: University of Chicago Press, 2016.
Melzer, Arthur M. *The Natural Goodness of Man: On the System of Rousseau's Thought*. Chicago: University of Chicago Press, 1990.
Melzer, Arthur M. "The Origin of the Counter-Enlightenment: Rousseau and the New Religion of Sincerity." *American Political Science Review* 90 (1996): 344–60.
Melzer, Arthur M. *Philosophy between the Lines: The Lost History of Esoteric Writing*. Chicago: University of Chicago Press, 2014.
Menin, Marco. *La morale sensitive de Rousseau: Le livre jamais écrit*. Paris: L'Harmattan, 2019.
Molesky, Mark. *This Gulf of Fire: The Great Lisbon Earthquake, or Apocalypse in the Age of Science and Reason*. New York: Knopf, 2015.
Montesquieu, Charles-Louis Secondat de. *The Spirit of the Laws*. Trans. Anne Choler, Basia Miller, and Harold Stone. Cambridge: Cambridge University Press, 1989.
Mostefai, Ourida. *Jean-Jacques Rousseau, écrivain polémique: Querelles, disputes et controverses au siècle des Lumières*. Leiden: Brill, 2016.
Neidleman, Jason. *Rousseau's Ethics of Truth: A Sublime Science of Simple Souls*. London: Routledge, 2017.
Neiman, Susan. *Evil in Modern Thought: An Alternative History of Philosophy*. 2nd ed. Princeton: Princeton University Press, 2015.
Neuhouser, Frederick. *Rousseau's Theodicy of Self-Love*. Oxford: Oxford University Press, 2008.
Nichols, Mary P. "Rousseau's Novel Education in *Emile*." *Political Theory* 13 (1985): 535–58.
O'Hagan, Timothy. "La morale sensitive de Jean-Jacques Rousseau." *Revue de théologie et de philosophie* 125 (1993): 343–57.
O'Hagan, Timothy. *Rousseau*. London: Routledge, 1999.
O'Hagan, Timothy. "Taking Rousseau Seriously." *History of Political Thought* 25 (2004): 73–85.
Pangle, Thomas L. *The Spirit of Modern Republicanism: The Moral Vision of the American Founders and the Philosophy of Locke*. Chicago: University of Chicago Press, 1990.
Pascal, Blaise. *Pensées and Other Writings*. Trans. Honor Levi. Oxford: Oxford University Press, 1995.
Philonenko, Alexis. *Jean-Jacques Rousseau et la pensée du malheur*. 3 vols. Paris: Vrin, 1984.
Plato. *Republic*. Trans. Allan Bloom. 2nd ed. New York: Basic Books, 1991.
Plattner, Marc F. *Rousseau's State of Nature: An Interpretation of the "Discourse on Inequality."* De Kalb: Northern Illinois University Press, 1979.
Pope, Alexander. *Essay on Man*. In *The Major Works*, ed. Pat Rogers, 278–308. Oxford: Oxford University Press.
Pufendorf, Samuel Freiherr von. *Of the Law of Nature and Nations*. Trans. Basil Kennett. N.p., 1729.

Pufendorf, Samuel Freiherr von. *On the Duty of Man and Citizen*. Trans. Michael Silverthorne. Ed. James Tully. Cambridge: Cambridge University Press, 1991.

Rapaczynski, Andrzej. *Nature and Politics: Liberalism in the Philosophies of Hobbes, Locke, and Rousseau*. Ithaca: Cornell University Press, 1987.

Riley, Patrick. *The General Will before Rousseau: The Transformation of the Divine into the Civic*. Princeton: Princeton University Press, 1986.

Roosevelt, Grace. *Reading Rousseau in the Nuclear Age*. Philadelphia: Temple University Press, 1990.

Rosenblatt, Helena. *Rousseau and Geneva: From the "First Discourse" to the "Social Contract," 1749–1762*. Cambridge: Cambridge University Press, 1997.

Schaeffer, Denise. *Rousseau on Education, Judgment, and Freedom*. University Park: Pennsylvania State University Press, 2014.

Schwartz, Joel. *The Sexual Politics of Jean-Jacques Rousseau*. Chicago: University of Chicago Press, 1984.

Schwarze, Michelle A., and John T. Scott. "Mutual Sympathy and the Moral Economy: Adam Smith Reviews Rousseau." *Journal of Politics* 81 (2019): 66–80.

Scott, John T. "The Theodicy of the *Second Discourse*: The 'Pure State of Nature' and Rousseau's Political Thought." *American Political Science Review* 86 (1992): 686–711.

Scott, John T. "Politics as the Imitation of the Divine in Rousseau's *Social Contract*." *Polity* 26 (1994): 473–501.

Scott, John T. "Rousseau and the Melodious Language of Freedom." *Journal of Politics* 59 (1997): 803–29.

Scott, John T. "'*La morale sensitive*' dans l'*Essai sur l'origine des langues* de Rousseau et ses sources." In *Langues de Rousseau*, ed. Charles Porset and Tanguy L'Aminot, 9–32. Études Jean-Jacques Rousseau, no. 16. Montmorency: Musée Jean-Jacques Rousseau, 2007.

Scott, John T. "Pride and Providence: Religion in Rousseau's *Letter to Voltaire*." In *Rousseau and l'Infâme: Religion, Toleration, and Fanaticism in the Age of Enlightenment*, ed. Ourida Mostefai and John T. Scott, 115–36. Amsterdam: Rodopi, 2009.

Scott, John T. "Between Religious Fanaticism and Philosophical Fanaticism: Rousseau's 'Profession of Faith of the Savoyard Vicar.'" In *Enlightenment and Secularism*, ed. Christopher Nadon, 189–98. Lanham, MD: Lexington Books, 2013.

Scott, John T. "En vertu de la bonté: Shaftesbury, Diderot et la bonté naturelle de l'homme." In *Philosophie de Rousseau*, ed. Bruno Bernardi, 233–47. Europe des Lumières 31. Paris: Classiques Garnier, 2014.

Scott, John T. *Rousseau's Reader: Strategies of Persuasion and Education*. Chicago: University of Chicago Press, 2020.

Sherover, Charles M. "Rousseau's Civil Religion." *Interpretation* 8 (1980): 114–22.

Shklar, Judith N. *Men and Citizens: A Study of Rousseau's Social Theory*. 2nd ed. Cambridge: Cambridge University Press, 1985.

Smith, Amy Elizabeth. "Naming the 'Un-Familiar': Formal Letters and Travel Narratives in Late-Seventeenth- and Early-Eighteenth-Century Britain." *Review of English Studies* 54 (2003): 178–201.

Spacks, Patricia Meyer. *Privacy: Concealing the Eighteenth-Century Self*. Chicago: University of Chicago Press, 2003.

Spector, Céline. *Rousseau*. Cambridge: Polity Press, 2019.

Starobinski, Jean. *Jean-Jacques Rousseau: Transparency and Obstruction*. Trans. Arthur Goldhammer. Chicago: University of Chicago Press, 1988. Originally published in French in 1957.

Stilz, Anna. *Liberal Loyalty: Freedom, Obligation, and the State*. Princeton: Princeton University Press, 2009.

Strauss, Leo. "On the Intention of Rousseau." *Social Research* 14 (1947): 455–87.
Strauss, Leo. *Natural Right and History*. Chicago: University of Chicago Press, 1953.
Strong, Tracy B. *Jean-Jacques Rousseau: The Politics of the Ordinary*. Thousand Oaks, CA: Sage, 1994.
Taylor, Charles. *Sources of the Self: The Making of Modern Identity*. Cambridge, MA: Harvard University Press, 1989.
Taylor, Charles. *The Ethics of Authenticity*. Cambridge, MA: Harvard University Press, 1991.
Trousson, Raymond. *Jean-Jacques Rousseau jugé par ses contemporains: Du "Discours sur les sciences et les arts" aux "Confessions."* Paris: Honoré Champion, 2000.
Tully, Kendra A., and John T. Scott. "Rousseau's *Observations* on Inequality and the Causes of Moral Corruption." *Political Research Quarterly* 73 (2020): 184–95.
Vargas, Yves. *Introduction à l'"Emile" de Rousseau*. Paris: Presses universitaires de France, 1995.
Velkley, Richard L. *Freedom and the End of Reason: On the Moral Foundation of Kant's Critical Philosophy*. Chicago: University of Chicago Press, 1989.
Velkley, Richard L. *Being after Rousseau: Philosophy and Culture in Question*. Chicago: University of Chicago Press, 2002.
Viroli, Maurizio. *Jean-Jacques Rousseau and the Well-Ordered Society*. Cambridge: Cambridge University Press, 1988.
Voltaire (François-Marie de Arouet). *Oeuvres complètes de Voltaire*. 205 vols. Oxford: Voltaire Foundation, 1968–2022.
Waksman, Vera. "'Les difficultés étaient dans la nature de la chose': De la religion, de l'homme et du citoyen." In *La théologie politique de Rousseau*, ed. Ghislain Waterlot, 91–108. Rennes: Presses universitaires de Rennes, 2010.
Ward, Lee. "'Gods Would Be Needed to Give Men Laws': Rousseau on the Modern Republican Legislator." *Perspectives on Politics* 43 (2014): 41–51.
Warner, John M. *Rousseau and the Problem of Human Relations*. University Park: Pennsylvania State University Press, 2016.
Waterlot, Ghislain. "Le discours des prosélytes du vicaire et sa contradiction." In *La religion, la liberté, la justice: Un commentaire des "Lettres écrites de la montagne" de Jean-Jacques Rousseau*, ed. Bruno Bernardi, Florent Guénard, and Gabriella Silvestrini, 49–66. Paris: Vrin, 2005.
Waterlot, Ghislain. "Rousseau démontre-t-il l'affirmation: 'Jamais peuple s'subsisté ni ne subsistera sans religion'?" In *La théologie politique de Rousseau*, ed. Ghislain Waterlot, 63–89. Rennes: Presses universitaires de Rennes, 2010.
Williams, David Lay. *Rousseau's Platonic Enlightenment*. University Park: Pennsylvania State University Press, 2007.
Williams, David Lay. *Rousseau's "Social Contract": An Introduction*. Cambridge: Cambridge University Press, 2014.
Wokler, Robert. "Rousseau's Two Concepts of Liberty." In *Lives, Liberties, and the Public Good: Essays in Political Theory for Maurice Cranston*, ed. G. Feaver and F. Rosen, 61–100. London: Macmillan, 1987.
Wokler, Robert. *Rousseau*. Oxford: Oxford University Press, 1995.
Yamashita, Masano. *Jean-Jacques Rousseau face au public: Problèmes d'identité*. Oxford: Voltaire Foundation, 2017.
Yamashita, Masano. "Fate and Consolation in the Late Rousseau." *Sens public*, September 30, 2019, 1–22.
Zaretsky, Robert, and John T. Scott. *The Philosophers' Quarrel: Rousseau, Hume, and the Limits of Human Understanding*. New Haven: Yale University Press, 2009.

INDEX

Academy of Dijon, 7, 20–22, 27, 59
Adam (biblical), 69
amour de soi (self-love), 58, 62–64, 77, 81, 123–24, 127, 181
amour-propre, 4, 17, 50, 58, 62–63, 77, 81, 119, 123–27, 135, 139–40, 165–67, 180–81, 190–91, 194. *See also* pride
Archimedes, 153
Aristotle, 64, 69, 96, 113
Ashley-Cooper, Anthony. *See* Shaftesbury, 3rd Earl of (Anthony Ashley-Cooper)
atheism, 27, 32, 35, 105, 154, 183, 185–86, 204, 214–15, 230
Augustine of Hippo, 6–7, 42

Bachofen, Blaise, 228
Bacon, Francis, 28
Barbeyrac, Jean, 66–67, 75, 113
Bayle, Pierre, 100–101, 185–86, 188, 214, 218, 223
Beaumont, Christophe de, 1, 41, 43–46, 49, 51–55, 127, 166, 195–96
Berman, Marshall, 10
Bernardi, Bruno, 206, 212, 224
Bolingbroke, 1st Viscount (Henry St. John), 88
Bonnet, Charles (pseud. Philopolis), 92, 109
Butterworth, Charles, 36

Caligula, 215
Calvinism, 10, 138, 150, 194, 200
Cassirer, Ernst, 5–6, 16, 57–58
Castel, Louis-Bertrand, 68–69
Catholicism, 11, 44–45, 49, 141, 150, 193, 198, 213, 220
Catiline, 178
Cato, 97
Christianity, 28, 31–32, 49, 51–54, 65, 186, 189, 193, 196, 200–204, 212–28
Cicero, 12, 97, 103
citizen(s), 1, 19, 27, 33, 41, 47–51, 71, 86, 120, 201–30
civil religion, 3, 19, 49, 51, 201–5, 210–13, 218, 221, 224–28
Clarke, Samuel, 152, 156–57
Condillac, Étienne Bonnot de, 80, 110, 112, 114, 122, 152
corruption, 2, 6–7, 15, 17, 19, 24–26, 29, 33, 42, 45–46, 80, 86, 94, 115, 118, 122, 139, 152, 177, 181, 190, 229
Crousaz, Jean-Pierre, 99
Cumberland, Richard, 71
custom(s), 33, 79, 153, 178, 181, 191, 205, 209–11

d'Alembert, Jean le Rond, 110, 122, 161
Derathé, Robert, 155
Descartes, René, 28, 61–62, 152–54, 158
d'Houdetot, Sophie, 13, 127–28
Diderot, Denis, 21, 75, 106, 164
dogma(s), 19, 27, 33, 35, 48–52, 107, 141, 153, 157, 162–63, 166, 190–91, 197–203, 210, 213, 215, 219, 221–28

INDEX

dualism, 8, 11, 17–18, 108, 112–13, 121–22, 127–28, 132–35, 151, 158, 169, 171, 173–74, 177, 179

Ellenburg, Stephen, 137
Encyclopedists, 5, 161
enlightenment (concept), 23–26, 30–31, 46, 65, 78, 83, 114–15
Enlightenment (era), 5–6, 8, 22, 34, 85, 189, 194
Epicureanism, 8, 133
equality, 122, 159, 201, 215
esotericism, 10, 14, 32
evil, 5–6, 16, 18, 26, 46, 51, 56–58, 70–79, 83–85, 90–105, 123–24, 128–29, 165–75, 204, 229

faith, 2, 10–11, 18, 27, 31–32, 36, 42–43, 45, 47–48, 51–54, 65, 85–86, 106–7, 127, 131–32, 141, 149–50, 153, 162–64, 169–74, 183, 188, 191–94, 196, 198–99, 202, 210, 211, 213–15, 223–28
fall of man, 10, 65–66, 117
fanaticism, 23, 50, 135, 181, 185–87, 202, 214–15
Formey, Johann Heinrich Samuel, 85
free will, 82, 110–12, 171–72
French Revolution, 57

Galileo Galilei, 61
general will, 205–7, 211, 228
Goldschmidt, Victor, 113
Gospel(s), 7, 16, 18, 28, 31, 49, 52–54, 188–89, 193–96, 198, 200, 203, 204, 206, 213, 219, 221, 227, 235
Gouhier, Henri, 11, 132
Gourevitch, Victor, 86–87, 99, 107
Grimsley, Ronald, 10–11, 156
Griswold, Charles, 225
Grotius, Hugo, 65
Guénard, Florent, 226

Hanley, Ryan, 122
heaven, 7, 29, 69, 164, 208, 210, 222
Helvétius, Claude Adrien, 159, 170
Hendel, Charles, 10
Hobbes, Thomas, 28, 50, 59, 65–66, 70–80, 114, 119, 126, 188, 217–18, 228

Hooker, Richard, 65
Hume, David, 114, 135

intolerance, 47, 50, 107, 194, 198–201, 215, 222, 225–27
Islam, 186, 217
Israel, Jonathan, 8

Jephthah, 216
Jesus, 31, 193–96, 216
Judaism, 31
justice, 2, 4, 42, 46, 48, 79, 84, 103, 105, 125–28, 139, 152, 169, 170, 173–78, 180, 192–95, 206, 224–25, 228
Justin Martyr, 31

Kant, Immanuel, 16, 56–58
Kavanagh, Thomas, 10
Kelly, Christopher, 34
knowledge, 4, 14, 25–26, 30, 41, 44, 59–60, 80, 95, 105, 110, 112–15, 126, 153–55, 157, 165, 174, 178, 190, 192

lawgiver, 10, 53, 106, 183, 201, 203–12, 216–17, 224
laws of nature, 4, 16, 58, 61, 65, 69, 87, 93, 96, 105, 106, 166, 168, 172, 192
Leibniz, Gottfried Wilhelm, 5, 90–92, 152, 156, 161
Lenne-Cornuez, Johanna, 144, 146
Le Roy, Charles-Georges, 97
Leszczyński, Stanisław (Stanislaus), 29–31
liberty, 162, 201, 208
Locke, John, 5, 8, 60, 65, 70–71, 80–81, 110, 112, 114, 152, 170, 178, 188
Lycurgus, 209

Machiavelli, Niccolò, 208–9, 221–23
Macy, Jeffrey, 184
Malebranche, Nicolas, 152, 161
Mandeville, Bernard, 28
Manicheans/Manicheaism, 57, 92–93, 166
Marx, Karl, 58
Masson, Pierre-Maurice, 10–11, 86
Masters, Roger, 11–12, 133
Meier, Heinrich, 138, 140, 175
Melzer, Arthur, 155, 158, 189

Mohammed, 209, 217
monotheism, 51, 193, 216–17
Montaigne, Michel de, 178
Montesquieu, Baron de La Brède et de (Charles-Louis de Secondat), 39, 71
Moses, 65, 192, 209–10, 216

natural goodness of man, 2–7, 12, 15–21, 41–45, 50, 58, 62, 64, 72–79, 82, 86, 93–98, 115, 117–19, 121–23, 126–34, 152, 165, 177, 181, 229
natural religion, 16, 48, 52–54, 129, 139, 147, 149, 156, 183, 190–94, 200, 219, 226–28
Neidleman, Jason, 10
Neuhouser, Frederick, 16, 58, 62–63
Newton, Isaac, 29, 57, 62, 68, 100, 156, 161
Numa Pompilius, 209

O'Hagan, Timothy, 11, 122
original sin, 2, 6–7, 15, 40, 42–43, 119, 136, 203
Orpheus, 147, 182–83

paganism, 28, 31, 49, 186, 209, 213–17, 221–22
paradise, 68, 97, 185
Pascal, Blaise, 6–7
perfectibility, 17, 50, 62, 70, 82–84, 92, 95, 109, 111–15, 121
Petrarch, Francesco, 13
Pharisees, 31
Philopolis. *See* Bonnet, Charles (pseud. Philopolis)
Plato, 60, 195
Pliny the Elder, 12
Plutarch, 34, 37
polytheism, 215–16, 226
Pope, Alexander, 57, 88, 90–93, 98–99, 101, 103
Poul-Serrho, 186, 214, 230–31
pride, 17–18, 22, 24, 25–27, 30–33, 44, 50, 65, 77, 81, 85–107, 115–16, 119, 129, 138–39, 152, 154–55, 165–68, 180, 187, 189–91, 194. See also *amour-propre*
Prometheus, 23, 29, 37
Protestantism, 1, 14, 45, 54, 141, 150, 194, 196–200, 218

providence, 3–4, 6, 16–17, 51, 56–57, 69, 72–74, 86–88, 90, 92–107, 129–30, 164, 168, 171–74, 222
Pufendorf, Samuel Freiherr von, 62, 65–67, 71, 73, 75, 113–14
pure state of nature, 4, 16–17, 58–69, 72–74, 78, 82–84, 87, 108–9, 115, 121–22
Pyrrhonism, 26, 30
Pythagoras, 32

Rosenblatt, Helena, 11
Rosier (Rozier), Abbé (Jean-Baptiste François), 37

Sadducees, 31
savage(s), 65, 68, 76, 78–79, 111, 114, 117, 135
self-love. See *amour de soi* (self-love)
Seneca, 12
sentiment(s), 2, 10, 15, 32, 35, 44–45, 48, 86, 105, 116, 120, 124–25, 134, 136, 148, 154, 170, 179–83, 190, 215, 218, 222, 224, 228
Shaftesbury, 3rd Earl of (Anthony Ashley-Cooper), 5, 102
Shklar, Judith, 106
sin, 7, 65, 75. See also original sin
sociability, 11, 62, 72–74, 113–14, 132, 180, 224
social contract, 117, 205–10, 221, 225–28
Socrates, 24–25, 28, 32–33, 60, 195
Solon, 34, 36, 40, 209
sovereign, 51, 201, 203, 206–8, 213, 217–18, 223–24, 226
sovereignty, 201, 205–6, 211
Spector, Céline, 63, 114, 138, 174, 227
Spinoza, Baruch, 8, 28, 66, 188, 216
Starobinski, Jean, 9–10
Stoicism, 8, 133, 172
Strauss, Leo, 10

Taylor, Charles, 10
theodicy, 3–4, 16–17, 56–84, 92–93, 108, 117, 168
Toland, John, 5
toleration, 14, 19, 52, 54, 188, 202
Tronchin, Théodore, 96

Vincennes, 21, 45
virtue, 2, 4, 14–15, 20–34, 37, 40, 46, 74–78, 83, 115, 122, 125–26, 129, 135, 139–41, 152, 156–57, 178–79, 185, 187, 195, 197, 205, 214, 221, 230
Voltaire (François-Marie Arouet), 3, 5–6, 10–11, 13, 16, 85–107, 154, 164, 188–89, 202, 217

Warburton, William, 209, 216, 218, 221, 223
Williams, David, 225

www.ingramcontent.com/pod-product-compliance
Lightning Source LLC
Chambersburg PA
CBHW022043290426
44109CB00014B/967